Suicide and Its Impact on the Criminal Justice System

Elizabeth Kelley and
Francesca Flood, Editors

AMERICAN BAR ASSOCIATION
ABA Publishing

Cover design by Elmarie Jara/ABA Design

Printed in the United States of America.

25 24 23 22 21 5 4 3 2 1

Library of Congress Cataloging-in-Publication Data
Names: Kelley, Elizabeth (Lawyer), editor. | Flood, Francesca, editor.
Title: Suicide and its impact on the criminal justice system / Elizabeth Kelley and Francesca Flood, editors.
Description: Chicago, Illinois : American Bar Association, 2021. | Includes index. | Summary: "The book is about NON-custodial suicide, i.e., people within the criminal justice system committing suicide, including defendants and lawyers"-- Provided by publisher.
Identifiers: LCCN 2021029624 (print) | LCCN 2021029625 (ebook) | ISBN 9781641059862 (paperback) | ISBN 9781641059879 (ebook)
Subjects: LCSH: Suicide--United States. | Criminal justice, Administration of--United States.
Classification: LCC HV6548.U6 S75 2021 (print) | LCC HV6548.U6 (ebook) | DDC 362.2802/4364--dc23
LC record available at https://lccn.loc.gov/2021029624
LC ebook record available at https://lccn.loc.gov/2021029625

Contents

Acknowledgments

We would like to acknowledge all the people who contributed to this book. First, we thank the authors of each chapter. We appreciate their expertise, insights, and time. We also thank those who peer-reviewed chapters: Dr. Eric Y. Drogin; Donna Lee Elm, Esq.; Dick Ginkowski, Esq.; Professor Brooks Holland; The Hon. Kathleen M. O'Connor; Dr. Michael Klausner; and Phillip Wetzel, Esq. We also would like to acknowledge Justin Murphy, Esq., co-chair of the ABA's *Criminal Justice Magazine* Editorial Board, and Erin Remotigue, editor, for their assistance with editing and publishing the article that led to this book. Finally, we thank John Palmer at the American Bar Association for his keen eye and rapid response.

Chapter

1

The Price of Empathy: Learning to Cope with Trauma in the Criminal Courtroom

Jennifer K. Johnson

As various chapters in this book show, any criminal justice professional who has been exposed to someone who has committed suicide is impacted long after the event. As a young public defender, Jennifer Johnson had a colleague whose client committed suicide. This chapter describes how that tragedy has stayed with her, as well as with the colleague and the judge who presided over the case. Attorney Johnson explores how she felt woefully unprepared and unequipped to deal with this. But as she now knows, she was not alone.

In recent years, the legal profession, led by the American Bar Association, has acknowledged that being a lawyer is stressful in countless ways—and not the helpful kind of stress that produces adrenaline and inspires excellence. Rather, chronic stress can begin in law school and adversely impact the way we practice, and the way we live. For criminal justice professionals, the feeling of impotence in a hopeless system for lawyers can create burnout and compassion fatigue for lawyers who care.

This chapter explores the unique demands of criminal practice; the neurobiology of stress and how it can lead to burnout and compassion fatigue; and explores possible solutions for building resilience across the profession.

One of the many takeaways of this chapter is that things do not have to be this way.

• • •

> We have not been directly exposed to the trauma scene, but we hear the story told with such intensity, or we hear similar stories so often, or we have the gift and curse of extreme empathy, and we suffer. We feel the feelings of our client. We experience their fears. We dream their dreams. Eventually, we lose a certain spark of optimism, humor and hope. We aren't sick, but we aren't ourselves.
>
> —C. Figley, 1995

When Ksenia "Kay" Tsenin took the bench of San Francisco's Department 15 in the 1990s, her courtroom seemed fairly typical. The procession of defendants standing before her faced charges of petty theft, drunk driving and prostitution. But within the span of a few years, Tsenin found herself presiding over a de facto mental health court. Her misdemeanor court, like others in San Francisco's Hall of Justice and across the nation, was increasingly home to men and women who had fallen through the cracks of our decimated mental health system. They were now cycling through our jails, our hospitals, and the streets, and their crimes could be traced directly to untreated mental health and addiction. Our outdated criminal courts were unprepared and ill-equipped for the onslaught of men and women who were—quite simply—in the wrong system. Long before therapeutic courtrooms became a regular feature of our criminal justice system Judge Tsenin realized she had to improvise.

To the delight of the defense bar and the frustration of the district attorney, Judge Tsenin launched a quiet end-run around the antiquated legal system. She began offering defendants in her courtroom an informal diversion that included a pathway to treatment and recovery, one that would result in a more just resolution of the charges. One that could offer healing and hope. Her process was not institutionalized, it was not replicated in other courtrooms, and it drew equal amounts of praise and criticism from her colleagues on the bench. Still, despite the judge's unconventional approach, the process seemed to be working for the growing number of defendants appearing on her special docket.

And then, a young woman named Sheila killed herself.

Judge Tsenin was devastated, as were all of the lawyers working in Department 15. I was one of them. The last thing we were expecting was for Sheila to commit suicide. She was a star student at UCLA who had been appearing regularly in court. She was smart. She had promise. She had bipolar disorder, and by all accounts, she was doing extremely well in her mental health treatment.

"I'm not very good at talking about things like this," Judge Tsenin said of that day in a recent interview for this piece. "What I remember is that we were all happy. We were expecting another good progress report. Instead, her case manager told us that she had killed herself the night before."

I was new to the Public Defender's Office and Sheila wasn't even my client. Yet decades later I still recall the uncomfortable tug of two competing feelings: a sense of powerlessness to have stopped this suicide, and an overwhelming regret at our failure to have done so. Because it wasn't just the judge who was invested in her. We *all* wanted to see her succeed—down to the court clerks, the bailiff, even the reluctant prosecutor. For many of us, it marked the first time we had been so close to suicide.

Not her. She was doing so well.

We were not prepared. We were also expected to walk back to the office from the Hall of Justice and keep working like nothing had happened. It affected all of us, but none more than Sheila's public defender, Scott Burrell. Along with Judge Tsenin and the rest of us in Department 15 that day, Burrell learned of Sheila's death in court. In that moment, and for years to come, he would replay the signs he realized too late that he had missed and imagine what he—her public defender—might have done differently.

"I had spoken to the program a couple of days before because I wanted to see her progress," Burrell recalled in a recent interview. "I knew some things were not going well and she had stopped going to counseling or classes. So, I knew that she was having some trouble and I knew they were afraid she wasn't taking medication. I tried to reach her a couple of days before just to talk to her and find out where she was. And I couldn't find her."

Most of all, Burrell said, he felt blindsided by his own lack of education.

"It never occurred to me until then that we were dealing with a person with a disease—a mental illness—that could kill them. Sheila's mental illness came back and won."

Judge Tsenin softened the blow. Even in a misdemeanor court overwhelmed by a high volume of defendants, Burrell said, "she, more than any other judge, was different … She valued them all as people." Judge Tsenin spoke of Sheila's death openly. She shared her own pain. But looking back on a full career in law, Burrell said, she proved to be the exception. When he walked out of that courtroom, it was "back to the office and next case up."

There was no counseling available—not for Burrell or for any of us—nor any process to seek supervision or guidance. Even if there had been, Burrell doubts he would have availed himself of it. That would have been viewed as a sign of weakness. *He* would have viewed it that way, because "trial lawyers are supposed to be indestructible." Just as police officers—even today—must be reminded over and over that it is okay to seek help when they've been exposed to trauma, Burrell said, trial lawyers need the same kind of reassurance.

With no formal resources to turn to, we were left to seek guidance from our more experienced colleagues in the misdemeanor unit, or the ultra-seasoned ones who had made it to the felony unit and had developed the tough exterior that comes with witnessing tragedies that most humans never see—that most never *should* see.

"My supervisor didn't have any reaction that was memorable," Burrell recalled. "I know what it *wasn't*. She didn't ask me how I was or tell me to take the day off. What I imagine her saying is, 'Oh, is that your first?'"

Although it has been more than two decades since Sheila's suicide, the culture of the profession has not changed much. Most lawyers practicing in the criminal justice system today are not prepared for the death of a client by suicide. Not because it is a shocking and unexpected tragedy—which it is. We are not prepared because no one has prepared us. We are not prepared because, from the time we are law students through the sunset of our careers as seasoned attorneys, we receive very little, if any, training that informs us that this can happen in our job—or worse yet, that it *might* happen. The suicide of a client is not commonplace. But that lack of preparedness for the stress and trauma we see on a daily basis is, sadly, all too common. We operate in a chronic state of psychic disrepair that does not afford us the emotional bandwidth to absorb shocking and unexpected tragedies such as suicide. In fact, the system that molds us, lays out the expectations for our behavior, and defines our successes and failures inherently counters and undermines our ability to respond in a healthy way.

Even today, we are not encouraged to seek help, and we lack proper training in mental health and addiction. This impacts our ability to understand our mentally ill and addicted clients, but it also impacts our own self-knowledge as we struggle with human responses to chronic stress. The stigma of mental health is so pervasive that lawyers often hide rather than disclose a disability, for fear of repercussions. The coping mechanisms that we have learned as lawyers not only don't help us, they likely cause further harm. We have been conditioned since law school to react to the trauma of what we witness in a way that is counterproductive and harmful to our own mental and physical health. And yet, we still have a duty to provide competent representation.

In this chapter, we use the premise of client suicide to take a deeper look into the structural failures that leave lawyers in criminal courtrooms unprepared to cope with trauma in a healthy way. In Part I, we examine a profession in crisis that puts us at a disadvantage when it comes to processing traumas such as client suicide. In Part II, we consider the neurobiology of stress and how it can lead to burnout and compassion fatigue. In Part III, we explore possible solutions—ways that we can build resilience in ourselves as individuals and in our profession as a whole.

I. The Legal Profession

> We are at a crossroads. To maintain public confidence in the profession, to meet the need for innovation in how we deliver legal services, to increase access to justice, and to reduce the level of toxicity that has allowed mental health and substance use disorders to fester among our colleagues, we have to act now. Change will require a wide-eyed and candid assessment of our members' state of being, accompanied by courageous commitment to re-envisioning what it means to live the life of a lawyer.
>
> —*Path to Lawyer Well-Being*, at 1

In 2017, the National Task Force on Lawyer Well-Being issued a comprehensive report on the state of the field, entitled *The Path to Lawyer Well Being: Practical Recommendations for Positive Change* (National Task Force on Lawyer Well-Being, *The Path to Lawyer Well-Being: Practical Recommendations for Positive Change* (2017), at 1; hereinafter *Path to Lawyer Well-Being*). This groundbreaking report found the legal profession to be at an inflection point: If it does not begin to prioritize the health and well-being of the workforce, it risks losing the public trust. The task force was assembled in 2016 in the wake of two studies that showed unusually high rates of chronic stress, substance abuse, and depression among both practicing lawyers and law students (P. R. Krill, R. Johnson, & L. Albert, *The Prevalence of Substance Use and Other Mental Health Concerns Among American Attorneys*, 10 J. Addiction Med. 46 (2016); J. M. Organ, D. Jaffe, & K. Bender, *Suffering in Silence: The Survey of Law Student Well-Being and the Reluctance of Law Students to Seek Help for Substance Use and Mental Health Concerns*, 66 J. Legal Educ. 116 (2016); hereinafter *Suffering in Silence*). As the report correctly pointed out, the rate of dysfunction in the profession is simply not sustainable: "This research suggests that the current state of lawyers' health cannot support a profession dedicated to client service and dependent on the public trust" (*Path to Lawyer Well-Being*, at 1).

This alarming information prompted a deep dive into the health of the profession and a commitment on the part of the legal community to prioritize the well-being of attorneys. To date, approximately 200 law firms, law schools, and other legal employers have signed onto the American Bar Association's "Well-Being Pledge." The signatories to the pledge acknowledge that substance use and mental health problems represent a significant challenge for the legal profession and commit to do more to improve the health and well-being of lawyers.

It is heartening and important that, as a profession, we have begun to address these institutional failures. But we have by no means arrived. The culture of the profession and the nature of the adversarial system make lawyers a tough population to reach, and the law a reluctant profession to reform. Understanding the factors that put law students and working attorneys at risk of distress—from client suicide and countless other lesser traumas—is key to making positive changes to our own behavior, and in holding our profession accountable.

It Starts in Law School

Law students tend to be competitive, academically oriented, driven people. Legal education encourages and rewards those high-achieving personality traits. Students learn early how to handle a heavy workload with little free time. They walk into class knowing they may be subjected to rigorous questioning by a professor using the Socratic method of teaching. Expectations are set high for law students and success is defined by external measures such as grades, on-campus interviews, and moot court and trial competitions. The emphasis on achievement in a high-pressure atmosphere is undoubtedly one of the reasons that law students graduate, pass the bar exam, and succeed in practice. However, something is clearly missing because our law students are suffering.

The conclusion drawn from the 2016 Survey of Law Student Well-Being is that "law students are among the most dissatisfied, demoralized, and depressed of any graduate student population" (*Path to Lawyer Well-Being*, at 34). The survey found disturbingly high rates of alcohol abuse, illegal drug use, anxiety, and depression among law students, as well as a reluctance to seek treatment. More than a quarter of participants were at risk for problem drinking, yet only 4% sought help (*Suffering in Silence*, at 140). Earlier studies on law students found relatively normal rates of depression before law school. Those levels skyrocket in the first year of law school, peak in the third year, and never return to baseline (Susan Swaim Daicoff, Lawyer, Know Thyself: A Psychological Analysis of Personality Strengths and Weaknesses 9 (American Psychological Association 2006) [hereinafter Daicoff]).

So, what is it about law school education that is producing such impaired young professionals? The answer is layered and complex. Law school may not be what students are expecting when they walk through those campus doors the first time. Portrayals of the law in media and entertainment do not comport with reality. Many students enter law school without a clearly defined career goal and find themselves directionless. The experience can be lonely and isolating. Students may also be disillusioned by the study of law. A common complaint from students is that there is a lack of positive feedback from professors. Beyond that, Burrell notes that "most" of his professors hadn't even practiced law; they'd been on an academic career path from the start. That ruled out any discussion of vicarious trauma, healthy coping, or other wisdom that would offer an avenue beyond the dark gallows humor that Burrell and others resorted to in order to "close yourself off from the feelings."

The stress in law school, meanwhile, is extreme. For students who are used to being at the top of the class, suddenly competing with academic equals can be both daunting and dispiriting. Furthermore, maintaining a front of confidence and control despite internal feelings of awkwardness and insecurity can create cognitive dissonance. Yet law students are expected to perform at the highest levels.

There is little counterbalance in law school to the high-pressure atmosphere and intense curriculum. The emphasis from the top down on external measures of success overshadows the importance of support for intrinsic rewards like community, personal growth, and emotional health. Students lack resources and avenues for support and also struggle with the stigma of needing help. We owe it to our new lawyers-to-be to teach them the value of self-care and to recognize the warning signs of distress. We owe nothing less to those already in the field.

Profile of a Lawyer: Individual Risk Factors

The qualities that got us through law school are the same ones we carry to the practice of law. We are competitive. We have a drive to achieve and to succeed. We work long hours under time pressure, with high caseloads and little relief. The stakes are particularly high for attorneys working in the criminal justice system. The population we serve has high social service needs and we are often divided in our mission. One side of the courtroom is tasked with protecting the rights and the liberty of the accused, the other side with seeking justice and ensuring public safety. In the broadest sense, that adversarial system leads to an emphasis on rights and obligations over emotions and interpersonal harmony. It also encourages dominance and aggression, which can impair relationships at work and at home. It is no surprise that, like law students, lawyers have higher than normal rates of depression and psychological distress (DAICOFF, at 9).

To complicate matters, lawyers have a duty to zealously advocate for all of their clients, and young lawyers have little choice in who they are assigned to represent. For both public defenders and district attorneys, that decision may be as simple as what day he or she happens to be in court. The restricted ability to choose our clients and cases can feel depersonalizing and the lack of agency can cause internal conflict and stress. The ethical duty to advocate for a person or a cause may force a lawyer to subordinate his or her own emotional response to the needs of the case. That takes a toll. "For some lawyers that have been doing this for a long time, you can tell that they are dealing with humans and human problems," Burrell said, "but they no longer see the clients as human. It's a defense mechanism."

Layered on top of the duty of zealous advocacy is the duty of confidentiality. Lawyers cannot discuss their cases or their clients outside the workplace. The attorney-client privilege is a sacred part of our legal system and those conversations, those communications are untouchable. The inability of a lawyer to share painful, disturbing, or even confusing information with close family or friends can contribute to mental health conditions. Burrell, for example, said he never talked to his longtime partner about Sheila's suicide. "I literally didn't talk to anybody at all," he said. The same went for other distressing cases that followed. "Our clients tell us difficult things," he said, and "you promise that you will keep it in confidence." Beyond that, Burrell said, "I didn't want to bring the darkness home." That had consequences for Burrell, who began to keep much more than client conversations to himself, keeping them from his partner, close family, and friends. "You even shut down things that have nothing to do with the law," he said. "I started ignoring my feelings. And instead, I just started trying to appear like a lawyer is supposed to appear."

In short, simply abiding by the oath that all attorneys take in order to practice law may make us more vulnerable to distress (L. Norton, J. Johnson, & G. Woods, *Burnout and Compassion Fatigue: What Lawyers Need to Know*, UMKC L. Rev. 84, no. 4 (2016) 987, at 996 [hereinafter "Norton et al."]. *See* ch. 12, Suicide in the Criminal Justice System: Ethical Considerations).

Profile of a Profession: Institutional Risk Factors

Our vulnerabilities as individual lawyers do not exist in a vacuum. Lawyers are part of an old and venerated profession that is steeped in tradition. As much as we are shaped by our own ambition, we are also shaped by the institution. To be sure, many of the stressors that lawyers face also exist in other professions: high workload, little time, pressure to perform. Yet criminal law is unique, as noted earlier, *because* of its adversarial nature. That takes a deeper toll than many attorneys realize. We spend most of our days engaged in active disputes, arguments, and confrontation in a public courtroom. The job we have chosen also exposes us to endless stories of loss, poverty, victimization, mental illness, and other human suffering—including, on some occasions, the shock of client suicide.

For criminal law practitioners who are in court daily, the relentlessly confrontational nature of the work can be destructive over the long term if it is not left in the courtroom when the lawyers walk out. While the gladiator mentality is necessary and useful in front of a jury, living in that adversarial state of mind and body has long term, negative physiological consequences. Dr. Lee Norton is a noted traumatologist and lead author of a 2016 law review article, to which I also contributed, entitled *Burnout and Compassion Fatigue: What Lawyers Need to Know*. She explains it this way:

> Adversarial thinking is useful in trials when the lines have already been drawn. But, when it prevails within the workplace, it undermines essential social engagement and fluid, generative problem solving. Habitual adversarial thinking often generates a chronic oppositional posture. This brittle stance is characterized by a black-and-white, either-or, good-bad, yes-no, win-lose world view that damages personal and professional relationships, is physically destructive, and leaves the affected individual at much higher risk for medical and emotional health conditions (Norton et al., at 995).

A barrage of trauma exposure complicates matters. Our justice system has been flooded with people who come from impoverished communities, are addicted to drugs and alcohol, and may suffer from both mental and physical health problems. Sometimes the criminal charges are the least of their worries. As a result, we become more than just defense lawyer, prosecutor, or judge: we are also social worker, therapist, and coach. The defendants, victims, and witnesses in our system of justice often do not understand the limitations on the lawyers or the constraints of the law. The criminal justice process is not swift, and constant delays and continuances can frustrate those who are not familiar with just how slowly the wheels of justice turn. Expectations of lawyers and judges in a criminal court are high, and our inability to deliver on those expectations can cause distress. As a society, we have watched our social safety network disappear. Treatment services that *should* be available to our clients are thin or often nonexistent. That can lead us to feel a deep sense of powerlessness and even guilt.

After Scott Burrell learned in court of his client's death, he walked back to his office and played his phone messages. There was one from Sheila. One he received too late. One that would torment him.

"I don't know if there's anything I could have or would have said that would have changed things, but it kills me that I didn't get the message," Burrell said. "That's what I thought about all day. I still think about it. She's deciding on ending her life and she called me—she called her lawyer." That feeling of "failure" is common, even if client suicide is not. Said Burrell: "We meet with people who are desperate and need us to save the day. Most of the time we can't save the day."

When we begin a career in criminal law we knowingly sign up for those realities. What we do not sign up for is walking into court without the tools to psychologically process the content of the work. The unique combination of both individual and institutional risk factors for lawyer distress makes us susceptible to suffering from both burnout and compassion fatigue. In part II, we explore the ways that unaddressed stress can lead to poor performance at work, relationship problems, mental illness, addiction, and medical problems.

II. The Neurobiology of Stress

> Chronic fight, flight, or freeze reactions become ingrained in our nervous system, making us inclined to perceive threat where it does not exist. This means we react instead of respond, act instead of reflect, speak instead of think, and accuse instead of consider, and that we do so in a way that is highly inflammatory to all aspects of our physical body. In short, we make ourselves mentally and physically ill.
>
> —Norton et al., at 992

The response of our bodies and brains to stress is an evolutionary adaptation for which we should all be thankful. Stress triggers a primitive physiological reaction that puts us into survival mode, and we remain in that excited state until the danger passes. However, when stress becomes chronic, our bodies are unable to return to a normal state of arousal. Advances in the scientific understanding of the neurobiology of chronic stress teach us that it has long-term consequences: physically, emotionally, and cognitively. Although a thorough examination of the neurobiology of stress is beyond the scope of this chapter, an overview of the science is helpful.

What Happens to a Body Under Stress?

When faced with a threat or a dispute, our nervous system goes into a state of high alert, activating a series of neurological and chemical reactions. The "fear center" of our brain, called the amygdala, activates our central stress response system. Those instinctive responses take place in our autonomic nervous system which is further divided into the sympathetic and the parasympathetic systems. The sympathetic nervous system acts as a gas pedal, increasing our heart rate, pulse, and respiration, and causing a spike in blood sugar. It increases blood flow to the muscles in our arms and legs, the pupils dilate, and we release the stress hormones adrenaline and cortisol. We are in "fight, flight, or freeze" mode.

When the threat has passed, our parasympathetic nervous system engages and acts as a brake, slowing down the heart rate, pulse, and respiration and conserving sugars that give us energy. The parasympathetic nervous system is governed by the vagus nerve, the longest and most complex of our cranial nerves. It runs from the brain through the face and thorax and down to the abdomen. It acts as a freeway carrying information between the organs of the body and the brain. The vagus nerve controls the body's relaxation system and counteracts the stress response produced by the sympathetic nervous system. The parasympathetic nervous system calms the stress hormones and puts us in a relative state of relaxation.

That reaction to stress is automatic and designed for our survival as a species. Under healthy conditions, threats are intermittent. But what if they are constant? For criminal lawyers, the workplace is permeated by the perception of threat. Every time we enter the courtroom and argue, fight, disagree, or blame, we activate that process. If stress becomes chronic and our relaxation mechanism does not have the time or opportunity to return the body to a resting state, we are at risk of living in that heightened state of arousal. Over time, the body's response can become generalized, putting us in a constant vigilant and reactive state.

Some lawyers have a natural or learned ability to regulate their autonomic nervous systems in a way that deflects and depersonalizes contentious situations. Most of us are not that fortunate. The consequences can be dire. That uncontrolled negative cycle eventually erodes our ability to solve problems and resolve conflicts—the very qualities we count on in the courtroom (*see generally* Norton et al.).

Understanding Burnout and Compassion Fatigue

Ignored or left unaddressed, chronic stress can wreak havoc on our bodies, our emotional well-being, and our ability to provide competent counsel to those we represent. We are at risk of developing both burnout and compassion fatigue—two related conditions that can exist individually or together. Understanding the nuances between them will help us recognize and address our symptoms.

Burnout is a state of emotional, mental, and physical exhaustion brought on by prolonged work stress. It stems from a gap between expectations and outcomes or situations where perceived demands are greater than perceived resources. Burnout is caused by a number of factors, including long hours, lack of support, lack of control over the job, high levels of scrutiny, unclear job expectations, and a lack of resources. The condition is characterized by a diminished interest in work, decreased sense of personal accomplishment, increased cynicism, and a loss of personal identity. It may result in fatigue, anxiety, loss of hope, feelings of detachment, and reduced performance and productivity. Burnout can happen in any job at any level and is connected to the demands rather than the nature of the job.

Compassion fatigue is the cumulative physical, emotional, and psychological effect of exposure to traumatic stories when working in a helping capacity. Unlike burnout, compassion fatigue is directly related to the *content of the material* rather than the job conditions. For those of us in the criminal legal system, witnessing a barrage of sadness, trauma, poverty, and mental illness—up to and including suicide—has come to define our day-to-day work in court. Burrell likens the accumulation of vicarious trauma to being slowly boiled like a frog: "You feel something, but you get used to it and you keep trying to work through it. And then you're cooked."

For years, he said, he "felt unhappy" professionally, "and I couldn't put my finger on it." It's only in retrospect that he realized "there's an aspect of dealing with people's problems and taking them home that impacted me."

Acknowledging that our own feelings of distress may be symptoms of compassion fatigue is critical to healing. For simplicity, they can be divided into three domains: emotional symptoms, physical symptoms, and cognitive symptoms. Emotional symptoms of compassion fatigue include chronic anxiety, self-doubt, inexplicable guilt and shame, withdrawal and isolation, irritability and anger, powerlessness, and a feeling of numbness. People suffering from compassion fatigue are overwhelmed by small challenges and may have persistent intrusive concern about cases and clients.

Physical symptoms of compassion fatigue include changes in breathing, changes in heart rate, difficulty sleeping, headaches, problems of the immune system, changes in appetite, decreased libido, headaches, and chronic musculoskeletal pain. These symptoms come about because of the overactivation of the autonomic nervous system we discussed above, which directs the body to produce adrenaline and cortisol, putting the body in that perpetual mode of fight, flight, or freeze.

Finally, and importantly, given the duties of our profession, cognitive symptoms include rigid black-and-white thinking, difficulty concentrating, confusion and memory loss, inability to recognize cause and effect, loss of sense of direction and purpose, minimization of problems, lack of insight and preoccupation with events and stressors that cannot be controlled (Norton et al., at 989).

Lawyers may not recognize symptoms of emotional, physical, or cognitive distress for what they are: possible signs of vicarious trauma. In fact, they may not realize anything is wrong at all. These conditions develop over time and happen quietly and incrementally. The symptoms may be subtle. Because our colleagues are responding in a similar way, both the symptoms and how we process them are normalized. As those signs of distress translate into poor coping strategies and maladaptive, self-destructive behaviors, the danger to our health becomes real.

The Consequences: All Paths Lead to Chronic Dysregulation

What lawyers too often do is excuse, minimize, or ignore the signs and symptoms of burnout and compassion fatigue and simply tough it out: *I always have trouble sleeping, I'm used to the stress, I can handle it, I don't have time to go to the doctor.* Lawyers are masterful at dodging and denying when faced with the potential that they themselves might need help. The profession conditions us this way and the culture of the criminal law reinforces it. But the danger of that lack of insight is serious. All paths lead to behavioral dysregulation; that is to say, we engage in self-destructive emotional regulation strategies that have long-term consequences. Specifically, lawyers are at risk of self-medication, relationship problems, poor health, and poor performance at work (*see generally* Norton et al.).

As we learned in Part I, lawyers are already vulnerable to using substances to mitigate work stress. They are more than three times more likely to suffer from depression and twice as likely to have an addiction to drugs or alcohol than non-lawyers. Adding burnout and compassion fatigue increases our vulnerability to using alcohol and drugs as a coping strategy. Lawyers may also engage in other forms of self-medication, such as sexual compulsions, reckless spending, gambling, and binge eating. Obviously, these behaviors can spell trouble on the job or at home. Although not the highest among professionals, lawyers have a divorce rate that hovers around 27% (Dan P. Ly, Seth A. Seabury, & Anupam B. Jena, *Divorce Among Physicians and Other Healthcare Professionals in the United States: Analysis of*

Census Survey Data, BMJ 350 [Feb. 18, 2015], https://doi.org/10.1136/bmj.h706). As for suicide rates, among lawyers they are six times that of the general population, making suicide the third leading cause of death in our profession (*The Lawyer's Epidemic: Depression, Suicide and Substance Abuse*, Abnormal Use [blog], http://abnormaluse.com/2012/03/the-lawyers-epidemic-depression-suicide-and-substance-abuse.html).

The number-one cause of death for lawyers is cancer, followed by heart disease—trends that underscore the medical consequences of chronic stress. The adrenaline and cortisol that are key to the fight, flight, or freeze response can turn on us, causing digestive problems like ulcers, acid reflux, ulcerative colitis, and irritable colon. Chronic stress affects the circulatory system, leading to high blood pressure, heart disease, high cholesterol, abnormal heart rhythms, and stroke. Our respiratory system is impacted, causing ailments like asthma, allergies, and pneumonia. Chronic inflammation caused by stress can result in musculoskeletal pain and injury and a compromised immune system.

Finally, and perhaps most distressingly, chronic dysregulation leads to poor job performance. If we don't recognize and address symptoms of distress, we will put our clients in jeopardy and we will put our jobs at risk.

Neuroscience shows us that chronic stress can have far-reaching consequences. But those consequences are not inevitable. Neuroscience also tells us how we can prevent, avoid, and mitigate the damage. In Part III, we discuss possible solutions: ways that we can build resistance in ourselves and in our profession.

III. Possible Solutions: Building Resilience

> To be a good lawyer, one has to be a healthy lawyer.
>
> —*Path to Lawyer Well-Being*, at 1

As criminal lawyers, we know the price of our empathy is high. We also know that in the courtrooms we inhabit, there is a relentless need for our compassion. Still, sometimes, our empathy and compassion are just not enough. In Department 15 in the late 1990s a group of young lawyers and an unconventional judge learned that hard lesson. Scott Burrell says he will never forget that day and that he has thought of Sheila, and that missed call, so often. Yet despite the span of more than two decades, he hasn't had the opportunity until now to explore the full context of his experience. "It is helpful to talk about it," he said. And that's why a cultural shift is so critical.

As criminal lawyers, we need to step up and make changes in the way we live—both at work and away from work. While setting reasonable expectations for ourselves and making time for self-care may not be our custom, it should be. We need to develop strong, supportive social networks outside of the office comprised of people who are not in the business of criminal law. We should also strive to incorporate non-work-related activities and hobbies during time away from the job. Interests and activities that use different skills and different parts of the brain provide a mental respite. In that vein, we also need to take time away from the office that is commensurate with the nature of the work, not based on outdated cultural norms (Norton et al., at 998-99).

But lawyers cannot do this alone. It's incumbent on the legal profession to make a concerted effort to prioritize the well-being of the lawyers in its employ. That effort needs to start in law school. In an encouraging trend, schools have begun to address this gap. In 2016, the same year the law student survey revealed its distressing findings and the Task Force on Lawyer Well-Being first convened, Stanford professor Ronald Tyler authored a law review article entitled *The First Thing We Do, Let's Heal All the Law Students: Incorporating Self-Care into a Criminal Defense Clinic* (R. Tyler, *Berkeley Journal of Criminal Law* 21, Issue 2 (2016), art. 1, at 1). Stanford has since created an innovative self-care curriculum in the Stanford Criminal Defense Clinic that encourages mindful self-reflection, teaches coping skills, and increases resilience. Meanwhile, in 2018, first- and second-year students at Berkeley Law launched a student-run Peer Wellness Coalition to encourage a conversation about wellness that would be woven throughout the three-year curriculum. These programs are promising.

For those who employ lawyers, *The Path to Lawyer Well-Being* report set forth five straightforward recommendations for employers that are intended to minimize lawyer dysfunction and reinforce the positive relationship between wellness and excellence in the practice of law: (1) identifying stakeholders and the role that each of us can play in reducing the level of toxicity in the profession; (2) ending the stigma surrounding help-seeking behaviors; (3) emphasizing that well-being is an indispensable part of a lawyer's duty of competence; (4) expanding educational outreach and programming on well-being issues; and (5) changing the tone of the profession one small step at a time (*Path to Lawyer Well-Being*, at 10-11).

Law offices and government agencies can and must develop a culture that establishes a hierarchy of well-being: self-care first, all else second. In the courtroom we argue, compete, bicker, fight, and withhold. But inside the office, we should be expected to be cooperative, helpful, open, compassionate, and nonjudgmental. By providing counterbalance to that heightened state of alert, we can allow lawyers to move back and forth between the sympathetic and the parasympathetic nervous systems in a way that gives our mind and body a break from constant conflict (Norton et al., at 1001).

True and lasting cultural change in our profession will come from within and will come from courageous and sometimes unconventional players in the criminal justice system. A few years after Sheila committed suicide, Judge Tsenin became the supervising judge of the criminal court. With the expanded reach of her authority, she gathered a reluctant group of stakeholders from across the criminal justice system to figure out how San Francisco could better serve people with mental illness. Her motivation stemmed in large part from Sheila's suicide. It led to the formation in 2002 of San Francisco's first collaborative mental health court. As Judge Tsenin recently explained, "I finally had the power to do something. And I did."

Behavioral Health Court's success in reducing recidivism, violence, and psychiatric hospitalizations has been recognized nationally. Mirroring a nationwide trend toward problem-solving courts, San Francisco now has expanded the concept into a community justice center, a neighborhood court, a veteran's court, and a young adult court.

The impact on defendants in collaborative court programs has been sweeping and overwhelmingly positive. But the benefits do not end there. Along with the core mission of addressing the root causes of criminal behavior, collaborative programs also serve the emotional health and well-being of the lawyers working in them. By turning down the temperature of the adversarial system, we allow lawyers to recover. The criminal legal system has long prized jury trial work over some of the less combative aspects of practice. As a profession, we should be encouraging the idea that therapeutic jurisprudence benefits not only those facing criminal charges, but the lawyers and judges in the courtroom as well.

Conclusion

Client suicides do not happen in isolation. The distress and sense of powerlessness experienced by the judge, the prosecutor, and that client's defender are almost always additive. They are layered on top of exposure to myriad other traumas, and occur against the backdrop of a work environment that counteracts healthy coping mechanisms. Viewed in this light, it is no surprise that a client suicide can sometimes push us to a breaking point. We will never come to expect or to accept the suicide of a client. However, we can and should be better prepared.

The culture of the legal professions runs deep, and it is difficult to change. One of the first steps is pulling back the cloak that has kept the dysfunction of the profession hidden from view. Going forward, it will be up to lawyers to challenge the norms of the profession, hold our agencies accountable, and insist that self-care remain a priority. By raising the standards of the profession, and prioritizing our own physical and mental health, we can strive to be healthy lawyers, which will make us better lawyers.

• • •

Jennifer K. Johnson is a partner in the Johnson Woods Group which provides education and consulting services at the intersection of mental health and law. For nearly two decades, she was a trial attorney at the San Francisco Public Defender's office where she specialized in representing clients with serious mental illness. From 2002 until 2016, she worked with a diverse group of community stakeholders to develop, implement, and supervise San Francisco's felony and misdemeanor Behavioral Health Courts. For more than 15 years, Ms. Johnson was the lead attorney in both courts while also representing clients with serious mental illness on homicide and attempted homicide charges.

In addition to her work in the courtroom, Ms. Johnson has helped shape mental health and criminal justice policy at the local, state, and national levels. She was a lead stakeholder in the development of the San Francisco Police Department's Crisis Intervention Team Training Program in 2011. She remains part of the CIT program where she focuses on the training curriculum. She is a Senior Consultant with SAMHSA's GAINS Center for Behavioral Health and Justice Transformation and conducts Sequential Intercept Mapping Workshops and trauma training throughout the country. She is a member of the Criminal Justice Advisory Panel for the Arc's National Center on Criminal Justice and Disability and a board member of San Francisco nonprofit Legal Assistance to the Elderly.

Ms. Johnson is a lecturer at Berkeley Law where she co-teaches a seminar in mental health and law with Dr. George Woods. She is the co-author of a number of articles, including *Burn Out and Compassion Fatigue: What Lawyers Need to Know*, UMKC Law Review, 84(4) (Summer 2016), and *Justice that Heals: Promoting Behavioral Health, Safeguarding the Public and Ending Our Overreliance on Jails* (June 2016). She recently authored a chapter on mental health courts in the American Bar Association publication, *Representing People with Mental Disabilities: A Practical Guide for Criminal Defense Lawyers* (Elizabeth Kelley, ed., American Bar Association, 2018).

Ms. Johnson has been recognized for her work with awards from the California State Association of Counties, the Council on Mentally Ill Offenders, Pioneer Institute, and the San Francisco Superior Court. She can be reached at jenniferkjohnson@comcast.net.

Complete citations are available from the author upon request.

Chapter

2

Pretrial/Noncustodial Client Suicide and Attorney Impact

Francesca Flood, Ed.D., and Elizabeth Kelley, Esq.

When an inmate at a local jail commits suicide, the media often covers the story, the public becomes concerned, an inquiry or investigation might be launched, and the matter is then dropped or fades from attention. We know about these people and they are counted, yet they may ultimately be forgotten. However, the people we don't know about are those who are free on bond waiting disposition of their case.

Both of us know anecdotally about individuals who have contemplated suicide or actually ended their own lives while on bond. We set out to learn more about what we have coined "noncustodial suicide." This chapter, which originally appeared in a shorter form in The ABA Criminal Justice Magazine, *describes the data we gathered as we sought to find and interview attorneys who had had clients who committed suicide while on bond. Common themes emerge, such as attorneys believing that the threat of mandatory sentences and the shame of a criminal indictment were too much for a client to bear. And to a person, virtually every criminal defense lawyer asked—some decades after a client had committed suicide—"How did I not see it coming?" and "What could I have done?"*

• • •

Each year, at least 4.9 million people are arrested in the United States (Prison Policy Initiative, 2019). The percentage of these individuals who think about suicide, attempt it, and/or take their own life is unknown (Flood & Kelley, 2019).[1] Defendants in the criminal justice system are not a sympathetic population, and as such, there is a paucity of research about pretrial/noncustodial (free on bail, bond, or own recognizance) client suicide. Beyond the individual's death, there is a larger wake of damage. Family and friends are affected, and there may be long-term effects, as suicide is more challenging to navigate than other types of deaths (Worden, 1996). If informed of the accused's death, victims may experience emotional upheaval (Hoffer, Shelton, Behnke, & Erdberg, 2010).

There are misperceptions concerning the suicide of a noncustodial client within the criminal justice system. A common belief is that only child sex offenders commit suicide pretrial. This assumption is an error. Additionally, while attorneys do not usually discuss client suicide, this does not mean they were not affected psychologically by the death. This chapter discusses the results of a study we conducted in 2019 to correct these misperceptions. Attorneys shared their experience with client suicide. Our research revealed that noncustodial suicide is more widespread and not restricted to child sex offenders. Moreover, attorneys discussed the psychological impact of client suicide.

Defense attorneys who represent pretrial/noncustodial individuals are affected, and the impact of a client's suicide is coming to light. While research on attorney suicide is emerging, it is a nascent topic slowly moving from the shadows. Given that attorneys are 3.6 times more prone to depression than nonattorneys, it is a subject needing attention (Flores & Arce, 2014). According to Achimalbe's 2016 study on the prevalence of substance abuse and mental health concerns with nearly 13,000 participating attorneys:

- Of all professions, attorneys have the highest rates of suicide.
- Between 21% and 36% qualify as problem drinkers.
- Approximately 28% experienced some level of depression symptoms.

According to Krill, Johnson, and Albert (2016), 18% reported elevated anxiety levels. When a client commits suicide, most defense attorneys

[1] Francesca Flood & Elizabeth Kelley, *Noncustodial Client Suicide: Prevention and Attorney Well-Being*, American Bar Association (Summer 2019).

feel the impact, and there are lingering effects. These effects can add to their depression and other maladaptive behaviors (Flood & Kelley, 2019). (*See* ch. 1, The Price of Empathy: Learning to Cope with Trauma in the Criminal Courtroom.)

Researching noncustodial client suicide is a difficult task given the gap in the literature. Deaths of individuals who are free on bail, bond, or their own recognizance pending adjudication do not fall under the purview of governmental statistics, and therefore their suicides are not accounted for in numbers such as inmate deaths. Without a central repository accounting for these deaths, the number of noncustodial individuals who have taken their own lives is virtually unknown. Only family members and their counsel are intimately aware of their deaths. The court is informed as a matter of formality to resolve the case, and the phenomenon remains silent.

Unless the death is associated with a high-profile case such as Aaron Swartz (computer genius and entrepreneur), Don Lapre (king of infomercials), or James Beckwith (president of Southern Vermont College), there is minimal, if any, news coverage or notice. The public is unaware, the broader criminal justice system is uninformed, and mental health experts are seldom brought in forensically to understand why. Nevertheless, without examination and understanding, preventing a client suicide becomes challenging. When a phenomenon such as client suicide is not given needed attention and research, it is perceived as an unimportant topic, and by association, its casualties are relegated to the sidelines as well. Without a centralized mechanism to record and account for these suicides, it is impossible to examine the breadth of this phenomenon. Researchers would be required to undertake a Sisyphean task of contacting every court to pinpoint cases, attempt to identify a family member, or reach out to defense counsel who would be willing to share their experience with the phenomenon to understand its scope fully.

Background

Studies on the pretrial suicide of alleged sex offenders (state and federal) have been published.[2] Though there is scant empirical evidence of the number of suicides within this population, it is clear that given their level

[2] James M. Byrne, Donald Rebovich, Arthur Lurigio, Karin Tusinski Miofsky, & Jacob Stowell, *Implementation and Impact of the Central District of California's Suicide Prevention Program for Federal Sex Crime Defendants*, 76 Fed. Probation J. 1 (June 2012), 3-13.

of anxiety, depression, fear, and hopelessness, there is a greater proclivity for this phenomenon (e.g., committing suicide before trial) (Hoffer et al., 2010). Responding to these suicides, two federal districts in California created a multidiscipline pilot program where mental health workers and the criminal justice system combined forces in crisis intervention. While Byrne et al. (2009) focused on those accused of child sex or pornography charges, the authors posited that defendants in other types of cases were just as likely to commit suicide. Our study set out to determine if this was true.

To better understand the range and context of pretrial/noncustodial suicide and its impact on defense counsel, we queried 69 defense attorneys from private practice and public defenders through online surveys. Subsequent discussion with 25 of these participants followed to gain greater detail. Attorneys who participated in the study had either experienced pretrial/noncustodial client suicide and/or had concerns that their client was at risk for doing so. While this descriptive study relied on the narrative of affected attorneys and is anecdotal, it nonetheless provided an intimate look at the experience and first-hand knowledge of the client's involvement with suicide; thus, we use direct quotes from the study report.

When we sought to find a home for publication, we were rejected by some targeted organizations which believed that the phenomenon was unique to child sex offenders, and further examination was not merited. Upon finishing the study, the findings did not support this hypothesis; the authors found evidence to the contrary. Based on input from attorney participants, pretrial/noncustodial suicide is not unique to child sex offense cases but relatively widespread. Moreover, counsel articulated the need for more identification education, discussed how attorneys are indeed adversely affected, and that the criminal justice system is a contributing factor to this phenomenon. This chapter offers an overview of this study related to pretrial/noncustodial suicide, the impact on defense counsel, the role criminal justice plays in this phenomenon, and potential solutions to reduce these suicides.

Client Suicide Demographics

In reviewing the data compiled in our study (Table 2.1), attorney participants ($N = 69$) reported a total of 85 client suicides. One of the most surprising data points was that some of the respondents had experienced more than one client suicide. The majority of suicides were White males. More

Table 2.1 Client Suicide Demographics

		N = 85			
	N	**%**		***N***	**%**
Gender			**Age**		
Male	70	82.35%	<20	3	4%
Female	14	16.47%	20–29	24	28%
Unidentified	1	1.18%	30–39	16	19%
			40–49	24	28%
			50–59	12	14%
			60+	6	7%
Race			**Veteran**		
	N	**%**		***N***	**%**
Black/African American	2	2%	Yes	13	15%
White/Caucasian	73	86%	No	50	59%
Asian or Pacific Islander	1	1%	Unknown	22	26%
American Native	2	2%			
Latino/Hispanic	5	6%			
Unknown	2	2%			

than half (64%) were between 20 and 49 years of age. While veteran suicide is highly prevalent in the general population, in this study the majority (59%) of client suicides had not served in the U.S. military. Attorneys also reported whether clients had a known history of mental illness and a substance abuse history. Although the number of clients who experienced suicidal thoughts is unknown, attorneys believe it to be pervasive. Attorneys disclosed that clients attempted suicide. However, these numbers are not accounted for here, as they did not result in death. Using their own words, we provide feedback from participants. Some attorneys stated that while their clients did not consciously attempt suicide, they abused drugs, alcohol, or attempted "death or suicide by cop." Moreover, several attorneys reported that their clients died from heart attacks which they believe were stress-induced. "He was physically ill all the time with fear."

Numerous attorney participants posited that despite the nature of the criminal charge, most clients experienced suicide ideation (wanting to take their own life or thinking about suicide) as the first step in the suicide

Table 2.2 Client Suicide Demographics

	N = 57	%	History	*N* = 81	%
Crime			**Mental Illness**		
White Collar	6	11%	Yes	30	37%
Rape	3	5%	No	30	37%
Robbery	1	2%	Unknown	21	26%
Child Sex	15	26%			
Pornography	12	21%	**Substance Abuse**	***N* = 81**	**%**
Drug Mfg.	3	5%	**Abuse History**		
Drug Possession	10	18%	Yes	45	56%
Murder		0%	No	23	28%
Attempted	1	2%	Unknown	13	16%
B & E	1	2%			
Weapons	5	9%			

trajectory. As one participant stated, "Suicide ideation is prevalent, and there are probably more attempts than we know about." Although attorneys could not recall the specific criminal charges for all 85 suicide events, they accounted for 57 completed suicides (Table 2.2). In addition to child sex crimes, attorneys have seen clients charged with white-collar crimes, domestic violence, DUI, drug possession and manufacturing, and a host of other charges. Attorneys believe clients experience emotional upheaval, fear of prison, despair, stigma, loss of status and identity, dehumanization, addiction, and mental disabilities—each of these plays a contributing role in the arc of suicide. Many attorney participants emphasized that while client suicide is a problem, it is an unexamined subject. "It's a problem we need to look at because I know other attorneys who also had clients kill themselves."

Once arrested or indicted, the accused faces significant social and financial turmoil, feeling disconnected from society. When a state or the people of the United States accuse an individual of wrongdoing, it sends a clear message: That person no longer belongs as a member. *Anomic suicide* is an excessive response by a person who experiences this turmoil (Durkheim, 1897). When the totality of a person's life is reduced to one point in time, a criminal charge, their sense of self is diminished. Identities are irrevocably altered and/or obliterated, and the individual sees no road back. As stated by one attorney respondent, "You really can't win ... and you don't get credit for the 50 years of good life you lived." Another noted, "they built a legitimate life for themselves to have it brought down by one mistake, one prosecution."

Indeed, several participants mentioned that even if their clients had been exonerated, the damage to the accused's reputation is irreparable. As former U.S. Secretary of Labor Raymond Donovan asked in 1987, after being acquitted, "Which office do I go to [to] get my reputation back?" The defendant's life is irreversibly altered. The catastrophic loss of reputation and shame, not guilt, can still lead an innocent person to suicide. "I ain't the only lawyer that had an innocent client, or that I believed he was innocent commit suicide."

Impact on Defense Attorneys

When a client commits suicide, their attorney is left with the aftermath. In the instant study (Flood & Kelley, 2019), more than 85% of the respondents were concerned about their client's suicide ideation, but only 35% felt skilled at dealing with it. Sadly, 65% experienced a client suicide without any warning—the client never said a word. In all cases, but especially when the client was silent, the attorney experiences a constellation of emotions ranging from guilt and inadequacy to trauma and depression. As one respondent summarized, "Most participants in the criminal justice system ... are woefully inept at identifying those at risk for suicide." During the interviews, attorneys spent more time sharing their personal and emotional processing. The majority echoed, "I didn't see it coming," "I kept asking what did I miss," and "Could it have been prevented?" All these statements reinforced a sense of guilt, sadness, and anger. Although defense attorneys are not typically included in the circle of survivors of suicide loss, at face value they should be, especially when the loss has been internalized with feelings of guilt at failure to recognize the signs, and/or profound sadness.

Survivors of suicide loss are at greater risk of developing depression, post-traumatic stress disorder, suicidal behaviors, and/or complicated grief—a prolonged sense of sorrow that does not improve over time (Survivors of Suicide Loss, 2020). Unfortunately, many attorney-survivors do not seek assistance because they do not recognize themselves as such, nor are they recognized by others. According to Cho (2016), "Besides the regular exposure to trauma, what makes things worse is that there is a lack of acknowledgment that such trauma can have an impact on the attorney. It's as if we're supposed to be robots, able to carry out our duties as lawyers with robotic precision and never have any emotional reaction." Defense attorneys are left on their own to deal with their emotions, suffering in silence. One participant stated, "Attorneys need to talk about it ... where it's safe to talk about it ..." There has been a long-standing and substantial stigma in this profession concerning certain emotions that are seen as weak. As one participant explained, "We can't cry in this profession, but we can drink." Mental health issues are swept under the rug, and discussing one's emotional state is frowned upon.[3]

Despite the attempt to stunt one's emotional response, we must process and make sense of events and the world around us as humans. Without proper assistance, many of the emotional challenges experienced will develop into maladaptive responses. As one respondent shared, "I'm already a functioning alcoholic." In comparison to other highly educated professions, 36.4% of attorneys screened higher for alcohol use when compared to doctors and surgeons at 15% (Cho, 2016). Maladaptive responses and coping mechanisms were shared during the interview process. Several comments from attorneys interviewed reinforce that the psychological challenges are real: "Drinking is the acceptable coping method," "You have to build walls to survive this, but sometimes they come crashing down," "I compartmentalize a lot. Otherwise, I would perpetually be on antidepressants and probably an alcoholic," and "drinking, drugs, other addictive behaviors, dangerous behaviors are not that uncommon. In the prosecutor's office as well. Our slow suicide."

The overall responsibilities of a defense attorney are daunting, filled with stress, and effectively require taking on others' problems. These attorneys take on the responsibility to retain their client's liberty, minimize the time of incarceration, and (in some instances) shield a client from the death penalty. All of these are a tremendous burden and challenges

---

[3] Mark S. Goldstein, *Scared. Ashamed. Crippled. How One Lawyer Overcame Living with Depression in Big Law*, Law.com (Feb. 2019), https://www.law.com/americanlawyer/2019/02/12/scared-ashamed-crippled-how-one-lawyer-overcame-living-with-depression-in-big-law/?slreturn=20210322193752.

that rest on the shoulders of counsel. "Well, you know this isn't a happy profession," shared a respondent.

Criminal Justice System Plays a Role

In speaking with participant attorneys, many suggested that factors within the criminal justice system contribute to this phenomenon. Overcriminalization, criminalizing mental health illness, racism, overzealous prosecutors, harsh sentences, dehumanization of the defendant, and a host of other elements were expressed as contributory. "It's really a brutal process ... our criminal justice system," said one respondent. There is a sense that law has been reduced to win or lose. Public defenders articulated that they do not have access to the same resources and funds as prosecutors.

Moreover, funds for mental health care are in woefully short supply. Effective prosecution requires removing the label of *human*. "Prosecutors need to remember they are dealing with humans," said one attorney. However, by limiting the perception of the individual to criminal, it is easier to see past the person. "The language of the court is designed to objectify: the defendant, accused, offender, and a whole list of other worse names," shared one attorney.

Like most professions, there are many good prosecutors and others who could use improvement. When one is overexposed to numerous and intense emotions, there is a tendency to distance others and displace certain emotions. This tendency results in compassion fatigue, indifference to a more charitable view, and straying from our better angels (Violanti & Gehrke, 2004). When we are perpetually exposed to an onslaught of nails protruding from wood, eventually every nail appears to need hammering. "I was the prosecutor, concerned I had contributed to it [defendant suicide]." When people are accused in the criminal justice system, it is easier to see them through the lens of guilt, criminal, and irredeemable. As one attorney offered, "Prosecutors do not see the accused/defendants as mothers, fathers, spouses, children—just as criminal—it is easy to dehumanize, to say mean things—to be mean. Defense lawyers can be guilty of it [dehumanization] too." (*See* ch. 6, Death Suggested, Cause Abated.)

Justice is swift and served when "[w]e believe people cannot be rehabilitated. So, lock them up and throw away the key," lamented one defense attorney. As with many demanding professions that involve stressful circumstances, disastrous scenarios, and even life-and-death outcomes, gallows humor can develop. Humor can serve as an emotional buffer or can be a component of compassion fatigue. As one outraged participant shared, "The prosecutor found it [suicide] funny and made a joke about it with the person's family sitting right behind him."

One of the most sacred tenets of the American criminal justice system is that a defendant is innocent unless proven guilty. However, many within the system do not believe that this principle is accurate. According to Phillips (2019), "Prosecutors usually assume the accused is guilty and offer a plea simply to move the calendar along. After all, the accused has been arrested, bail has been set, the police have provided the prosecutor their report and the case is moving towards trial." The axiom that smoke is always indicative of fire enables prosecutors to vilipend the accused's character, solidifying guilt. "Our system is guilty until proven innocent," stated another participant. And still another said, "Our system of justice is that we really don't look for justice for our defendants." Indeed, many nonattorneys mistakenly believe that a not guilty verdict means innocence. Even if acquitted in the justice system, the taint of guilt is permanently affixed.

An additional question concerning the presumption of innocence is raised through suicide. Do only guilty people kill themselves? According to Miller (2018), "[t]he New Jersey Supreme Court determined evidence of attempted suicide is admissible to show consciousness of guilt but requires the trial court to hold a hearing outside the presence of the jury to evaluate whether evidence of the suicide attempt supports an inference that the defendant was seeking to avoid prosecution."[4] Is suicide simply a "consciousness of guilt," or a psychological breaking point, even for an innocent person? An emotional participant stated, "I believe he was innocent. And still, he committed suicide."

Examining Mental Health

Negative life events (NLEs) are highly correlated with suicide attempts. Being confronted by the prospects of trial, prison sentence, legal fees, penalties, family embarrassment, public humiliation, and being labeled a criminal can lead to pretrial/noncustodial suicide. "It can be argued that

[4] Colin Miller, *Should Evidence of a Defendant's Suicide Attempt While Awaiting Trial Be Admissible?* Law Professor Blogs Network (Oct. 2018).

every white-collar criminal is a suspect for suicide as they all experience NLEs during the proceedings of the case" (Brody & Perri, 2016, at 789). When there is hopelessness, anguish, and fear, suicide is often the impulsive act used to end the suffering (Raison, 2012).

According to James and Glaze (2006), 40% to 60% of the *incarcerated* population have presented symptoms of a *Diagnostic and Statistical Manual of Mental Disorders IV* (*DSM-IV*) diagnosis, compared to 26.2% of the general population. Adults with mental illness, behavioral health disorders, substance use/addiction, and other maladies are overrepresented in the criminal justice system. Nearly 26% of jail inmates display signs of severe psychological distress, and there is a high rate of mental illness (e.g., depression, anxiety, bipolar, and/or schizophrenia spectrum disorder (Bronson & Berzofsky, 2017). Mental illness and/or substance use are linked to a higher incidence of arrests and incarceration.

The criminal justice system has become the primary point of contact and prison the primary warehouse for those with mental illnesses and substance use disorders. Psychological autopsies revealed that most people who died by suicide had suffered from mental health challenges (Bradvik, 2018; *see also* ch. 5, Psychological Autopsies). When threatened with incarceration and the fallout of involvement with the criminal justice system, any mental disturbance can be exacerbated (Collier, 2014). Attorney respondents who knew their clients had a previous history of mental health issues stated that the illness caused the associated crimes. "We have criminalized mental illness." Mental illness, when combined with impoverishment, predisposes a criminal response. "People with mental illness that trespass and steal are homeless."

The criminal justice system and, by extension, prisons have become the de facto solution to a vulnerable population: the mentally ill. In an article by Bao (2020), the author relates a story about a gentleman diagnosed with bipolar disorder. He refused to take his medication, and without understanding the consequences, continually broke the terms of a restraining order. Believing the man would receive better mental healthcare there, a judge ordered him to prison. Before transfer, the man hung himself in his jail cell. When individuals who are predisposed to mental illness are in pretrial/noncustodial status, the opportunity for suicide increases. However, this does not suggest that such persons should be confined pending adjudication. As one participant stated, "We need to look at mental health as the underlying issue and not how we can lock them away."

The deinstitutionalization and shifting of the mentally ill from long-term healthcare institutions to the justice system assumed that patients would receive better care and reduce state expenses. The outcome of this thought process has long been debated. Incarcerating those with mental disorders did not reduce care expenses, nor did it address the problem ethically. "A substantial portion of the prison population is not receiving treatment for mental health conditions. This treatment discontinuity has the potential to affect both recidivism and health care costs on release from prison" (Gonzalez & Connell, 2014, at 2328). Without adequate care, a desperate cycle of emotional turmoil is created: not only for the individuals, their families, and the community, but also for the attorneys who will ultimately be called upon to represent these individuals.

Potential Solutions

Suicide and its prevention have been studied extensively. This knowledge must be applied to the pretrial/noncustodial population, offering their defense counsel and family the appropriate tools to ameliorate the loss of life and the collateral fallout of suicide. Evidence suggests that the intersection of suicidal behavior and thoughts that encourage suicide, combined with depression and hopelessness, produce suicidal ideation (Mills & Kroner, 2008). Training defense attorneys to assist clients who are suicidal was identified as a topic for continuing legal education. "I probably did have clients [ideate], but I didn't think they were serious." Nearly 97% agreed that identifying suicidality and learning how to navigate it would be a welcome addition to the curriculum. More than half of the participants stated that they were unsure if they were equipped to deal with client suicide ideation. "We need to put our legal hats aside sometimes to find out what's best for someone's human life ... find a way ... without breaking ethical rules." (*See* ch. 10, Suicide in the Criminal Justice System.)

Many attorneys (88%) referred the client to a mental health professional even when suicide was not discussed. However, several stated that while they believed their client would benefit from a therapist, the money was not available. Some informed the client that they should not say anything about suicide. "If you say suicide, you're going to be locked up in a cell somewhere wearing a paper jumpsuit." Concern over attorney-client privilege was raised: "If you're making the family aware, you're violating attorney-client privilege in the worst way." Several participants stated they were unclear or unsure how to respond to suicide ideation in terms of reporting. Given the attorneys' disparate response to their clients, it is a subject that bears further exploration for ethical implications and perhaps further guidance for consistency. (*See* ch. 12, Suicide in the Criminal Justice System: Ethical Considerations.)

In concert with many law firms, the American Bar Association has recognized the need to address the psychological, emotional, and physical toll of the profession. Many are addressing attorney wellness, removing the stigma associated with mental health issues by creating a safe space for attorneys to discuss their concerns and challenges. Attorneys must learn to seek help when it is needed. "There are multiple crises going on. We don't ask for help," shared a participant. Trauma experiences such as client suicides can have lingering effects. "It's been 20 years ago. I still remember." Even a lack of attorney response—"I'm embarrassed to say it didn't affect me at all"—should be explored, to ensure that emotions are not erroneously blunted. When counsel can see that their disclosure will not be held against them or thwart their careers, more are likely to take advantage of systems designed to promote wellness.

The term *mass incarceration* has been widely used, discussed, researched, and the subject of much activism. Still, the United States is the world's leader as a carceral state, with 5% of the global population and 25% of its prisoners. "The U.S. locks up more people per capita than any other nation, at the staggering rate of 698 per 100,000 residents. El Salvador follows this at 614 per 100,000 and Turkmenistan at 583 per 100,000" (Prison Policy, 2020). Nearly every attorney interviewed voiced concerns about overcriminalization. As one attorney offered, "There are … other ways to handle this … other than prison." As a nation, we should re-examine the incarceration of individuals who would better serve their punishment through community service, seek alternatives to locking up juveniles, question why the aged and dying are languishing in prison, and address the disproportionate number of inmates with mental illness. Each participant expressed some flaw in our criminal justice system and the need to address these failings. Several participants suggested that more alternative courts be established for drug-related crimes, DUIs, and veterans. As a society that seeks punitive measures, we must recognize and accept that the cost of sending as many people as we do to jail/prison has a negative return on investment in both financial and human costs.

Conclusion

Research to predict and prevent suicide death of pretrial/noncustodial clients is needed. While society at large may be unsympathetic to this population and not make them a primary concern, these individuals matter to their family and their attorneys. An accounting of this phenomenon should be centralized and published. It is only through measurement that we can understand the problem's size and pervasiveness. Defense attorneys who may be in a unique position to identify a client's suicidality should receive continuing legal education for identification and management.

Attorney care and wellness are essential. Given the work's rigors and stress, attorneys are at greater risk for mental health challenges. Client suicide exacerbates the mental state of an already overburdened attorney. The stigma associated with mental health care must be eliminated. Environments that encourage dialogue, provide therapeutic assistance, and assure no repercussions for seeking help must be created.

Changes to our criminal justice system will not occur overnight, if at all. However, incremental changes can and should be made. We should seek to redirect the flow of the accused who are mentally ill or suffer from addictions. Those who served this country may be better served through mental health care than incarceration. Finally, we should ask ourselves if we are sending individuals to prison for no other reason than retribution or punitive motive. Is there a better solution for some individuals to recompense society without incarceration?

Chapter

3

Suicide in Prison

Kimberly Dawn Dodson

There are very few silver linings to the global pandemic cloud. However, one is that because of the outbreak of COVID in our jails and prisons, the public has been made more aware of the horrible conditions in these institutions. The public is shocked—shocked!—to learn that prisons are unhealthy, unsafe, and understaffed. Moreover, the public now seems to comprehend in a way it did not before that except for inmates sentenced to life in prison, virtually all will be released back into our communities. The barbaric conditions will not only further damage those who were already damaged going in, but also damage those who were not. We must dispel the myth that inmates are coddled.

This chapter by Professor Kimberly Dodson shows that jails and prisons, because of their dehumanizing environment, cause a shameful number of those incarcerated, as well as those merely accused, to believe that taking their lives is the only answer. The chapter also discusses how some populations are particularly vulnerable. Prosecutors and courts should be mindful of this data when prosecuting cases and imposing sentence. Defense lawyers should use this data to argue for mitigated sentences or, if possible, to divert clients away from a custodial sentence.

• • •

Prisons are undoubtedly a high-risk location for suicide attempts and suicide. Individuals who are justice-involved face a multitude of stressors that may exacerbate thoughts of suicide. First, individuals caught up in the criminal justice system must confront the fact that they will carry the label "criminal" or "offender," possibly for the rest of their lives. In many instances, their crimes have received a considerable amount of media attention and public scrutiny. As a result, incarcerated individuals also must face the fact that their reputations in the community have been irrevocably damaged. Public notoriety and backlash mean their families and friends may be the focus of harassment, judgment, and ridicule. Certainly, this can place a great deal of strain on the offender and his or her social support system.

Prisoners, particularly those with long sentences, must come to terms with the reality that the world will move on without them, and this may be anxiety-inducing. They must confront the fact that they will miss out on special life events, such as holidays, birthdays, anniversaries, graduations, and weddings. In addition, they will not be there to offer support to their children, resolve marital or relationship issues, or comfort or say goodbye to a dying loved one (Tartaro, 2018). These circumstances may intensify their feelings of loneliness, helplessness, and despair.

The nature of certain crimes often carries serious negative consequences once an individual is incarcerated. For example, the offenses of child molestation and rape, compared to burglary and theft, are considered taboo and viewed as widely unacceptable. In addition, such offenses garner substantial disapproval and condemnation from correctional staff and other prisoners. Prisoners may experience a significant amount of guilt and shame surrounding the nature of their crimes, which are added sources of emotional stress and psychological anxiety. Prisoners convicted of sexual offenses also may fear being physically injured, sexually assaulted, or killed while serving their sentences (James, 2015). This fear is not completely unfounded when one considers data gathered by the Associated Press that examined inmate deaths at San Quentin Prison in California. Data shows that male sex offenders are disproportionately murdered in comparison to the general prison population. Specifically, "male sex offenders made up about 15% of the prison population but accounted for nearly 30% of homicide victims" (*The Guardian*, 2015, Feb. 16, para. 4). Nevertheless, most prisoners, regardless of their crimes, reported that their number-one concern is physical safety, and this is especially true for first-time offenders (Listwan & Hanley, 2012). Research conducted by Fagan et al. (1993) suggests these safety concerns may be warranted, as first-time offenders are more vulnerable to violent victimization.

The presence of any of these factors may motivate offenders to contemplate or attempt suicide. Even individuals with strong coping skills may find it difficult to deal with the "pains of imprisonment," including the "deprivation of liberty, autonomy, security, heterosexual relationships, and goods and services" (Sykes, 1958, at 286-294). However, many individuals who end up behind bars often lack appropriate coping skills and do not have the capacity to resolve conflicts or stressors in prosocial ways. For instance, prior to incarceration, individuals may abuse alcohol and drugs to cope with stress or to self-medicate a mental health condition. Others may resort to violence to cope with stress and strain. Individuals carry these maladaptive coping skills with them when they enter prison.

It is incumbent on correctional staff and clinicians to identify and treat the serious medical needs of inmates (*Estelle v. Gamble*, 429 U.S. 97 (1976)), including mental health disorders (*Bowring v. Godwin*, 551 F.2d 4 (4th Cir. 1977)). The state of one's mental health is inexorably tied to suicidal ideations. Because suicide is one of the leading causes of death in prison, preventative measures must be put in place to reduce the likelihood of suicide. This chapter includes a discussion of the prevalence of suicide in prison, methods of suicide used by prisoners and what happens when a suicide occurs in prison, suicide risk and protective factors, and vulnerable populations. The chapter also discusses the importance of suicide risk assessments and screenings, the development and implementation of preventative practices, civil liability issues related to suicide, common causes of prison litigation, and how to avoid civil liability.

The Prevalence of Suicide in Detention

Annually, about 4,500 individuals die in state and federal prisons across the United States (Carson & Cowhig, 2020; Dodson, 2018). Suicide is the leading cause of death in juvenile facilities and jails and the fifth leading cause of death in prison (Noonan & Rohloff, 2015). Between 2000 and 2014, 4,134 jail inmates committed suicide, which represents 34% of all jail inmate deaths (Noonan & Rohloff, 2015). Between 2006 and 2016, 2,353 state prison inmates died by suicide (Statista Research Department, 2021). Although the data for jail inmates covers a 14-year time period and the prison inmates examines a 10-year period, the data demonstrates that suicide is a serious concern for those who are incarcerated. Recent data shows that the total rate of suicide among jail inmates is 47 per 100,000 individuals compared to 14 per 100,000 prison inmates (National Institute of Corrections, 2017).

The greater frequency of jail suicides compared to prisons suicides is related to the transient nature of jail populations in comparison to prison populations. Jails will experience a great deal of inmate turnover, resulting in close to 11 million admissions to jails each year (Sawyer & Wagner, 2020). The fact that jails deal with more prisoners naturally translates into a greater number of individuals who may commit suicide. Correctional staff in prisons have the opportunity to spend more time observing and getting to know the routines of those they supervise. This gives prison staff a distinct advantage because it is more likely they will recognize unusual behavior that may indicate an inmate is experiencing emotional distress and at an increased risk of suicide (Tartaro, 2018).

Methods of Committing Suicide While in Custody

The most common form of suicide among prisoners is and continues to be hanging or asphyxiation (Hayes, 2010). The reason for this is straightforward: this method and the instruments needed to commit suicide are readily available to inmates. Shoestrings, bedsheets, and clothing can be fashioned into makeshift nooses, and ligature or tie-off points are easy to locate in a prison cell. In fact, prisoners' cells seem to be the preferred location for committing suicide, with data showing that 87% of prisoners' suicides occurred in their cells (Mumola, 2005). Many suicides by hanging may go undetected because inmates have learned they can sit upright in their beds and still complete an act of suicide. A passing officer doing a bed check may not realize the inmate has committed suicide because it appears that the inmate is merely sitting on the bunk.

There are cases in which inmates have jumped from top tiers of housing units to kill themselves, but most facilities have instituted measures to prevent this as a method of suicide. Sharp-edged instruments, such as razors and "shanks" (homemade, knife-like weapons) also can be used to attempt or commit suicide, although this method is more easily detected by correctional officers making their rounds because of the presence of blood. In addition, cutting one's wrist rarely results in suicide completion (Tartaro, 2018), and inmates determined to commit suicide may know this information. Inmates may attempt to hide pills they receive during medical visits, but if they plan to overdose, it would mean they would have to hoard pills for weeks undetected. This, too, is unlikely because correctional officers routinely conduct cell searches for contraband. Therefore, hanging or asphyxiation remain the most practical options for committing suicide in prison.

What Happens When Suicide Occurs?

When a corrections officer discovers an inmate hanging in their cell, the officer attempts to determine if the inmate has vital signs or is able to be revived. If there are no signs of life, the cell is designated a crime scene and an investigation is launched. Typically, an outside agency will conduct the investigation. For example, if a federal inmate dies while in custody, the Federal Bureau of Investigation (FBI) will handle the case. In Texas, if an inmate dies in a state-run correctional facility, the Texas Rangers are called in to conduct the investigation. The investigators will document the scene with photographs, and in some instances, sketches of the scene will be completed. Once the documentation of the scene is complete, the individual's body is removed from the cell and transferred to a medical examiner's office for autopsy. For surviving friends and family, this is a difficult time. It may take months to receive the final autopsy report, and even then questions may linger about their loved one's death.

Family and friends on the outside are not the only ones grieving the passing of a loved one. The suicide of an inmate can have a ripple effect in the prison. Inmate-friends want the opportunity to grieve and honor the person who has passed. Allowing inmates to hold a memorial service gives them a positive outlet for their grief. Some prisons in the United States allow inmates to participate in every aspect of the memorial and/or funeral services. For example, in Louisiana, at Angola Prison, an inmate's coffin is made in the prison woodshop by a master prison carpenter. Inmates also create shrouds to adorn the coffin during the memorial and burial services. Finally, inmates also perform the memorial and burial services on the prison grounds for those who have passed but have no one to claim their bodies (Cain, 2012).

Correctional staff and mental health counselors must understand that the loss of a fellow inmate contributes to maladaptive coping strategies for the inmates left behind. For instance, an inmate may assault another inmate or staff member because anger is easier to express than sadness.

In the eyes of the inmates, anger shows strength and tears show weakness, the latter of which may leave them feeling vulnerable. The death of an inmate, especially by suicide, may create mental health crises for other inmates. It may not be unusual for those left behind to also contemplate suicide because they may have difficulty dealing with the pain and loss. (*See* ch. 16, Case Study: An Insider's View of Suicide in Prison.)

After a suicide occurs, prison wardens and administrators take a three-pronged approach to review suicide cases that includes an administrative review, a clinical mortality review, and a psychological autopsy (National Commission on Correctional Health Care [NCCHC], 2018). An administrative review evaluates correctional and emergency responses to an inmate's death. It involves a review of the incident and facility procedures used, training received by involved staff, and emergency response. The review may conclude with recommendations for changes in policy, training, physical environment, medical or mental health services, and/or operational procedures. The NCCHC (2018) recommends that correctional staff, not just administrators, participate in the review.

A clinical mortality review includes an assessment of the incident and facility procedures that were implemented, training received by the staff involved, relevant medical and mental health services records, and reports involving the inmate. Like the administrative review, the clinical mortality review should include recommendations for changes in policy, training, physical environment, medical or mental health services, and operational procedures as necessary. A *psychological autopsy* is a written reconstruction of a person's life emphasizing factors that may have led up to or contributed to the death. A psychologist or other qualified mental health professional performs the clinical autopsy that is based on a thorough review of all of the inmate's file information, a careful examination of the suicide site, and interviews with staff and inmates acquainted with the deceased. (*See* ch. 5, Psychological Autopsies.) The NCCHC (2018) requires the reviews to be completed within 30 days following an inmate suicide or death.

Suicide Risk Factors in Prison

Much of what we know about who commits suicide in prison mirrors who commits suicide in the general population. For example, men are more likely to commit suicide than women (Noonan & Rohloff, 2015).

In comparison, Whites attempt and complete suicide more often than Blacks and Hispanics (Kochanek et al., 2016). Older individuals, those over 50 years of age, also are at a greater risk for suicide attempts and completions (Barry et al., 2017; Carson & Cowhig, 2020). In addition, prisoners serving life sentences are more likely than other prisoners to commit suicide (Myslimaj & Dervishi, 2016).

Utilizing demographic characteristics alone to predict who will attempt or commit suicide is discouraged because this information may lead to false positives and false negatives (Pompili et al., 2009). False positives occur when inmates are identified as suicidal when, in fact, they are not. Conversely, false negatives occur when inmates are not identified as suicidal, but in reality they are suicidal. Correctional facilities often have limited resources to adequately supervise prisoners. Correctional staff and clinicians may overlook the false negatives because they are busy dedicating their time and attention to the false positives. Obviously, this is not an ideal situation, because correctional and medical staff may miss an opportunity to prevent an inmate's suicide.

There are other individual characteristics beyond demographic factors that provide clinicians with a more accurate picture of the risk of suicide. Suicide risk factors are classified into two categories: static and dynamic. Static factors are unchangeable or immutable. Demographic characteristics, such as gender, race, age, and sentence length, are static factors, but, again, they do not provide clinicians with all of the information they need to assess the risk of suicide. Other static factors that are useful include one's history of substance abuse, violence, self-harming behavior, prior suicide attempts, and present and past mental health diagnoses (Reeves & Tamburello, 2014).

Unlike static factors, dynamic factors are changeable or mutable. Dynamic factors in prison include receipt of bad news from home or court, disciplinary charges, incarceration-related conflicts, administrative segregation or housing changes, recent self-harming behaviors, and recent suicidal ideations and attempts (Tartaro, 2018). Research indicates that an inmate's coping ability is another dynamic factor, and targeting this ability for intervention may aid inmates in changing their perceptions and response to personal and institutional stressors and strains (Howells et al., 1999). Table 3.1 presents a detailed list of prison suicide risk factors, including demographic, historical, clinical, social and health-related, and environmental causes.

Table 3.1 Prison Suicide Risk Factors

Demographic Factors	Historical Factors	Clinical Factors	Social and Health-Related Factors	Environmental Factors
Age (i.e., > 50)	History of psychiatric treatment and/or mental illness	Hopelessness, worthlessness, or helplessness	Recent life crisis (e.g., bad news, loss of support, family conflict, death and bereavement)	Segregated housing unit, solitary confinement, or single cell
Gender (i.e., male)	Past inpatient psychiatric treatment	Suicidal ideas	Recent punitive sanctions (e.g., disciplinary reports, loss of privileges, and/or new charges)	Accessibility of ligature points
Gender identity	History of substance abuse	Anxiety, agitation, or irritation	Lengthy or unexpected sentence	Accessibility of instruments of self-harm (e.g., plastic utensils, bedsheets, shoelaces)
Race (i.e., White)	History of traumatic life events (e.g., childhood physical or sexual abuse, abandonment)	Impulsive, aggressive behaviors	Recent harassment (e.g., peer conflict, bullying, humiliation, and/or sexual assault)	
Sexual orientation	Past suicide attempts	Unwilling to accept help	No social or family visits	
Marital status (single, separated, divorced, or widowed)	Family history of suicide	Depression or agitated or dysphoric depression	Loneliness	
Low educational attainment	Conviction of a violent crime against a person (e.g., homicide, rape, child molestation)	Personality disorder	Disability	
	First incarceration	Psychosis or psychosis with delusions of impending doom	Chronic physical or terminal illness	

Suicide Protective Factors in Prison

Although the identification of suicide risk factors is important, it also is important to recognize protective factors that reduce the risk of suicide. Table 3.2 lists some of the factors that are associated with a lower risk of suicide.

It may seem counterintuitive that inmates can express hopefulness and optimism, but their participation in rehabilitation and treatment programs can help them foster positive coping skills. Individual and group counseling encourages inmates to accept responsibility for their crimes, while helping to alleviate the guilt or shame they carry with them about the nature of their crimes and/or their incarceration. The ability to cite reasons for living and making plans for the future demonstrate an optimistic view of life, which reduces the likelihood of suicide. Connections with family, friends, and the community help inmates to feel supported as well as making them feel they are valued as human beings.

Everyone needs to feel they have a purpose in life. This may be especially true for those behind bars. Inmates often are assigned jobs during incarceration that may include food service, maintenance, grounds keeping, and industrial manufacturing. These purposeful activities, as with social support, make prisoners feel they have value as human beings and they have a reason to make it through another day of incarceration.

Table 3.2 Prison Suicide Protective Factors

- Hopefulness, optimism
- Future-oriented thinking, behavior, and plans
- Ability to cite reasons for living
- Good social support
- Purposeful activity
- Cultural or religious beliefs that discourage suicide
- Willingness to accept help and/or treatment
- Compliance with effective treatment (e.g., adherence to medication regimes, treatment appointments)
- Stable mood or low symptom severity
- Absence of suicidal ideas or intent

Participating in faith-based (Dodson et al., 2011) and educational programs (Braswell et al., 2017) also helps inmates cope with incarceration.

Inmates who are willing to accept help for mental illness and adhere to medical treatment plans report lower levels of anxiety and depression, which reduces the chances of suicidal ideations and attempts (Alexopoulos et al., 2009). Treatment compliance results in the stabilization of mood disorders and reduces the severity of mental health symptoms, thus working together to decrease suicidal ideations and attempts (Pompili et al., 2014). A suicide risk assessment performed by qualified clinicians and mental health care providers is a crucial step in suicide prevention.

Vulnerable Populations

Correctional policies may be detrimental to transgender inmates because of limited access to transgender-related medical care (Drakeford, 2018). Correctional policies also may result in transgender inmates being exposed to greater levels of gender-based victimization. Transgender inmates often have magnified adjustment issues to incarceration because correctional policies fail to address appropriate housing arrangements for this population. When inmates are sent to a correctional facility, they are assigned to prisons based on their assigned sex at birth, not their gender identity. Transgender women who end up in prisons for men experience physical and sexual violence more often in comparison to other inmates. For instance, a study of California prisons found that 60% of transgender inmates reported that they had been sexually assaulted compared to 5% of incarcerated men (Jenness et al., 2007). Related research shows that inmates also are targeted for physical and sexual violence based on their sexual orientation, particularly male inmates who are smaller in stature and have effeminate characteristics (Tewskbury, 1989).

Sexual assault victims in prisons report increased psychological distress, including anxiety, depression, crying, flashbacks, sleep difficulty, and nightmares (Wolff & Shi, 2009). Physical and psychological trauma coupled with mental health issues is a recipe for suicide. A study conducted by Drakeford (2018) found that transgender inmates who experienced gender-based victimization are more likely to report lifetime suicide attempts. Lesbian, gay, bisexual, transgender, queer, and intersex (LGBTQI) prisoners have higher levels of anxiety and depression and higher rates of suicide and suicide attempts (National Institute of Corrections, 2011). Suicide among LGBTQI individuals is exacerbated by the use of protective custody or administrative segregation. Segregated housing units have the highest rates of suicides and suicide attempts (Marksamer & Tobin, 2013). However, it seems correctional facilities use segregated units/cells as the default solution for LGBTQI housing. Gender identity, gender expression, and sexual orientation are not legitimate reasons to segregate these inmates from the general prison population. Correctional administrators and staff must create policies and practices that are nondiscriminatory as well as providing for the safety and security of those housed in prison.

Suicide Prevention in Prison

Today, much is known about the risk factors related to suicide. As previously discussed, we know there are static and dynamic factors that play a significant role in identifying inmates at risk of committing suicide. Research tells us that the first month of incarceration is the most critical period when inmates may decide to kill themselves (Mumola, 2005). We also know that the most common form of suicide in prison involves hanging or asphyxiation and that inmates typically attempt or commit suicide in their cells. With this knowledge, correctional facilities can develop, implement, and utilize preventative practices.

Suicide Risk Assessment and Screening

A prisoner's denial of suicidal intent is an inadequate assessment of the risk of suicide. Instead, a systematic risk assessment that includes several diagnostic instruments/methods must be utilized. Also, psychiatrists or clinicians should conduct a psychiatric risk assessment of client-inmates contemporaneous with their admission to a correctional facility. Suicide and suicide attempts frequently occur within the first 30 days of confinement (Rabuy, 2016), although there is some empirical evidence suggesting that the first week of confinement is the most critical (Mumola, 2005). Therefore, mental health practitioners working in prison settings must act quickly to assess the prisoners' suicide risk.

The most popular risk assessment tool used in correctional settings is the Chronological Assessment of Suicide Events (CASE) interview method. The CASE interview aids clinicians in gathering crucial data from four proximate time periods: 1) presenting suicidal ideation/behavior, (2) recent suicidal ideation/behaviors, (3) past suicidal ideation/behaviors, and (4) immediate suicidal ideation (Knoll, 2010; Shea, 1998). The strength of the CASE interview is that it leads clinicians toward a more comprehensive, reliable interview that reduces the probability of omitting important information or questions. Clinicians begin with an extensive exploration of the presenting event (e.g., self-harm and/or suicide attempt) over the past two days. Next, the evaluator shifts the focus to any self-harming or suicidal behaviors within the past two months. Previous suicide attempts are explored with a focus on the most serious attempts. Finally, the evaluator returns to the immediate situation and examines the patient's present suicidal intent and plans. Table 3.3 includes sample interview questions that may be used by clinicians to assess suicide risk. Although the interview questions were designed for people in the general population, they are certainly relevant in a prison setting.

Table 3.3 CASE Suicide Risk Interview Questions

Initial questions

- Have you ever felt that life was not worth living? (Follow up with specific questions that ask about thoughts of death, self-harm, or suicide.)
- How does the future look to you?
- Have things ever reached the point that you've thought of harming yourself?

After acknowledgment of suicidal ideation

- What led up to the thoughts (e.g., losses or symptoms)?
- How often have those thoughts occurred (frequency, intensity, controllability)?
- How close have you come to acting on those thoughts?
- How likely do you think it is that you will act on them in the future?
- What do you envision happening if you actually killed yourself (e.g., escape, reunion with significant other, rebirth, reactions of others)?
- Have you made a specific plan to harm or kill yourself? (If so, what does the plan include?)
- Do you have access to any means to kill yourself (pills or razor blades)?
- Have you made any preparations (e.g., hoarding pills, writing a note, taking steps to avoid discovery, rehearsing)?
- What things would lead you to feel more (or less) hopeful about the future (e.g., treatment, reconciliation of relationship, resolution of stressors)?
- What things would make it more (or less) likely that you would try to kill yourself?

Table 3.3 CASE Suicide Risk Interview Questions (*Continued*)

- What things in your life make you want to go on living?
- If you began to have thoughts of harming or killing yourself again, what would you do?

After attempted suicide or self-harm

- Can you describe what happened (e.g., circumstances, precipitants, view of future, use of substances, method, intent, seriousness of injury)?
- What thoughts were you having beforehand that led up to the attempt?
- What did you think would happen (e.g., going to sleep vs. injury vs. dying, getting a reaction out of a particular person)?
- Were other people present at the time?
- Did you seek help afterward yourself, or did someone get help for you?
- Had you planned to be discovered, or were you found accidentally?
- How did you feel afterward (e.g., relief vs. regret at being alive)?

For repeated suicidal ideas or attempts

- About how often have you tried to harm (or kill) yourself?
- When was the most recent time?
- Can you describe your thoughts at the time that you were thinking most seriously about suicide?
- When was your most serious attempt at harming or killing yourself?
- What led up to it, and what happened afterward?

Adapted from the American Psychiatric Association's *Practice Guideline for Assessment and Treatment of Patients with Suicidal Behaviors*, 2010.

A one-on-one interview gives clinicians an opportunity to demonstrate empathy toward their clients and build trust and rapport. CASE describes this interviewing technique as "shame attenuation" (Shea, 1998, at 59). Clinicians who utilize shame attenuation increase the likelihood that clients will be honest about their mental health histories as well as their present mental health concerns. Clinicians must learn to ask questions that are non-threatening and attempt to see things through the eyes of their patients. In doing so, the clinician decreases the hesitancy clients may have about sharing personal information (Knoll, 2010). Clinicians must have an awareness of the underlying defense mechanisms and distortions in thinking of their clients and when asking them questions. For example, instead of asking, "Do you have a bad temper and tend to pick fights?" the clinician using shame attenuation might ask, "Do you find others tend to pick fights with you, when you are just trying to do your own time?" (Knoll, 2010, at 193). The revised version of the original question is non-threatening and, in all likelihood, will result in the disclosure of the information the clinician will use to assess the inmate-client.

Ideally, screening would be conducted by a trained psychiatrist or clinician, but the scarce resources in many correctional facilities prohibits this possibility. Screening instruments that are suitable for use in a correctional setting should be short and simple. After completing a training course, corrections officers or other non-mental health staff members should be able to administer simple evaluations (Teplin & Swartz, 1989). The Referral Decision Scale (RDS) is specifically designed for incarcerated populations, but serious questions remain about its validity (Veysey et al., 1998). The Brief Jail Mental Health Survey (BJMHS) is one response to questions about the validity of the RDS. The BJMHS gathers data on more current indicators of crisis compared to RDS. Also, the BJMHS includes more information about dynamic risk factors. The BJMHS consists of eight items. Studies of the validity of the BJMHS are more favorable compared to the RDS (Kroner et al., 2011). Other promising tools are The Suicide Potential Scale (9 items), the Suicide Checklist (25 items), The Suicide Concerns for Offenders in Prison Environment (SCOPE) (28 items), and The Suicide Probability Scale (36 items). Each of these instruments has been tested with correctional populations, with varying results, although most produce valid measures of suicide risk (Perry et al., 2010).

It is important to note that inmates who are experiencing a crisis or a mental health problem that affects their functioning need to be assessed with more in-depth methods. This includes working with a mental health professional and undergoing more extensive evaluations. Ideally, each inmate would receive full evaluations at the time of admission, but that is not always practical. Tartaro (2018, at 243) notes that, "Instead, a recommended practice is to view the short instruments as screening tools for triage purposes." For instance, the Texas Department of Criminal Justice (TDCJ) uses standardized diagnostic interviews to evaluate inmates for symptoms of psychiatric illness, current suicidal ideation, prior suicidal behavior, and history of mental health treatment or hospitalizations (Tartaro, 2018). Following the screening, staff members may feel the need to refer inmates for a full mental health evaluation with a master's-level mental health professional or practitioner (Bailargeon et al., 2009). The American Psychiatric Association (2000) recommends referring inmates in need of further assessment to a psychiatrist or an appropriately licensed mental health professional. In some situations, it may be clinically necessary to forego the brief mental health assessment and go straight to the comprehensive examination. (*See* ch. 10, Suicide in the Criminal Justice System.)

Civil Liability in Prison Suicide Cases

For many Americans, the alleged suicide of Sandra Bland in the Waller County Jail in Hempstead, Texas, put inmate suicide at the center of national conversations about the treatment of those in custody. Sandra Bland was pulled over for failing to signal during a lane change. She was pulled over by Trooper Brian Encinia and issued a ticket for the violation. However, the encounter between the two escalated into a verbal argument and Encinia instructed Bland to exit her vehicle. She refused his initial request and he threatened to use a taser if she did not comply. Bland exited the vehicle and Encinia alleged that she kicked him and she was charged with "assaulting a public servant" (Collister, 2017, Sept. 16, para. 4). On intake, jail personnel asked her whether she was having thoughts of suicide. Records show she indicated that she had attempted suicide in the past, but she was not currently having such thoughts (Montgomery, 2019). However, she did disclose that she had a history of depression and that she was feeling depressed at the time of her booking. Three days later she allegedly hanged herself in her cell. Her family filed a wrongful death suit and they were awarded a $1.9 million settlement (Montgomery, 2019). Although Bland died in a county lockup, other high-profile prison suicides have grabbed national headlines, including the suicides of former NFL player Aaron Hernandez and financier Jeffrey Epstein. As with the Sandra Bland case, lawsuits for deliberate indifference or wrongful death can cost correctional facilities millions of dollars.

Deliberate indifference lawsuits are litigated in federal courts under Title 42 of the United States Code (U.S.C.), § 1983, commonly known as *1983 claims*. In the majority of lawsuits for cases involving suicide in prison, plaintiffs claim that the reckless disregard of the inmate's mental health and physical safety constituted a violation of the Eighth Amendment's guarantee against "cruel and unusual punishment." In such lawsuits, plaintiffs must demonstrate, by a preponderance of the evidence, that the actions of correctional staff and/or prison medical personnel showed "deliberate indifference" (*Estelle v. Gamble*, 429 U.S. 97 (1976)). Deliberate indifference is a high legal hurdle to surmount because mere negligence is not sufficient to establish deliberate indifference. The negligence standard only requires that a person should have done something, and did not. Deliberate indifference, in contrast, requires the plaintiffs to demonstrate that an inmate faced the possibility of serious harm and officials disregarded the obvious risk of such serious harm. This legal standard does not require proof of intent to harm, nor that prison personnel explicitly meant for the prisoner to die. Rather, plaintiffs must show not only that prison personnel failed to do what was necessary to prevent a prisoner's suicide, but also that they knew the prisoner was at risk and deliberately avoided clearly established standard procedures to intervene or prevent it from happening. The preventative steps do not necessarily have to be the best precautions, but they must be reasonable (Denton, 2019).

In *Bowring v. Godwin* (551 F.2d 4 (4th Cir. 1977)), a federal court ruled that there is no fundamental distinction between the right to medical care for physical illness or psychological or psychiatric illness. Serious mental health conditions include any serious disorder of thought or mood that substantially impairs one's judgment, behavior, capacity to recognize reality, or cope with everyday demands of life in a prison environment (consent decree, *Dunn v. Voinovich*, Docket 93-0166 (S.D. Ohio 1995); 42 U.S.C. § 1983). A professionally diagnosed mental illness is considered "serious" if the symptoms can be alleviated and it represents substantial harm if left untreated (Daniel, 2009). Prison mental health practitioners and clinicians are expected to exercise the same due care they would for patients in the community (*Stepakoff v. Kantar*, 393 Mass. 836 (1983)). A dispute between an inmate-client and a mental health professional regarding diagnosis or choice of treatment is not considered a constitutional violation. Similarly, a difference of opinion between two mental health professionals about a diagnosis or treatment decision does not represent a constitutional violation (Daniel, 2009).

Prison or jail officials, governmental agencies, and private service providers can be held liable for deliberate indifference (*Monell v. New York Department of Social Services*, 436 U.S. 658 (1978)). Psychiatrists employed by departments of corrections are not immune to liability. Also, part-time employees, consultants, or contract physicians do not have blanket immunity because these healthcare professionals are acting under the authority of state law. Unlike mental health and medical professionals working in a prison, psychiatrists working in mental health facilities have qualified immunity for cases involving negligence. *Qualified immunity* is a type of legal immunity. In essence, "[q]ualified immunity balances two important interests—the need to hold public officials accountable when they exercise power irresponsibly and the need to shield officials from harassment, distraction, and liability when they perform their duties reasonably" (*Pearson v. Callahan*, 494 F.3d 891 (10th Cir. 2009), at 897).

Common Causes for Litigation Related to Prisoner Suicide

An examination of several court decisions reveals some common failures in prison settings regarding suicide that leave them vulnerable to civil liability claims under 42 U.S.C. § 1983. Such failures can occur at multiple points along a continuum of care that includes identifying risk of self-harm or suicide, diagnosis and treatment of mental health conditions and disorders, and administrative responsibilities. Table 3.4 presents some of the most common failures of care that result in litigation.

Table 3.4 Prison Litigation Related to Suicide

- An inadequate mental health and psychiatric examination (*Comstock v. McCrary*, 273 F.3d 693 (6th Cir. 2001); *Steele v. Shah*, 87 F.3d 1266 (11th Cir. 1996)).
- Failure to consider clear and substantial risk factors in assessing an inmate's potential for suicide (*Williams v. Mehra*, 186 F.3d 686 (6th Cir. 1999)).
- Failure to place an inmate on suicide watch or administer suicide precautions once it is obvious that there is a substantial risk (*Holland v. City of Atmore,* 168 F. Supp. 2d 1303 (S.D. Ala. 2001)).
- Failure to communicate medical treatment or actions taken by treatment providers (*Woodward v. Myres*, No. 00 C 6010, 99 C 0290 (N.D. Ill. Dec. 4, 2002)) or to custody and correctional staff.
- Failure to adequately monitor an inmate on suicide watch and maintain an appropriate observation log (*Brown v. Plata,* 563 U.S. 493 (2011)).
- Discontinuation of suicide watch for an inmate despite the prior knowledge of suicidal behavior or potential continued risk (*Brown v. Plata,* 563 U.S. 493 (2011)).

Table 3.4 Prison Litigation Related to Suicide (*Continued*)

- Failure to follow policies and procedures related to suicide risk assessment (*Woodward v. Myres*. No. 00 C 6010, 99 C 0290 (N.D. Ill. Dec. 4, 2002)), intervention, and prevention.
- Failure to provide adequate training to correctional officers and staff (*Thomas v. Cumberland County Correctional Facility,* No. 1:2009cv01323, Document 167 (D.N.J. 2012)).
- Abrupt discontinuation of psychotropic medications for inmates who are known to have made a serious suicide attempt in the recent past (*Washington v. Walter Harper,* 494 U.S. 210 (1990)).
- Grossly inadequate treatment by professional standards or the lack of treatment plans, policies, procedures, or staff, creating a "grossly inadequate mental health care" system (*Plata v. Brown,* 427 F. Supp. 3d 1211 (N.D. Cal. 2013)).
- Repeated instances of delayed or denied medical or mental health treatment (*Estelle v. Gamble*, 429 U.S. 97 (1976)).

Avoiding Liability

The court decisions reviewed here are instructive for developing risk-management strategies for administrative, clinical, and correctional staff. The development and implementation of a set of comprehensive suicide prevention policies and practices is the best defense against civil liability. Mental health and suicide prevention training are essential components of any comprehensive set of policies and practices for reducing the likelihood of lawsuits. In 2007, the World Health Organization created guidelines for correctional facilities to follow in an effort to decrease the number of inmate suicides worldwide. Today, these guidelines continue to be used to develop and implement evidence-based practices and policies for the prevention of suicide in prison. Prison administrators must be on the forefront of developing suicide prevention policies and practices. Suicide prevention policies must clearly and consistently communicate to all correctional personnel the expectations for the implementation and application of the policies. Prison administrators also must provide the resources needed to support corrections officers and medical personnel who will be on the front lines of suicide prevention. Table 3.5 presents a list of strategies that can be useful for suicide prevention and avoiding civil liability.

Table 3.5 Suicide Prevention Strategies

- Provide suicide prevention training and periodic refresher courses for all administrative, clinical, and correctional staff.
- Consider suicide risk in inmate housing, cell placement, and work assignments.
- Ensure prompt transfer of mental health records of high-risk inmates between facilities and obtain detailed information from jails at the time of admission to prisons.
- Develop measures for handling verbal and nonverbal communications of intent to commit suicide.
- Provide 24-hour access to emergency medical and mental health care.
- Place inmates on suicide watch in the line of sight or a special observation cell.
- Rigorously maintain a suicide watch observation log.
- Obtain written clearance from mental health staff before transferring an inmate who has been on suicide watch to general population or to another housing location.

Conclusion

Suicide in prison is a serious issue and it demands attention. Prisoners are more likely to report childhood physical and sexual abuse, neglect, homelessness, job instability, unstable relationships, substance abuse, mental health disorders, and past suicidal ideations and suicide attempts. It is important that correctional staff and medical professionals working in prisons understand the historical, social, and clinical factors that culminated in the incarceration of those they serve. Corrections officers and medical personnel should be trained to identify inmates at risk for suicide, especially vulnerable populations, and how to respond appropriately to a mental health crisis. Correctional facilities should have comprehensive plans, policies, and practices in place to ensure that they have effective measures to identify suicidal inmates and prevent suicide. A comprehensive prevention strategy serves two important purposes: the likelihood of inmate suicide is significantly reduced, and correctional administrators and personnel are less likely to be the target of civil litigation.

• • •

Kimberly Dodson is an Associate Professor and Criminology Program Director in the Department of Social and Cultural Sciences at the University of Houston-Clear Lake. She earned her Ph.D. in criminology from Indiana University of Pennsylvania. Prior to working in academia, Dr. Dodson was a deputy sheriff and criminal investigator for the Greene County Sheriff's Department in Greeneville, Tennessee. As a criminal investigator, she worked cases primarily involving the sexual abuse and exploitation of juveniles. Her research interests include correctional policy and program evaluation and justice-involved individuals with special needs. Dr. Dodson is a member of the Academic Offenders Program at UHCL and she teaches at the Ramsey Unit in Rosharon, Texas. In addition, she is currently consulting on a Texas death penalty case for a death-row inmate who has special needs. Professor Dodson's email is dodsonk@ uhcl.edu.

Complete citations are available from the author upon request.

Chapter

4

Recognizing and Addressing the Problem of Suicide Following Incarceration

Tracy D. Gunter
Kyle D. Webster
Sandra K. Antoniak

In his compelling book Halfway Home: Race, Punishment, and the Afterlife of Mass Incarceration, *Reuben Jonathan Miller meticulously describes the obstacles faced by individuals who have been released from prison and jail. Miller shows that for all too many, try as they might, there is simply no escape from the collateral consequences of conviction. This chapter by Drs. Tracy D. Gunter, Kyle D. Webster, and Sandra K. Antoniak continues that discussion. For most, the emotional scars of incarceration are permanent. Indeed, many entered institutions already scarred, whether by poverty, mental illness, substance abuse, or trauma. As such, they are uniquely vulnerable to suicide.*

As a nation, we are closely examining ways to appropriately reduce our jail and prison populations. Given the large numbers of those who are incarcerated, facilitating a smooth reentry with material as well as psychological support for individuals reentering society is imperative.

• • •

The experience of incarceration is far more common in the adult population in the United States than many people realize. Each year in the U.S., over 7 million people are released from jails, and over half a million people are released from prisons (https://www.healthypeople.gov/2020/topics-objectives/topic/social-determinants-health/interventions-resources/incarceration). Overall, one in 100 adults has been incarcerated in a prison or jail (Maruschak & Minton, 2020).

The burden of incarceration is not distributed evenly in the population. People who become incarcerated have often experienced significant health disparities and social inequalities prior to incarceration (Western & Pettit 2010). In particular, incarcerated people are more likely to suffer from infectious disease, mental health disorders, and substance use disorders than people who have not been incarcerated (American Academy of Family Physicians, 2015); and, even with this increased disease burden, are more likely to be medically underserved (Dumont et al., 2012). People who have been incarcerated are also more likely to have lower incomes, less education, and be unemployed (Rabuy & Kopf, 2015).

Although correctional facilities provide some services, they are often stressful places to live and are ill-equipped to address this disadvantaged and medically underserved population; thus, incarceration appears to only worsen the plight of an already disadvantaged population (National Research Council, 2014; Prison Policy Initiative, 2015). For some inmates, placement in a facility may offer some protection by providing safe housing, limited access to substances of abuse, predictable meals, and access to health screenings and basic health care. However, rates of suicide during periods of incarceration are much higher than for the general population (Dixon et al., 2020), and this increased risk of death persists after release. Any protection or advantage offered by incarceration quickly erodes after release because jails and prisons frequently return former inmates to the community with minimal financial resources, no job, no housing, and no health care. The newly released persons must then find housing, employment, and ways to meet their basic needs, in addition to integrating themselves into the families and communities from which they have been absent. Following incarceration, returning citizens are more likely to look for jobs and less likely to be employed than people in the general population (Prison Policy Initiative, 2018).

The process of entering the community after a period of confinement is difficult and one manifestation of this difficulty is the high risk of death following release from secure confinement (Kouyoumdjian et al., 2016; Phillips et al., 2017; Prison Policy Initiative, 2017; Webb et al., 2011). Incarceration is estimated to shorten life expectancy by more than 4 years for men and more than 10 years for women (Kouyoumdjian et al., 2016). Independent risk factors for increased mortality after release from confinement include homelessness, substance use disorders, and the use of psychiatric medications while incarcerated (Binswanger et al., 2016). See Table 4.1 for an overview of some of the risk factors associated with death after incarceration. The majority of these deaths are due to violence and substance-related causes, (van Dooren, Kinner, & Forsyth, 2013), including overdoses, transportation accidents, suicide, and homicide

Table 4.1 Selected Studies Demonstrating Excess Risk of Death After Incarceration

Source	Modifier/Variable	Increase in Risk for Death by Any Cause
Binswanger (2007)	White	3.8
	Black	2.3
	Male	3.3
	Female	5.5
	Age 18–24 years old	3.4
	Age ≥ 45 years old	2.7
Spittal (2017)	Opiate use	2.2
	Two or more sentences	1.5
	Problematic alcohol use	1.5
	Antidepressant prescription confinement	1.9
Binswanger (2016)	Homelessness	1.5
	Injection drug use	1.5
	Tobacco use	1.5
	Cirrhosis (liver disease)	4.4
	Psychiatric medication prescribed at release	2.3
Chang (2015)	Substance use disorders	1.6
Wildeman & Anderson (2020)	Solitary confinement	4.5

Table 4.2 Selected Studies Demonstrating Excess Risk of Death by Suicide After Incarceration

Source	Modifier/Variable	Increase in Risk for Death by Suicide
Pratt (2010)	Released from jail	2.3
	History of alcohol misuse	2.4
	History of self-harm	2.0
	Any psych diagnosis	2.1
Spittal (2014)	# Prior imprisonment(s)	3.1
	≥ 5 marriages	0.4*
Haglund (2014)	Any previous psych history	3.5
	Prior suicide attempt	3.6
	Psychotic disorder	2.4
	Substance use history	3.1
Brinkley-Rubinstein (2019)	Restrictive housing	1.7

*When increased risk is less than 1.0, the factor decreases risk.

(Hakannson & Berglund, 2013). Of these causes of death, suicide is generally thought to be the most common cause of non-natural death among people recently released from jails and prisons (Binswanger et al., 2011; Phillips et al., 2017). See Table 4.2 for an overview of some of the risk factors associated with suicide after confinement.

Although deaths that occur in facilities are rather extensively investigated using standard protocols, most deaths that occur in the community are not examined beyond a determination of cause of death. Thus, less is known about what happens to people who die after they return to the community after confinement. All too often, people assume that the former inmate will somehow find their place in a society that will accept their reentry. Former inmates, however, commonly were not integrated into their communities prior to incarceration, and continue to experience trauma and lack resources at the time of reentry (Pettus-Davis, Renn, & Kennedy 2020). This cumulative burden contributes to the high death rate after confinement. (*See* ch. 9, Pretrial, Probation, and Parole.)

The study of preventable death after confinement has become more frequent in the past 25 years, and suicide has been noted to be a major contributor to this phenomenon. In this chapter, we shall focus on death by suicide after confinement and summarize the known demographic, mental health, and criminal justice system risk factors associated with suicide following confinement. We will then move to a discussion of interventions that may mitigate the risk of death by suicide following confinement and conclude with ways to improve the understanding of suicide after confinement. We firmly believe that the things that would mitigate the risk of suicide after incarceration would also result in fewer deaths of former inmates by all causes and less criminal recidivism.

Demographic Factors

There are several broad categories of risk factors that impact the statistical likelihood that a person will die by suicide after incarceration. Most people who die by suicide following release from confinement in the United States are unmarried Caucasian men, usually either young adults or of advancing years (Barry et al., 2017; Pratt et al., 2006; Rosen et al., 2008; Spittal et al., 2014; Spittal et al., 2017; van Dooren et al., 2013; Webb et al., 2011; Zlodre & Fazel, 2012).

The data concerning race and gender, in part, reflects the greater proportion of Caucasian men in society overall and in confinement. Women and members of minority groups have lower baseline rates of death by suicide in the general population, but incarceration dramatically increases their risks of death by suicide following release from confinement (Binswanger et al., 2007; Pratt et al., 2006; Sirdifield, Brooker, & Marples, 2020; Spittal et al., 2014; Zlodre & Fazel, 2012). Incarceration differentially impacts persons of color, and the experience of incarceration dramatically raises their risk of death by suicide over their never-incarcerated similarly aged peers.

Men are more likely to be held in prisons and women are more likely to be held in jails (Prison Policy Institute, 2019). Jails generally are places of crisis and have shorter lengths of stay, less information about the people being admitted, and fewer resources than prisons for evaluating and treating those who are incarcerated. The rate of death by suicide is higher in jails than prisons, as is the death rate following release. Whether incarcerated in jail or prison, women who have been incarcerated are far more likely to die by suicide than their community matched peers. The burdens of disadvantage, trauma, substance use, and mental illness are greater for incarcerated women than for incarcerated men, and the increased risk of suicide is much higher for previously incarcerated women than for previously incarcerated men.

Former inmates who die by suicide are also frequently homeless (Lim et al., 2012) and are statistically more likely to live in poverty, be unemployed, suffer from addiction and mental illness, and struggle with physical illness than people who have not been incarcerated. Reports generally suggest that employment and access to health care should be protective, but no data were available on the impact of health care and employment on the rate of death by suicide after confinement.

Marriage is the most robust demographic factor known to be a protective factor against suicide after confinement (Sirdifield, Brooker, & Marples 2020; Spittal et al., 2014), but not universally identified as a protective factor. Having health insurance following release from confinement has been associated with decreased suicidal ideation following release (Yu et al., 2013).

Mental Health Risk Factors

Perhaps unsurprisingly, histories of traumatic life experience, personality disorders, substance use disorders, mental illness, and suicide-related behavior prior to incarceration are associated with increased risk of suicide-related behavior and death by suicide after release (Gunter et al., 2011; Haglund et al., 2014; Pratt et al., 2010; Spittal et al., 2017).

Individuals who have a history of substance use disorder prior to incarceration are at increased risk of dying by suicide following release from confinement, regardless of the particular substance abused (Haglund et al., 2014). Incarcerated persons who suffer from a mood disorder (depression, bipolar disorder, etc.) and/or a psychotic disorder (schizophrenia, schizoaffective disorder, etc.) are three to five times more likely to die as the result of suicide following incarceration than other releasees (Pratt et al., 2010; Sirdifield, Brooker, & Marples 2020).

People with prior suicide attempts and prior acts of self-injury are also at elevated risk of dying by suicide when compared to other releasees who do not have a history of suicide-related behavior (Spittal et al., 2017). The risk of death by suicide following release is also heightened when symptoms related to medical and mental health problems are severe enough to attract staff attention or require care during incarceration (King et al., 2015; Pratt et al., 2010; Spittal et al., 2017).

Criminal Justice Risk Factors

Risk factors for death by suicide following release from confinement are also related to criminal justice history. Individuals who have been in jails have higher rates of death following release than those still in jails (Alex et al., 2017) and those released from prisons (Pratt et al., 2010). Frequent incarceration and short duration of incarceration are risk factors for increased risk of death by suicide following release, particularly for former jail inmates (Thigpen et al., 2010). Longer duration of incarceration and past experience of incarceration mitigate the risk of death by suicide following release from confinement, particularly for prison inmates.

Individuals who have histories of impulsive or violent behavior are more likely than other incarcerated people to die by suicide following release from confinement. If someone spent time in restrictive housing, they were more likely to die by non-natural causes following release than someone who had not spent time in solitary confinement, and this risk increases with the number of stays in solitary confinement and the total length of time spent in solitary confinement (Brinkely-Rubenstein et al., 2019; Luigi et al., 2020; Wildeman & Anderson, 2020).

While incarcerated persons have a constitutional right to health care, they also often bring with them higher levels of healthcare needs resulting from cumulative care disparities experienced prior to confinement. Jail and prison administrators may lack knowledge or experience in running health systems, may have varying resources to pay the costs of interventions, and may be in locations in which resources are unavailable. These factors limit the amount and quality of care that is available to each incarcerated individual in need of health services (Freudenberg & Heller, 2016; National Research Council, 2014).

There were no studies located for this review that specifically examine whether health care rendered in-facility is evidence-based or would be generally accepted as meeting the community standard of care (The Pew Charitable Trusts, 2017). However, anecdotal evidence suggests that only a minority of people who receive treatment while incarcerated receive evidence-based care and appropriate wrap-around services following release from confinement (Prison Policy Initiative, 2020). Incarceration is generally associated with decreased life expectancy, with life expectancy falling with each year of incarceration (Prison Policy Initiative, 2017).

Once released, the formerly incarcerated individual no longer has a constitutional right to health care and is left to negotiate a fragmented and short-staffed system of care in the community, often with minimal resources to overcome barriers such as transportation, medical fees, and medication costs (Marks & Turner, 2014). Additionally, the record of health care received by individuals in the community frequently does not accompany them into confinement, nor does the record of health care received in the facility follow the person back to the community after release from confinement (National Research Council, 2014).

Discussion

The criminal justice system supervises some of society's most disadvantaged people, and incarcerated persons are among the most disadvantaged. People who have been incarcerated typically have lower educational achievement, poorer job skills, and fewer social attachments. Factors such as homelessness, substance use disorders, and mental illness are common in low-income communities and are all associated with both incarceration and reincarceration, frequently on misdemeanors, nonviolent crimes, and rule infractions (Chan et al., 2020). Improvements in access to safe stable housing, nutritious food, educational opportunities, health care, and employment may well lower the rates of crime and incarceration, thus preventing the initial legal involvement and the cascade of poor health outcomes that follow. Currently, however, we must align what we do know about people who have been incarcerated with services to address their reintegration into the community as we improve our understanding of the phenomenon of suicide after confinement through changes in data acquisition and analysis.

Pre-Release Planning

Once a person becomes incarcerated, systems must assess and address mental health, substance-related, and incarceration-specific risk factors associated with death by suicide, both in the facility and after discharge to the community. Interventions to reduce suicide risk following incarceration occur at the time of release planning and during community reintegration. People released from secure settings are much more likely to suffer from a variety of adverse health outcomes, including death by suicide, when compared to people who have not resided in secure settings. Since there is no single intervention that can be applied to everyone to reduce the risk of death by suicide, individualized release planning for incarcerated persons at increased risk of death by suicide following incarceration should begin early in confinement.

Risk factors such as low educational achievement, lack of job skills, unemployment, homelessness, substance use, mental illness, physical illness, prior suicide-related behavior, and lack of social connections could all usefully trigger an early needs assessment that would form the foundation for an individualized discharge plan. Individualized discharge planning would necessarily include referral to community-based medical and mental health services with the capacity to deliver care based on the previously incarcerated individual's unique needs (National Research Council, 2014).

Programs such as reentry courts and institution-specific pre-release programs have been helpful in assisting some former inmates as they reenter the community, and the interventions used by these programs are also likely to be helpful in reducing their risk of death by suicide. Specific steps used by many of these programs prior to release include securing appropriate identification, investigating safe stable housing options, and thinking through how the individual will afford subsistence and health care after release. Although it is tempting to transfer the responsibility of supervising former inmates to community corrections, we would argue that community corrections is also not a care system; people on community corrections supervision have an elevated risk for death by suicide that exceeds the prison death rate (Sirdifield, Brooker, & Marples 2020). Additionally, highly structured supervision and technical rule infractions serve to maintain repeated incarcerations; consequently, we believe that all corrections-supervised populations should be reduced (Jacobson et al., 2017; Pettus-Davis & Veeh, 2021; Prison Policy Institute, 2020).

Some incarcerated individuals qualified for public assistance benefits prior to their confinement (Freudenberg & Heller, 2016), and leveraging resources available to these individuals could be helpful. In recent years, the Social Security Administration became more active in reaching out to incarcerated individuals by providing resources such as "What Prisoners Need to Know" and "Entering the Community After Incarceration—How We Can Help." These resources emphasize the need to begin pre-release procedures when institutions have pre-release agreements with the Social Security Administration. Implementing strategies to get these forms of support in place simultaneous with release could improve post-release outcomes.

Both the timing and precipitating events associated with preventable death following release from confinement may vary among jurisdictions and over time. It is important for professionals doing pre-release planning to be familiar with current local data to best assist offenders reentering the community in obtaining necessary health care and support (Fox, Binswanger, & Kinner, 2019).

Transition to the Community

Opportunities for discharge planning and community transition are greater in prisons than in jails and lockups owing to the longer length of stay and relatively low turnover in prisons. However, it is people being released from jails who are often most in need of support services. Programming to facilitate post-release housing, employment, and health care are growing areas of intervention that may be associated with better outcomes following release from confinement (Freudenberg & Heller, 2016; Lim et al., 2012). Although we often refer to this process as reentry or reintegration, the reality for many formerly incarcerated persons is that they may not have experienced successful social or community integration prior to confinement and so will be going through a process of social learning to master community integration after confinement (Johns, 2018).

With regard particularly to health care, providing former inmates who have used mental health and medical services during incarceration with crisis contact information and scheduled appointments in the community to which they are returning could improve engagement in services following release. Additionally, giving the person and/or the anticipated providers summaries of medical and mental health care during confinement could prove valuable in breaking down the barriers to treatment often encountered by individuals leaving secure custody (Marks & Turner, 2014).

Connecting institutional care records with community health records, as part of the discharge process, would also enable clinicians serving recently released people to better understand each person's unique conditions of confinement and health needs (Freudenberg & Heller, 2016; Marks & Turner, 2014). Making appointments prior to release may also be a useful surveillance tool, because missed appointments after release may be an important indicator of increasing suicide risk (Sirdifield, Brooker, & Marples, 2020).

Addressing the problem of suicide following release from incarceration may include addressing issues such as employer discrimination by enacting consistent expungement, incentivizing employers to hire former inmates by offering insurance or tax benefits for those hiring formerly incarcerated persons, and preventing employers from asking about legal history (Prison Policy Initiative, 2018). Some people leaving incarceration would also be benefited by changing licensing requirements for occupational licenses, so that background checks are not required beyond that which is directly related to essential job duties.

Improving the Understanding of Suicide After Incarceration

Although there are some data about the risk factors that impact the likelihood of death by suicide after release from incarceration, the data themselves are incomplete (Freudenberg & Heller, 2016). The available data often classify people in overly broad categories, such as male or female, White or non-White, U.S.-born or foreign-born, and single or married. Because there have not historically been consistent person-centered ways to facilitate accurate classification of people, misclassification and/or exclusion of people of minority identities has occurred (Rockett et al., 2010), resulting in missed opportunities for intervention.

There is no standard process for evaluating deaths that occur in the community following release from confinement, as there is for evaluating deaths that occur during confinement (Pew Research Foundation, 2017; Philips et al., 2017). Whether deaths caused by lack of medical care, overdose, and accidents are categorized as intentional deaths or unintentional deaths may be largely a subjective determination by the death evaluator, further complicating data interpretation. A requirement to investigate deaths occurring within 28 days of release from jail or prison confinement, and using uniform criteria for death classification, would address this void (Phillips et al., 2017).

Reducing the risk of death by suicide following confinement at the population level will require improvements in data acquisition and pooling (Binswanger et al., 2019; Freudenberg & Heller, 2016). Such improvements could facilitate the development of prediction tools to identify those people at greatest risk of death following incarceration and to guide care, both during incarceration and in the post-release periods (Borschmann et al., 2019). Resources to address the concerns raised in this chapter are too few and frequently inadequately funded (Freudenberg & Heller, 2016) when compared to the magnitude of the need. The development of inexpensive and scalable tools to identify those people at greatest risk to die by suicide after release from confinement, match interventions, and rigorously evaluate outcomes could provide invaluable information to inform law and policy around incarceration and release.

Conclusion

Over 10 million people are arrested in the United States each year and over 6 million people are under some form of correctional supervision (Maruschak & Minton, 2020). People who are involved with the criminal justice system have frequently experienced racial disparities, economic disparities, and health disparities (Western & Pettit, 2010). Incarceration appears to only worsen the plight of this already disadvantaged population (National Research Council, 2014). The high rates of death by suicide following confinement are only one manifestation of this cumulative disease burden caused by the social inequality often experienced by this group. Individualized needs assessment, combined with appropriate community resource matching, is a necessary first step in the prevention of suicide after incarceration. Addressing this problem will also require consistently and uniformly assessing the needs of this population through more complete and refined data collection and analyses, developing systems to connect people at risk of death by suicide with the community resources necessary to meet their basic needs, and providing access to adequate health care as these individuals transition from incarceration back into the community. Public policy focused on the larger issues of improved housing, food security, health care, opportunity, and employment in general may also help reduce the occurrence of crimes that lead to incarceration, which would in turn help reduce the impact of incarceration on individuals and communities after people are released from incarceration, including the risk of death by suicide.

• • •

Dr. Tracy D. Gunter is Professor of Clinical Psychiatry at Indiana University School of Medicine. She completed her training at the University of South Carolina and worked in the areas of competence restoration and dual diagnosis after training. She was previously Director of the Outpatient Forensic Evaluation Service for the South Carolina Department of Mental Health and was Director of Forensic Services for the University of Iowa. She has served as a mental health consultant and service provider to the South Carolina Department of Juvenile Justice, South Carolina Department of Corrections, Iowa Department of Corrections, and Saint Louis County Jail. She has previously served as a consulting expert in litigation involving jails and prisons. She is certified by the American Board of Psychiatry and Neurology in General Adult and Forensic Psychiatry. She maintains an active clinical and forensic psychiatry consulting practice. She has taught in medical schools and law schools and provided continuing legal education and continuing medical education in the areas of mental health law, neuroscience and law, and health care in corrections. Her areas of interest include correctional health care research, suicide risk assessment and prevention, and wellness in medical and legal professionals. She may be reached at tdgunter@gmail.com.

Kyle D. Webster, DO, PhD, is a first-year resident in psychiatry at Indiana University School of Medicine. He obtained his PhD from Loyola University Chicago and his DO from Michigan State College of Osteopathic Medicine. His areas of interest are forensic psychiatry, first-episode psychosis, and cultural psychiatry. His previous research has focused on socioemotional adjustment in Ugandan children/adolescents with and without HIV and caregiver socioemotional health as a determinant of child well-being in school-aged and adolescent Ugandan children with and without perinatal HIV exposure.

Sandra K. Antoniak, MD, MFS, CCHP-P, is certified by the American Board of Psychiatry and Neurology in Child and Adolescent and Forensic Psychiatry. She is also a Certified Correctional Health Provider-Physician through the National Commission on Correctional Health Care. She has worked in a variety of correctional settings and serves as a forensic consultant to various governmental and community agencies. She may be reached through Impavida Forensic Consulting at santoniak.impavida@gmail.com.
Complete citations are available from the authors upon request.

Chapter

5

Psychological Autopsies

Christopher Caulkins

The term psychological autopsy *is probably the most exotic term in this book. As such, many legal practitioners may be unfamiliar with it. This chapter by Dr. Chris Caulkins describes the purposes, processes, and uses of a psychological autopsy. Psychological autopsies are not widely used in criminal litigation, and neither the editors nor the ABA take a position on its use. However, it may be a tool which prosecutors and criminal defense lawyers might use in the appropriate circumstances. Accordingly, judges will have to rule on its admissibility.*

• • •

Like the infamous 1991 storm that wreaked havoc on the U.S. East Coast and sank the *Andrea Gail* (National Park Service, n.d.), suicide is the result of the "Perfect [horrible] Storm." Like the Perfect Storm, suicide is so rarely the result of one thing. It is a combination of several conditions—biological, cultural, and psychological—that chip away at one's psyche.

Often, there is a significant factor that arises shortly before death, which is held out as the singular cause. Suicide is not like a homicide, where a person can be identified as being solely responsible for the death. Suicide is not that neat, and the ingredients of the Perfect Storm vary from person to person. Life is a subjective experience and what causes one individual distress may not be as impactful to someone else in the same situation (Shneidman, 1993). Generally, suicide is not about wanting to die; it is about desperately wanting to stop pain, referred to as a *psychache*, with the belief that there is no way to do so except by self-destruction (Shneidman, 1993, at 51).

There are three types of pain, all of which are registered in an area of the brain called the cingulate cortex (Lieberman & Eisenberger, 2015). These pain types are physical, psychological (Cacioppo & Patrick, 2008; Eisenberger, Lieberman, & Williams), and social (Selby et al., 2013) in nature. Physical pain is the reason people leaped to their deaths from the World Trade Center Towers on 9/11. Psychological pain may be inflicted by abuse, profound loss, or mental illness. Social pain may result from being bullied or socially isolated. All of these pain types are capable of contributing to psychache.

When applied to a known suicide death, the psychological autopsy investigation (PAI) breaks the Perfect Storm down into its causal parts. Of course, like any other phenomenon, there are likely to be factors that remain hidden or are discovered much later.

Purpose of the Psychological Autopsy

In addition to being used as a tool to understand a known death due to suicide, the psychological autopsy (PA) has other purposes. The psychological autopsy may aid in the determination of manner of death, such as homicide or accident versus suicide, where the manner is equivocal or unclear. Those initiating a PAI may include employers, the military, family of the deceased, and attorneys. The PAI has also been used in suicide prevention research and initiatives, as well as investigation of clusters of suicides in geographic, temporal, or digital proximity.

An attorney may find the determination of manner of death via PA a useful tool for the resolution of insurance claims, estate and contested will issues, malpractice claims, product liability, and worker's compensation claims, among others. The PA has also been used in the prosecution of criminal cases, such as in South Dakota (*State v. Guthrie*), where a husband was found to have killed his wife after staging her death as a suicide.[1]

---

[1] Editors' Note: During the course of editing this chapter, we learned of a capital case in Arizona in which Attorney D. Jesse Smith used a psychological autopsy to prove that the victim died by suicide rather than at the hands of his client. Arizona v. Larry Statz, 1982. Conversation with Attorney Smith, March 25, 2021.

History of the PA

The psychological autopsy was developed in the early 1950s by Dr. Edwin Shneidman and his associates on the request of the Chief Medical Examiner (ME) and Coroner for the County of Los Angeles (Shneidman, 2004). The original purpose was to allow the ME to rule on the manner of death among the dead referred to his office (at 31). However, Dr. Avery Weisman extended the PA to research the lives of people known to have died by suicide (Weisman, 1974).

Shneidman went on to establish the American Association of Suicidology (AAS) in 1968. As of this writing, the AAS is the only known organization credentialing people as Certified Psychological Autopsy Investigators. As of this writing, there are only 24 AAS-certified PAIs in the world, although hundreds have taken the course. The term *psychological autopsy* is sometimes co-opted by noncertified persons and can mean something very different than the procedure I outline in this chapter.

Methods and Procedures

A PA is a retroactive, evidence-based approach to death investigation with the aim of ruling suicide in or out as a manner of death. The findings result in an informed and educated expert opinion with scientific value (Young, 1992). At a base level, the PA is conducted in a similar manner among those who are AAS educated in the procedure. These commonalities include a review of records and a series of semi-structured interviews. The goal is to identify risk and protective factors in an attempt to rule evidence of suicide in or out.

While the basics of how the PA is conducted is the same between PAIs, how they conduct their study differs. The process I describe here is my method influenced by my life path. Other PAIs may or may not spend as much time and may not submit their results in a report that is of academic quality. As a serious suicidologist, whose wife and brother both died by suicide, I hold myself to a high standard. As a peer of mine so aptly put it, suicidologists who are bereaved by suicide themselves take a more "rich and meaningful approach" to the field of suicidology (Caulkins et al., 2017). Ask a lot of questions, if you are considering having a PA conducted, to ensure the process and level of thoroughness is sufficient to get the information you seek.

Upon receiving a request to conduct a PA, I meet with the person commissioning the study to explain the process, understand any needs unique to the particular case, and develop a strategy (list of needed documents, people to interview, etc.). It is helpful if I can see where the decedent lived and view any belongings available. I have seen everything from massive knife and gun collections and death-themed art, to walls covered with Marilyn Monroe memorabilia (Monroe died by suicide in 1962).

I review documents—paper, electronic, audio, video, photos—as they arrive. These may include medical records, therapist notes, final messages, ME investigation and autopsy findings, law enforcement records (reports, dispatch notes, 9-1-1 audio, etc.), ambulance reports, obituaries (including comments if online), news coverage, journals, social media postings, song playlists, telephone and text messages, school records, criminal history, e-mails, etc. It is not uncommon to discover extensive online browsing histories for suicide methods and obsessions with famous people who died by suicide.

The semi-structured interviews come next. I interview a series of people who knew the decedent. Ideally, three or more interviews take place. The accuracy of the information tends to improve as the number of interviews increases. I prefer to interview people from as many parts of the decedent's life as possible. This may include an array of family members, friends, clergy, coaches, co-workers, teachers, etc. The interviews typically take 60-90 minutes and are a conversation based on a set of standardized questions. The interviews may take place in person or by an online video technology. I prefer to audio-record the interviews so that no important information is missed.

After documents are collected and interviews have been transcribed from recordings, I upload into a qualitative analysis software package—like Atlas.ti or NVivo—and code the data. To code data, I create categories of risk and protective factors, such as "substance use," "mood changes," or "anxiety." The software allows me to highlight areas relating to these categories and tag them. Using substance use as an example, a report can be run on the categories, and all information relating to substance use across all documents and interviews is produced. This report makes searching for themes and patterns much easier and reduces the chance of overlooking important information.

The next step is to draw conclusions and write the final report. I attempt to triangulate or verify information from two or more sources to inform my conclusions. Triangulation reduces the chance of misunderstanding a part of the decedent's life circumstances. When writing the report, I cite and reference any research my observations and assertions are based on.

The last step in the process is meeting with the person who requested the PAI and any others they may choose to invite. I provide the written report, orally present the information, and answer any questions to the best of my ability. Sometimes people want to know things like "was my family member conscious or in pain while dying?" As a paramedic, I am uniquely qualified to answer questions such as this. I always respond to these types of questions by saying, "I answer questions like this honestly. The answer may not be pleasant. Do you still want me to answer?" More often than not, the answer is "yes."

Because the subject matter of the PA deals with sensitive issues, it is possible that an interview subject may experience some degree of psychological discomfort, or even crisis, as a result of participation. For this reason, the investigator must be prepared to alter, suspend, or terminate the interview as appropriate, and assist the subject in seeking professional help (AAS, 2013). Having said this, I have only ever had one case where the person interviewed experienced emotional distress. In that case it was a few hours after the interview, when the person unsuccessfully attempted to convince another family member to get interviewed and ended up in a heated exchange of words. My experience is also backed up by research showing that PAs do not "open old wounds" and that PAs are often received positively because there are limited venues to discuss thoughts and feelings about the suicide of a loved one without being judged (Cook, 2001; Dyregrov, 2004; Dyregrov et al., 2010-2011).

Protection of Interview Subjects

Three main precautions to protect interview subjects include the timing of an interview, the relative anonymity, and the voluntary nature of the interview. While it is best to conduct interviews within the first year, sometimes that is not possible. Interviews completed further out tend to diminish in value, as recall becomes more difficult. To respect some period of bereavement, interviews are not generally conducted right away unless there is some highly compelling reason to do so (AAS, 2013). Researchers have found that the quality of information remains the same between 2 and 6 months after the death (Brent et al., 1988).

Anonymity is another precaution. The identity of an interview subject will be known only to the PA investigator and the support team. The investigation team shares the goal of keeping the subject's identity anonymous. For legal and ethical reasons, there are exceptions to the anonymity rule. An example of an exception is if an interview subject makes a suicidal or other self-harm statement. A subject making such statement must be referred to an appropriate, third-party mental health professional. If an exception arises, the interview is gently terminated.

Finally, interviews are strictly voluntary. Under no circumstances should an investigator, a member of the investigation team, or any third party compel an individual to participate in the PA. Before an interview begins, its voluntary nature is explained, and the subject must acknowledge that their participation is completely voluntary. Voluntary participation also means that the interview subject is free to terminate the interview at any time and may withdraw all statements made prior to completion of the study. Such requests are honored without prejudice.

Research Metrics

The PA process retroactively identifies evidence-based risk factors. Central to this is the mnemonic, IS-PATH-WARM, which prompts investigators to remember suicidal ideation, substance abuse, purposelessness, feeling trapped (in a situation or place), hopelessness, withdrawing from social circles and activities, excessive anger, recklessness, and mood swings (AAS, 2013). In addition to IS-PATH-WARM, other factors are identified, including sleep disorders, mental health problems, perfectionism, obsessions with death, family history of mental illness and/or suicide, and others (AAS, 2013). I borrow from the field of anthropology and construct a kinship chart, also known as a family tree. In the way of an example, Figure 5.1 is a kinship chart of a case I worked on. It should be noted that the family granted written permission to share elements of their PA.

Death Classifications

Manner, cause, and method of death are often confused with one another. *Manner* is comprised of five categories. NASHI may be a helpful mnemonic to remember the manners, which are natural, accident, suicide, homicide, and indeterminate (equivocal, unknown, undecided). It is important to

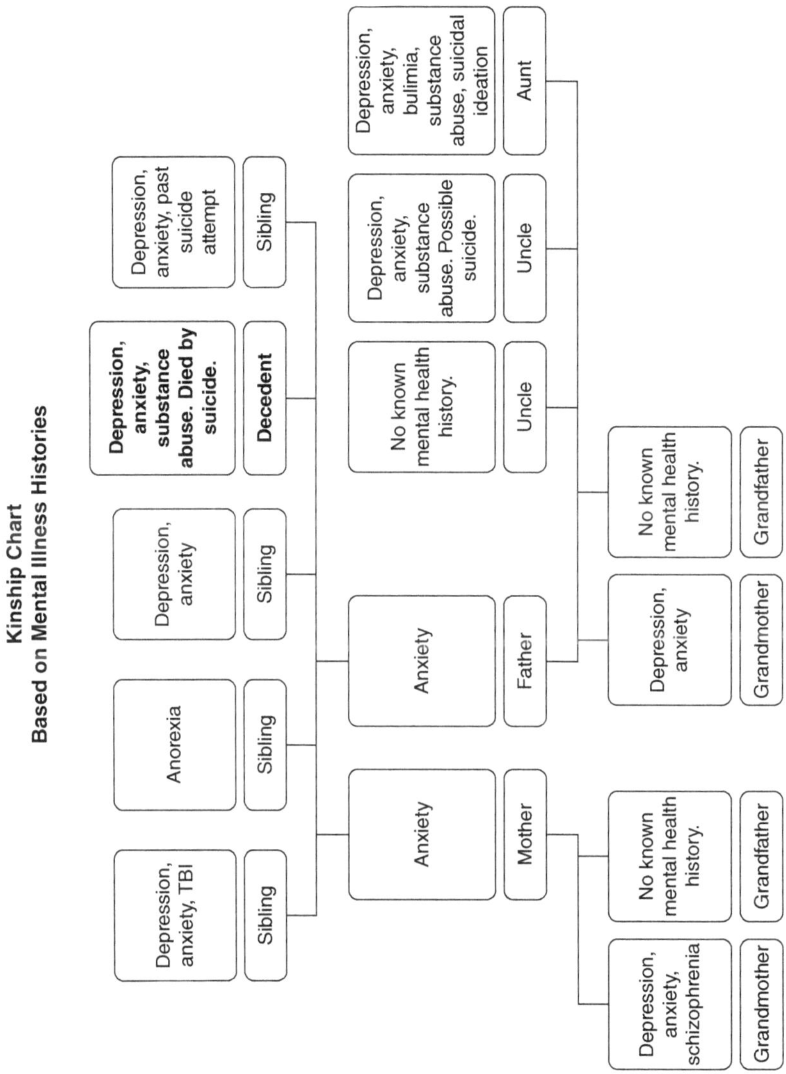

FIGURE 5.1 Kinship Chart

note that *homicide* is the act of a person killing another person, regardless of intent. *Murder* is the criminal element of homicide. Thus, a murder is a homicide, but a homicide is not necessarily a murder.

Method, also known as *means of death*, refers to how a person killed themselves or others. Examples of methods include firearm, hanging, and poisoning. *Cause of death* is what physiological process occurred that resulted in the death. Causes may be categorized into primary and secondary or contributing. Examples of cause of death include sharp force trauma (cuts, lacerations, or stab wounds), lung cancer, and myocardial infarction (heart attack).

The following is a fictitious example, but it is based on countless 9-1-1 calls that I have responded to in my almost three decades of working as a paramedic. I often find that examples help me understand concepts better, and I hope this scenario will serve that purpose for you as well.

It is a clear and sunny winter day. An ambulance responds to a 9-1-1 call for a car that veered off the road and struck a concrete bridge abutment. On arrival, the paramedics determine that the driver has suffered a massive amount of injury and is dead with no chance of resuscitation. It is noted that the driver had not been wearing a seatbelt. The paramedics complete their report and the police and ME take over the scene.

The law enforcement investigators find that there were no skid marks to indicate that the driver applied the brakes and that the road was dry and ice-free. An inspection of the car reveals no obvious mechanical problems or evidence of tampering. Police find no suicide note; however, suicide notes are only left in about 15%-20% of suicide deaths (Holmes & Holmes, 2005; O'Donnell, Farmer, & Catalan, 1993). None of the victim's family members indicate known suicidal thoughts or attempts.

The ME finds no evidence of knife or gunshot wounds and identifies no clogged heart vessels or underlying disease conditions. The lab results on blood and tissue samples fail to find any drugs in the driver's system and do not reveal low blood sugar level or other imbalances. The ME records the death as an undetermined manner with the primary cause as blunt force trauma.

The question before us in regard to the manner is whether there was a natural cause that went undetected by the ME (unlikely), an accident (driver swerved to avoid a deer or was distracted somehow), a suicide (intentionally drove into the abutment with intent to die), or a homicide (another person intentionally ran the driver off the road). A PA could shed light on this death investigation. Were this case ruled a suicide, the method would be vehicle crash.

Suicide Defined

Defining what is a death by suicide, and what is not, seems like a pretty straightforward thing to do. In reality, there are many philosophies as to how *suicide* is defined. Concepts such as suicide-by-other, rational suicide, and chronic suicide are bandied about. Earlier I mentioned the 9/11 deaths due to jumping. Those deaths were officially classified as homicides. There are many valid arguments for both homicide and suicide. From a literal standpoint, a human jumped to end their life (suicide). From a more nuanced viewpoint, acts of other humans created an environment where a person would have to choose between dying in a fire or hastening their death in hopes of eliminating a painful end to life (homicide).

For many PAs, the central question in manner-of-death classification revolves around intent. Did the person's act or omission (e.g., failure to self-rescue) have the express goal of death as an outcome? This would eliminate the debate around most conditions, such as obesity or long-term substance use, as being considered a type of "chronic suicide." We would be hard-pressed to find a person who at several times during their life did not knowingly do something that shortened their life.

The definition of suicide is not consistent even among MEs. In one case I investigated, a young person tied an object around their neck and leaned forward with the object attached to an unmovable anchor. The following is what I wrote in the final report:

> The question before us is one of intent. The decedent either intentionally strangled himself in an act of suicide or was an unwitting victim of the "choking game" gone wrong. If it is the latter, the intent was to gain a high from the decreased blood and oxygen flow to the brain, [and] the result would be an accidental death. The medical examiner's (ME) office that handled the case and determined the manner of death as suicide, was contacted to see how manner of death is determined in cases where the choking game is a possibility. The ME office responded that "realistically, a single individual couldn't partake in the choking game" and for that reason "we don't think that it's even a viable situation." This demonstrates a clear lack of understanding of the choking game. Loss of consciousness results in 13-18 seconds with the majority of the fatalities being males performing the act alone 96% of the time (Andrew, MacNab, & Russell, 2009).

When I inquired in another jurisdiction as to their opinion, the agency advised that the choking game in this scenario would be classified as an accident had they conducted the investigation. Given this ME's response, one could reasonably anticipate that auto-erotic asphyxiation and deaths from nonsuicidal self-injuries (NSSIs) would garner a similar response.

In another misclassification scenario, in spite of evidence to suggest that up to 36% of deaths after an officer-involved shooting are actually suicide-by-cop situations, these deaths get recorded, in most if not all jurisdictions, as homicides (Mohandie, Meloy, & Collins, 2009). In spite of the legal designation as homicide, I would consider suicide-by-cop a suicide. In these cases, the officer is the method or weapon. The same would be true in a suicide-by-other situation in which one person intentionally angered another person, knowing what the outcome might be. Then there are many known cases of a person killing their terminally ill spouse (sometimes at the spouse's request) and then themselves. Perhaps there is a need for the creation of an additional death-manner category of "mixed manner," and the dual manner is stated as a primary and secondary class of method (for example, primary suicide and secondary homicide).

There is the proverbial soldier who throws themselves on a grenade to save others in the platoon, or the parent who fights off a bear to save their child, knowing they will likely die. This type of death meets the definition of an altruistic suicide that sociologist Emile Durkheim (1897/1951) wrote about.

Last, suicide determination is often predicated on the presence or absence of a mental health disorder. The statistics and research do not support this strategy. This is not to say that mental illness is not a major contributor in many cases; it is just not a universal given.

Forensic Testimony and Evidence

There are two basic legal standards used to determine whether someone is an expert in their field and whether their testimony is valid—the *Frye*[2] and the *Daubert*[3] standards. The standard used varies by state and

[2] Frye v. United States, 293 F. 1013 (D.C. Cir. 1923).

[3] Daubert v. Merrell Dow Pharms., 509 U.S. 579 (1993).

there are sometimes two other standards—*Joiner*[4] and *Kumho Tire*[5]—that expand upon *Daubert* (Bernstein & Jackson, 2004). There are less than a handful of states that have their own test that is neither *Frye* nor *Daubert* (Bernstein & Jackson, 2004, at 6).

PAIs meet the *Frye* standard, but not the *Daubert* standard, because a known error rate is nearly impossible to determine, as the person is not alive to question and find out if the PA was right or not (AAS, 2013).

Under the *Frye* standard, evidence is admissible if it has "general acceptance" within the scientific community and the methods are seen as valid by those in the applicable field (Steadman & Konigsberg, 2016). Additionally, the judge does not rule on whether or not evidence is appropriate for submission under the *Frye* standard; rather, it is a point of debate between legal counsel on both sides of the case (Steadman & Konigsberg, 2016, at 63).

The judge, who makes the decision concerning admissibility, applies the *Daubert* standard. Criteria to meet the *Daubert* standard include whether the scientific methodology is relevant, reliable, peer-reviewed, has a known error rate, and is replicable (*id.*, at 63). In contrast, those satisfying the *Frye* standard would only be required to point out "consistencies between antemortem and postmortem data" rather than back up assertions with odds ratio statistics as required under *Daubert* (*id.*, at 65). Adhering to *Frye* standards for identification, rather than *Daubert*, would allow in more circumstantial (presumptive) evidence rather than direct (positive) evidence backed up with scrutiny of the scientific method (Wiersema, Love, & Naul, 2016). It is important to remember that the PA is an expert opinion with scientific value (Young, 1992).

Psychological Autopsy Certification Training (PACT)

I am currently on an AAS committee that is focused on improving the PA in many ways, including the education program, qualifications, and data collection, which means some of the information I relay here may have changed by the time you read this. Having said this, the following are the requirements for PAI certification at the time of this writing.

---

[4] General Elec. Co. v. Joiner, 522 U.S. 136 (1997).

[5] Kumho Tire Co. v. Carmichael, 526 U.S. 137 (1999).

Eligibility

> Registrants must possess a minimum of a Masters [*sic*] degree in a social sciences/behavioral health field OR alternative training in interviewing skills and a behavioral science background OR current employment/volunteer activities consistent with the opportunity to conduct psychological autopsies (a curriculum vitae (CV) or resume is required with this application), e.g. [*sic*] law enforcement, medical examiner system, etc. (AAS, n.d.).

Certification

The classroom portion of PACT typically takes about two full days to complete. To gain certification, the PAI candidate must independently perform a PA and submit it to the AAS PA coordinator. The PA grants PAI certification upon evaluation of the PA to ensure adherence to protocol.

Certification Renewal

Initial certification is good for three years. A fee of $300 is charged to maintain certification ($100 per year). In order to remain in good standing for the fourth through sixth years, a certified Psychological Autopsy Investigator must submit a second case within the first three-year period of certification. Once this is approved, the certification is good for a second three-year period. During the second three-year period, a PAI must submit a case to be renewed for five more years. Thereafter, PAIs must submit a case every five years (AAS, n.d.).

Mental Illness and Suicide

Claims of mental illness, by PA as a diagnostic means, should receive all due scrutiny. The work of psychiatrist Emil Kraepelin is hailed by many as the beginning of the shift to the medicalization of mental health disorders (Endstrom & Kendler, 2015). While this shift gave rise to important advancements in the diagnoses and treatment of many psychiatric maladies, it has also been appropriated to exclude other nonmedical possibilities and unnecessarily constrict our view of mental health. Shneidman (2005) warned about considering mental health disorders, such as depression, to be the same as suicide. Shneidman stated, "it may well be time to dekraeplinaize suicide" (at 11). As John Muir observed (1911, at 110), "When we try to pick out anything by itself, we find it hitched to everything else in the universe."

Aggregate PA data has been used by researchers to assert that 90% of those who die by suicide have a mental illness (Hjemeland et al., 2012). Consider the findings of CDC research that 54% of those who died by suicide had no documented history of mental health disorder (Stone et al., 2018). This lack of diagnosed mental illness in a large number of those who commit suicide is also evident in other countries (Shahtahmasebi, 2013).

Suicide is not classified as a mental disorder in the *Diagnostic and Statistical Manual of Mental Disorders, Fifth Edition* (*DSM-5*), although suicide appears repeatedly as being associated with certain disorders, as a symptom or a risk of the disorder (American Psychiatric Association, 2013). The American Psychiatric Association (APA) does leave a placeholder for the possibility of suicidal behavioral disorder (SBD) as a condition for further research (*DSM-5*, at 801). Similar to or building on this, other researchers have proposed the defining of a suicide crisis syndrome (SCS) (Schuck et al., 2019) or acute suicidal affective disturbance (ASAD) (Rogers, Chu, & Joiner, 2018).

While not dismissing the possibility that these newly proposed disorders are valid, the question that comes to my mind is whether SBD, SCS, and ASAD are efforts to medicalize suicide. Would a new disorder that fits the "those who die by suicide are nearly always mentally ill" narrative steer us perilously away from the study of suicide through a nonmedical lens? Would the new disorders give the fields of psychology and psychiatry unwarranted claims of jurisdiction over a critical public health issue that is so interdisciplinary? Should we medicalize homicide—another category of manner of death—if suicide is medicalized?

The purpose of the PA is not to retroactively diagnose a mental health disorder, and given that PAIs do not have to be mental health professionals, it would seem obvious that doing so is fraught with problems. Even if the PA is conducted by a mental health professional, I would argue that secondary sources of information are a poor substitute for direct patient interaction.

Summary

The psychological autopsy is a method of death investigation that complements and augments medical examiner and law enforcement investigations. The PA may also be used for suicide research and prevention initiatives. In cases of a death with an unknown or equivocal manner, the PA may be used to rule suicide in or out, as opposed to accident or homicide. Attorneys may find the PA of use in a variety of civil and criminal cases.

Developed in the 1950s by Dr. Edwin Shneidman and his associates, the PA has evolved over time. The American Association of Suicidology continues to credential professionals as psychological autopsy investigators and is the only known credentialing body at this time. There are experience and education prerequisites necessary to take the PA training, with periodic renewal required.

The PA consists of a review of records, a series of semi-structured interviews with those close to the decedent, and inspection of personal effects. This may include photos, artwork, music selections, movie interests, and favored literature. Every effort is made to corroborate findings with additional sources. Metrics applied include evidence-based suicide risk and protective factors.

A death should be classified as suicide with intent in mind. If a person intends to end their life, it is suicide. If a person engaged in risky behavior without intent to die, it should be classified as a manner other than suicide. Unfortunately, medical examiner work is sometimes as much a philosophy as it is science, so intent is ignored.

Another factor in misclassification of deaths is the false assumption that mental illness is a precursor to suicide. I have concern that the medicalization of suicide will not only negatively impact PA findings and ME determinations, but that it will also create a barrier to effective research into this deadly phenomenon. Suicide is not a mental disorder in and of itself. It is the tragic outcome of a series of events, conditions, and circumstances. The PA is not intended to retroactively diagnose mental illnesses.

Whether a PA or PAI testimony is admissible in court depends on the standards used in a state. The PA meets the *Frye* standard, but not the *Daubert* standard. This is predominantly because a known error rate cannot be calculated at this time. At the end of the day, the PA findings are an educated evidence-based opinion.

• • •

Christopher Caulkins, EdD, MPH, MA is a suicidologist and psychological autopsy investigator, and has researched, presented, and published on suicide at the state, national, and international levels. Dr. Caulkins is a practicing paramedic and emergency medical services educator with almost 30 years of experience responding to 9-1-1 calls for suicidal ideation, attempts, and—sadly—deaths. Full-time, Dr. Caulkins is faculty at a community college and teaches in the emergency medical services and health sciences programs.

Dr. Caulkins became a suicidologist after the suicide death of his wife, which intensified after the suicide of his brother and 11 EMS colleagues. For over 15 years, Dr. Caulkins has run a peer support group for those bereaved by suicide. Dr. Caulkins sits on suicide-related committees of the Minnesota Department of Health, the National Action Alliance on Suicide Prevention, the International Association of Suicide Prevention, the American Association of Suicidology, and the Minnesota Ambulance Association.

Dr. Caulkins can be reached at c.caulkins@mnsuicidology.org and his website is https://MNsuicidology.org.

Complete citations are available from the author upon request.

Chapter

6

Death Suggested, Cause Abated

Andrea D. Lyon

Andrea Lyon is a lawyer's lawyer. Because of her speaking and writing, in addition to her courtroom battles, she is legendary among the criminal defense bar. Many of us, after hearing one of her presentations, vowed, "I'm going to be like that one day." But as this chapter shows, even an experienced, intuitive attorney like Lyon can miss the signals that a client is going to commit suicide.

This chapter details Lyon's appointment to represent a woman accused of murdering her abusive husband through the day when Lyon walked into the courtroom and the prosecutor announced in open court that her client had killed herself. To this day, Lyon is angered by the callousness of the prosecutor and haunted by the fact that she did not see this tragedy coming.

• • •

I didn't see it. I have looked back on that many times. How could I have missed it?

I had been doing criminal defense, specifically in the homicide task force of the public defender's office in Chicago, for years. I knew how much trauma most of my clients had experienced, I had been delving into their lives in order to save them from being sentenced to death. I had studied, read, and consulted with experts. I liked to think I was good with clients, that I could hear the emotional subtext beneath their words.

But this I missed.

Carolyn Jackson[1] was not the first battered woman I had represented in a homicide. At the time I represented her, I had had about a half-dozen cases where battered women had killed their abusers, and nearly a perfect acquittal record. I had learned a lot about the syndrome, and had learned how to communicate it to juries and judges in a way that would answer the question that was always underlying such a case. Whether the client had acted in self-defense or not—which was most often the defense—what the judge and jury would want to know first is why did she stay? After all, it makes little visceral sense to most people, that someone who was being physically and psychologically abused would stay with her abuser.

I have written about this syndrome before, once with Dr. Helen Morrison for the National Association of Criminal Defense Lawyers magazine, *The Champion*[2] and once with my former law student and now law professor Emily Hughes and our client Juanita Thomas.[3] This chapter is not intended to restate those articles or to examine in any detail battered spouse syndrome, but it may be helpful to have an overview.

> Battered woman syndrome (BWS) is a psychological condition and describes a pattern of behavior that develops in victims of domestic violence as a result of serious, long-term abuse. BWS is dangerous primarily because it can lead to what some scholars say is "learned helplessness"—or psychological paralysis—where the victim becomes so depressed, defeated, and passive that she believes she is incapable of leaving her abuser.
>
> This gripping fear feels absolutely real to the victim. Feeling weak, and possibly holding out hope that her abuser will stop hurting her, the victim remains in the abusive situation. This continues the cycle of domestic violence and strengthens the BWS grip.
>
> BWS has been recognized by many state courts, and there are support systems available to domestic violence and BWS victims. Some states also take BWS into account when addressing violent outbursts by victims of domestic violence. If you or someone you know is afraid of speaking to authorities about an abuser, there may be ways to avoid punishment. … BWS begins as an abusive cycle with three stages. First, the abuser engages

---

1 I have changed the names of everyone for this chapter and am relying on my memory and the little bit of the file I still possess for this chapter. I do so to protect my former client's privacy, and so that I may speak candidly about some of the various participants of the criminal court system.

2 Andrea D. Lyon & Helen Morrison, M.D., *Self-Defense and Battered Spouse Syndrome: A Legal and Psychological Perspective*, Criminal Defense 9(3) (May-June 1984).

3 Andrea D. Lyon, Emily Hughes, & Juanita Thomas, The People v. Juanita Thomas: *A Battered Woman's Journey to Freedom*, Women & Crim. Justice 13(1) (2001).

> in behaviors that create relationship tension. Second, the tension explodes when the abuser commits some form of abuse: physical, psychological, emotional, sexual, or otherwise. Third, the abuser tries to fix his wrongdoing and apologizes. This third stage is frequently referred to as the "honeymoon" stage, and involves the abuser making amends for his bad behavior. During the honeymoon stage, the abuser is forgiven, and the cycle starts all over again.
>
> As the cycle continues, the victim starts to feel that the abuse is her own fault. When the victim takes responsibility for her own abuse, this develops into "learned helplessness." The victim feels helpless because she has convinced herself that the abuse is her own fault, yet she cannot understand why the abuse continues if it's her own fault. She becomes convinced of her helplessness and that the abuse cannot be escaped, absent the most drastic measures. Thus is born the psychology of BWS.[4]

It is therefore unsurprising for a traumatized woman (or man) who has ended up defending herself to be in shock, to be preternaturally quiet, and to take time to open up to her lawyer, especially one who was appointed to her rather than chosen by her, as is the case with being represented by a lawyer from the public defender's office.[5]

When I met Carolyn, it was in the lockup behind Branch 66 of the Cook County court system. Branch 66 was the courtroom that met daily at noon for preliminary hearings (or more often being told your client had been indicted by the grand jury) on sexual assault cases and homicides. As a member of the Homicide Task Force, I would go to that courtroom once a week, and if it was my turn up at bat and someone was charged with a homicide who could not afford their own lawyer (which was nearly everybody), I would become that defendant's lawyer. My assigned day was Monday, which meant there seldom was a day I didn't end up picking up a new case.

The clerk called out "People v. Carolyn Jackson—custody." The sheriff went back to the women's lockup to get her. I was next up, so this would be my case if the family hadn't hired anyone, so I listened carefully. Carolyn walked out in a jumpsuit that made her seem very frail.

---

[4] FindLaw, *Battered Woman Syndrome*, https://family.findlaw.com/domestic-violence/battered-women-s-syndrome.html.

[5] This is not unique to defending battered women; public defenders are often viewed with suspicion by their clients and their clients' families. It takes time to build up trust. *See, e.g.*, Lisa J. McIntyre, The Public Defender (University of Chicago Press 1987).

She was African American, maybe 5′4″, and maybe 120 pounds. Her hair was messy, her head bowed, her steps uncertain.

"Are you Miss Jackson?" asked Judge O'Meara, when she stood before him. She mumbled something in return, still not looking up. "Speak up!" said the judge. The sheriff, known as "Big Mike," a brown buddha of a man, nudged her (not unkindly, I noticed) and she looked up and nodded and said, quietly, "Yes."

"Miss Jackson, you are charged with the first-degree murder of one Alfonso Jackson." I wasn't surprised. Unlike what television and movies tell us, most homicides occur between people who know and love each other. I figured it was her husband. "Do you have your own lawyer?" the judge continued. She shook her head *no*. "PD!" he said. I really hated that. No matter how many times I and others tried talking to Judge O'Meara about how that "call-out" hurt relationships with our clients, who were convinced public defenders weren't lawyers, I couldn't get him to change.

I stepped up to the bench next to Carolyn Jackson. "Your Honor, Andrea Lyon, attorney at law, from the law office of the public defender's office for Ms. Jackson." If he wouldn't do it, I would make sure my client—and her family if they were in the audience—would know that in fact I was a lawyer. I handed her my card, but she dropped it. I picked it up. "Ms. Jackson waives formal reading of the charges, Your Honor, and pleads not guilty," I said. This was par for the course: one always pleads not guilty at the beginning of the case. I felt rather than saw Carolyn start next to me and she seemed like she was going to speak. I leaned over and whispered to her that we would talk and she should now talk only to me, that the rest of the system was not to be trusted.

"Assistant State's Attorney Jim Mahoney for the People," said the prosecutor standing to my right. Mahoney was a true believer: there was good and evil, he was on the side of good and our clients were evil, and by extension so were those who represented them. "The People ask that the current order of no bail stand, and ask for a continuance date for preliminary matters." I knew this meant that she would be indicted for first-degree even if she shouldn't be charged with that high of an offense. It gave the prosecution more leverage, as the minimum sentence was 20 years on that charge and could go as high as life without parole or the death penalty depending on the circumstances.

The judge asked for a recitation of the facts as known to the prosecution. "Two nights ago, Your Honor, the defendant did with malice and intent to kill or cause great bodily harm, stab her husband Alfonso Jackson with a knife." The prosecutor paused and looked at what I presumed was a police report. "The deceased was stabbed four times by the defendant," he continued, "which stab wounds caused his death. The defendant then called for an ambulance." Mahoney shook his head as he said this; this didn't sound like what a cold-blooded killer would do, and undercut his request for a no-bail order.

Judge O'Meara asked the prosecutor if Carolyn had a criminal record, and he replied that she did not. I would find out soon that there *were* police reports about her—as the victim. I told the judge that as this was a woman with no record, and it appeared she sought help for her husband, a no-bail order wasn't appropriate. The judge agreed, and set bail at $100,000, which was the same as no bail for a poor woman. The judge continued the case for three weeks, and Miss Jackson was taken back to the lockup by the sheriff. I followed them back there and talked to her with the cell bars between us.

"Ms. Jackson," I said, "let me re-introduce myself to you. My name is Andrea Lyon, and I am the lawyer who has been appointed to represent you." I explained my role, slowly, and told her I would be over to the women's jail to see her on Wednesday, two days from now. I didn't like to have a real conversation in a lockup with lots of people listening. "Do you have family I should get in touch with?" I asked.

"They don't wanna talk to me," she said, nearly unintelligibly. I knew that might have been the original reaction, but in my experience that would change. So, I asked her for names and phone numbers, and told her I would just let them know how to reach me, and when her next court date was. I cautioned her not to talk to anyone in the jail, that only our conversations were privileged. I did not get the sense that a lot of this was getting through, but that didn't surprise me either. She had all the earmarks of a battered woman, and she was in shock besides.

She was not able to meet my eyes in these few minutes, and clearly was somewhere else in her head, but I figured our next conversation would be better. I was wrong.

One of the bitter lessons of experience is that it tells you that you know what to expect because of that experience. Having represented battered spouses before, I thought she would be ready to talk to me a little about her relationship, or her children, or the event, or maybe even all three. But when I went over to Division 2 of the jail two days later, she just didn't want to talk. Carolyn's voice sounded raspy, like it does after you do a lot of crying, and she looked down most of the time. The only time she perked up at all was when she was telling me about her two daughters, but then a curtain came down over her eyes, and she stopped mid-sentence. I tried again to get her talking, but I could see she was exhausted. "Miss Jackson," I said, "I will stop by next week too, and see how you are." She looked up at me and said, "I ain't gonna be much better."

"You don't have to be," I told her. "I am here for *you* to fight for you." I smiled. "I don't need every answer all at once. Truly, we can take our time." I briefly put my hand over hers as I got up from the bleach-smelling table. I had spoken with her daughters by this time, and they had told me of the abuse at home by their father of their mother. Not in great detail, but that would come.

I went back the next week, and didn't get much further, but it seemed to me that she was feeling more comfortable than she had the first two times, so I was comforted. I shouldn't have been. I let her know that the next time I would see her was in a week—I had a vacation planned, so I would see her at the next court date. She nodded, and I left.

I got back from vacation the Sunday before court, unpacked, did laundry, all the things one does. The next day I appeared in Branch 66 to receive the expected indictment. I was a couple of minutes late getting there, so court was already in session. Mahoney caught my eye. He looked, well, smug. What had happened, I wondered?

Judge O'Meara called the case. I stepped up, and suddenly realized I hadn't heard the clerk say "custody." My stomach got tight. Something was wrong.

"Assistant State's Attorney Jim Mahoney, for the People." He was grinning. "Your honor, death suggested, cause abated." That is a phrase used when a party dies, thus nullifying the case. I looked around. Everyone seemed to know but me.

"What happened?" I asked, knowing, without wanting to, the answer.

"Well," said Mahoney, "your client saved the State of Illinois a lot of money. She killed herself last night." I stood, stunned.

"What?" I said again. No one was looking at me but the prosecutor.

"Yup," he said, "she decided to save us all from a trial and your bleeding-heart pleas." He looked around for all the world like he was expecting someone to laugh and say "good one!"

I whirled on him. "You, sir, must have been raised by wolves." I could hear crying behind me; her daughters were in court, as we had previously arranged. They hadn't known! Why hadn't anyone been called? I stood stock-still, looking at Judge O'Meara, who apparently had found something fascinating to look at on the bench. His clerk was also unaccountably busy.

Then I felt a gentle hand on my left shoulder. It was the sheriff, Big Mike. He leaned in and whispered to me that I should go see after her daughters. That shook me from my spot, and I walked toward the back of the courtroom, Mike beside me. Then I turned to him. "How?" I asked. I had to know.

"She swallowed her sheet," he said, his voice nearly cracking. "To suffocate herself, you know." I went to talk to her daughters, apologizing for not having known about this ahead of time, expressing my condolences, and privately seething about the needlessly heartless way this had been revealed.

I got back to my office, somehow. I sat down and kept asking myself, why hadn't I seen it? Was there something I could have done? There must have been, right?

She must have *really* wanted to die to force a sheet down her throat. She must have been desperately sad and hopeless. I hadn't seen. I hadn't helped. I hadn't *seen*.

Now I ask about suicidal thoughts, even if it might seem melodramatic. I look as well as listen, I ask for help if I feel there's any impediment to communication with a client. As the great poet Wanda Coleman said, "every shut eye ain't sleep." I know now that every open eye doesn't see.

You have to look. (*See* ch. 3, Suicide in Prison; ch. 10, Suicide in the Criminal Justice System; ch. 15, Case Study: Transformation; and ch. 16, Case Study: An Insider's View of Suicide in Prison.)

• • •

Andrea D. Lyon is a renowned lawyer, author, speaker, professor, and former Dean of the Valparaiso University Law School, who has been featured on national news and media outlets. Dubbed "The Angel of Death Row" by the *Chicago Tribune*, she was the first woman to serve as lead attorney in a death penalty case, and she holds an unparalleled 19 wins in 19 capital cases.

Ms. Lyon has dedicated her career to advocating and upholding justice for all. Her legal work began in the Cook County Public Defender's Office, where she rose to become Chief of the Homicide Task Force. Managing a 22-lawyer unit, she tried over 130 homicide cases and defended more than 30 potential capital cases at the trial level, including taking 19 capital cases through penalty phase. In 1990, Ms. Lyon founded and directed the Illinois Capital Resource Center representing all of the death-row inmates in Illinois.

Ms. Lyon is a leader of academic reforms in both curriculum development and mentoring diversity in law school student and faculty populations. She brought her depth of criminal justice experience to enrich legal education at University of Michigan Law School as assistant clinical professor; DePaul University College of Law as clinical professor of law, Associate Dean of Clinical Programs, and Director of the Center for Justice in Capital Cases; and as Dean of Valparaiso University Law School.

In January 2015, Ms. Lyon was awarded Operation Push's Rev. Dr. Martin Luther King, Jr. and President Lyndon B. Johnson Dream-Makers Award. A winner of the prestigious National Legal Aid and Defender Association's Reginald Heber Smith Award for best advocate for the poor in the country, she is a nationally recognized expert in the field of death penalty defense and a frequent Continuing Legal Education (CLE) teacher throughout the country. She has been designated as learned counsel in the federal defense system.

Ms. Lyon received her undergraduate degree from Rutgers University and her law degree from Antioch School of Law. Her publications include over 50 law review articles, and over 10 practice manuals and books, including *The Feminine Sixth: Women in Criminal Defense* (NACDL Press, 2018), *The Death Penalty: What's Keeping It Alive* (Rowman & Littlefield, 2015), *Team Defense in Criminal Cases* (with Mortimer Smith; ABA, 2014), and *Angel of Death Row: My Life as a Death Penalty Defense Lawyer* (Kaplan, 2010).

Ms. Lyon can be reached at andrea@andrealyon.com and her website is https://www.andrealyon.com.

Complete citations are available from the author upon request.

Chapter

7

When Judges Cry: Dealing with a Defendant's Death by Suicide

The Honorable Stephen R. Bough

Twenty-five years ago, no judge—particularly a federal judge—would have written a chapter titled "When Judges Cry." Thankfully, the world has changed and continues to change.

In this chapter by The Honorable Stephen R. Bough of the Western District of Missouri, we learn of the impact of criminal cases on a jurist like him who is unabashedly human. He grapples with the confines of sentencing laws, the realities of defendants' lives, and the devastation suffered by victims. This is a judge who wants to do the right thing and who understands the awesome power of his role. With all this comes the responsibility of looking after his own emotional well-being. Judge Bough encourages other lawyers to do as he has done: to use the myriad resources now available to promote wellness and combat burnout.

• • •

"Sentencing is the hardest thing for most judges (as it should be)."[1] The federal statute governing criminal sentencing says that a sentence should

[1] Christina Reiss, Guide to Judicial Well-Being (Federal Judicial Center 2013), 5.

be sufficient but not greater than necessary.[2] At no point in making that determination have I ever thought death was necessary. Sadly, I know that some defendants standing in front of me have had that thought. Judges are emotionally invested in their jobs and in individual cases. We are heartened by a defendant's success and saddened by their setbacks. The entire sentencing process, along with the possibility that you can get it wrong, is enough to make a judge cry.[3]

I was asked to write about my own experience with an individual who died by suicide pre-incarceration. Because the emotions stemming from the murder of an individual while on supervised release were similar, I discuss both experiences here, as well as a similar experience that occurred in my courthouse. In writing this chapter, I also felt compelled to put the role of a federal district judge regarding sentencing into perspective, including discussing some of the resources available to judges dealing with the stresses of this job. Talking about the mental health of defendants, lawyers, and judges is always a good conversation to have.

I. My Experience with the Death of Defendants

The first case where I had a defendant die involved a young man named William.[4] The resentence report (PSR)[5] noted that he had pled guilty to being a felon in possession of a firearm.[6] This PSR did not shock me; William had three prior felonies for stealing electronics from stores in rural Missouri, but they were all small-time thefts for a few hundred dollars. He had no history of violence. William had dropped out of school in tenth grade to work in his father's construction business and as a

[2] 18 U.S.C. § 3553.

[3] Melinda Henneberger, *Even the Judge Cried at Innocence Hearing for KCK Postman Now Free After 12 Years*, The Kansas City Star, November 6, 2020, https://www.kansascity.com/opinion/opn-columns-blogs/melinda-henneberger/article247008317.html.

[4] William is not this young man's real name. For a more extensive discussion of William and my journey in learning how to sentence a defendant, please read *Getting to Know a Felon: One Judge's Attempt at Imposing Sentences That Are Sufficient, But Not Greater Than Necessary*, UMKC L. Rev. 87(1), 25–33 (Fall 2018).

[5] For each defendant facing a federal sentence, the sentencing judge is provided a confidential PSR detailing, among other things, the defendant's personal and family history, criminal background, and the details of the underlying criminal offense. Section II of this chapter discusses the content and function of a PSR in greater detail.

[6] Step one of sentencing is to properly calculate the guidelines range. Step two is to apply the § 3553 factors.

maintenance worker at an apartment complex. This 22-year-old gentleman, who recently celebrated his birthday in prison, had already been in custody for 10 months at the time of his sentencing. Prior to this charge, the longest William had been in prison was 30 days. William's guideline range was 30 to 37 months. Using my best judgment, I determined that one year and a day in prison was sufficient but not greater than necessary for him. With good-time credit, this sentence meant he would be released almost immediately. But shortly after his release, William stopped reporting to his probation officer (PO). When his PO went looking for him, we learned that William had been murdered in a motel. The last entry on his docket was a horribly named "Notification of Death." I can say with great confidence that no judge ever wants this type of tragic outcome to befall a defendant under his or her supervision.

Losing William was hard on me, but it was nothing compared to the loss his family felt. William was in many ways a good man. He had a plan, a plan that did not include getting murdered. At my last check, no one has been charged in his death. After learning of William's death, I had a lot of doubts about the sentence I had given him. Maybe I should have separated him from his past for a longer period. Maybe I should have placed him on a location monitor. Maybe I should have made him report to his probation officer every week. Maybe I should have given him more time in prison. Or maybe I did everything right (though probably not).

The first time I had a case involving an individual who died by suicide was a defendant facing child pornography charges. The defendant was out on pretrial release (a decision made by a magistrate judge) and had pled guilty to a crime that involved a lengthy mandatory minimum sentence in the Federal Bureau of Prisons. I was dreading the sentencing hearing, including having to potentially hear testimony from the victim's family and trying to determine a just sentence. As the hearing approached, I can only imagine the weight of dread the defendant must have felt. "The notion of sex offenders as pariahs in correctional settings is not without foundation. Like the rest of society, prison culture is not immune to condemning those who engage in criminal sexual misconduct, especially in cases involving acting out against children."[7] Right before sentencing, we were informed by counsel that the defendant had died by suicide. Just like

[7] Alan Ellis & J. Michael Henderson, Federal Prison Guidebook: Sentencing and Post-Conviction Remedies 102 (4th rev., James Publishing, 2017).

the death of William, this case has stuck with me. While I was disgusted by the crime the defendant had committed, death never entered my mind as a viable sentence. What could we have done differently? Should more individuals be detained pre-sentencing? Was there something unique about this crime that made a person more susceptible to suicide? And, more broadly, what type of care and treatment envisioned by § 3553(a) needs to be considered pretrial?

This last example, while not my own case, nevertheless impacts the way I view this issue and my role in the sentencing process. The United States District Court for the Western District of Missouri had a defendant die by suicide right after the jury rendered its verdict. The defendant had been charged with a white-collar crime. After the jury returned a guilty verdict, and at the request of the defense counsel, the judge allowed the defense lawyer to escort the individual to the United States Marshal's office. On the way downstairs, the defendant swallowed some pills he had brought with him that day. Although an ambulance was called, efforts to medically intervene failed and the person ultimately died by his own hand. Prior to trial, the defendant had been out on pretrial release.[8] My colleague presiding over the trial was genuinely saddened, and the defendant's family was deservedly distraught. No one saw this coming. The people who work in our court were also upset; employees of the federal court system take their jobs seriously and work diligently to achieve justice. Several individuals, from the clerk's office to chambers staff, expressed how difficult the experience was and the toll it took on their emotional health.

In each of these cases, the stress on the families of those who died had to be devastating. However, the impact of those losses on judges and others involved in the administration of justice is also meaningful. Judges do cry. Life is sacred. The human connections between judges, lawyers, clients, and probation officers are real. I have concerns about my own ability to not bring my past experiences with defendant death into the next case. Part of me wonders if I should ever let a defendant self-report to the Marshal's office, even though allowing them to do so lets them hug their family one last time before they go to prison. When a defendant dies or takes their own life, the natural inclination is to think I did something wrong. It is one thing for a statute to tell you to view each case

[8] Pretrial release is determined on a case-by-case basis, subject to statutory requirements, a burden of proof, and recommendations by the United States Probation Office, U.S. Attorney's Office, and the Federal Public Defender.

individually; it's another thing not to carry the baggage of one horrible experience to the next similar case. It is often difficult, if not impossible, to fully process the human tragedies that play out in court while watching victims, defendants, and witnesses work through a case. But as the judge who hands down the sentence, I often forget that these experiences also affect my staff. When my courtroom deputy and court reporter must be escorted to their cars by U.S. Marshals due to a violent felon's family hanging out in front of the courthouse, the stress on my chambers staff is real. Judges, their families, and their staff are all partners in the very stressful, and often emotionally tragic, pursuit of justice. In short, the ripple effect of a defendant's death is far greater than one might expect. (*See* ch. 1, The Price of Empathy: Learning to Cope with Trauma in the Criminal Courtroom.)

I've tried to come up with a few lessons from these three deaths for myself. The first lesson is to *talk to a peer*. There are some things that, as judicial officers, we are not to able share with others due to judicial ethics concerns. For me, talking to a fellow judge allows me to fully open up to the extent to which I am comfortable and helps me process the things I see and encounter on the bench. In the Western District of Missouri there are several judges who provide me advice, guidance, and a listening ear. Senior judges are especially important because they have seen it all. While not everyone can go bend the ear of a Senior United States District Judge, we all need to find that mentor in our life who can listen, understand, and support our journey.

The second lesson is to *not make assumptions about people*. We all have implicit biases, even judges, and as a sentencing judge I particularly need to be aware of my own biases. For me, I strive to be acutely aware of not taking the stress or sorrow of one difficult sentencing and applying it to a similarly situated defendant. (For example, another young man, like William, charged with being a felon in possession of a firearm.)

Finally, I've learned the importance of taking a step back from a situation to *gain perspective*. For me, getting out of my courthouse to take a walk and get fresh air is essential to relieving the stress that comes with my position. Taking just a few minutes (or an entire lunch hour) to clear my head makes me more able to more fairly judge the next case. While the loss of these three defendants cannot be undone, the lessons I have drawn from these experiences impact how I approach the fair and equitable administration of justice and help give meaning to their untimely deaths.

II. Federal Judges and Sentencing

Some readers may be surprised to learn the amount of stress judges experience when sentencing criminal defendants. From my own experience, I am enormously impressed with the caliber of judges in the federal judiciary and the seriousness with which they approach criminal matters pending before them, particularly sentencing. A common criticism levied against judges is that they "tend toward narrow, formalistic forms of reasoning, they do little broad reading, and they live upper class lives with relatively little daily contact with poor people or cultures other than their own."[9] That may be a valid criticism, though that reasoning likely applies to any American making more than $100,000 per year. What I can tell you is that the vast majority of judges work extremely hard to administer justice for each defendant, a feat which is increasingly difficult given their large caseloads and often limited resources.

Federal judges are busy. In 2019, the average federal trial judge was assigned 528 civil cases and 168 criminal defendants (or 126 criminal cases).[10] In October of 2020, I had 107 criminal cases assigned to my docket, most of which had multiple defendants involved in drug conspiracies. In talking to my Missouri state court peers, I understand they have even larger caseloads. And, unlike my state trial court colleagues, federal trial judges have at least two law clerks helping them (mostly on civil matters, but these attorneys are always available to research a difficult criminal issue). The stress and pressure of equitably applying justice to each of those defendants is cumulative and, at times, daunting. To better understand the stress that judges experience, I think it is helpful to know a little about what is takes for a federal judge to sentence a defendant.

To sentence a federal court defendant, a federal judge must first properly calculate the sentencing guidelines and then apply the 18 U.S.C. § 3553(a) factors,[11] which include:

---

[9] Richard Delgado and Jean Stefancic, *Do Judges Cry? An Essay on Empathy and Fellow-Feeling*, Case W. Reserve L. Rev. 70 (no. 1) (2019), 50. My thanks to the authors for the inspiration for the title to this chapter.

[10] *Judicial Facts and Figures 2019*, United States Courts (Sept. 30, 2019), https://www.uscourts.gov/statistics-reports/judicial-facts-and-figures-2019. These national averages are based upon the total number of authorized judgeships, and can vary dramatically by each particular district.

[11] Gall v. United States, 522 U.S. 38, 49 (2007) (holding that the "Guidelines are the starting point and initial benchmark" and that the sentencing court "should consider all of the § 3553(a) factors").

- The nature and circumstance of the offense and the history and characteristics of the defendant;
- The need for the sentence imposed—
  - to reflect the seriousness of the offense, to promote respect for the law, and to provide just punishment for the offense;
  - to afford adequate deterrence to criminal conduct;
  - to protect the public from further crimes of the defendant; and
  - to provide the defendant with needed education or vocational training, medical care, or other correctional treatment in the most effective manner;
- The kinds of sentences available and the sentencing range[.]

To help me calculate the guidelines and to apply the § 3553 factors, the probation office prepares an extensive presentencing report. The PSR digs into the individual's family history, educational background, criminal history, addictions, facts regarding the incident, and just about every aspect of a person's life. I also require both the prosecutor and the defendant to file sentencing memorandums explaining why a particular sentence is warranted under the circumstances or whether there are mitigating facts I should consider. After I have read the PSR and the competing memorandum, I then hold a sentencing hearing, typically ranging from 30 minutes to an hour. The last person I hear from is the defendant, who has a right to tell me anything they want before I hand down a sentence. At the end of the hearing, I have to say these words: "It is the judgment of this Court that the defendant is sentenced to the Bureau of Prisons [BOP] for_____ months."

While the defendant and I are staring at each other, and after reading about an individual's history, family, education, and criminal history, I am often faced with a range of emotions—anger, disgust, empathy. In some cases, I am close to tears. Sentencing is difficult and is an exercise in keeping my emotions in check. In many cases, I ask myself: *How did this individual get here? Why did society allow this person to try heroin at age 12?* Most defendants before me lack even a high-school degree. Many struggle with lifelong mental health and drug addiction issues. Sadly, many have been raised to be federal felons by a parent who also used drugs or demonstrated criminal behavior, and asking a human to cast judgment on a drug felon is an incredibly difficult task. How can our society allow an innocent child to be raised like this? And how am I to know what is sufficient punishment: Will probation be enough? If prison time is warranted, how long should that sentence be? And how can I force the BOP to provide training, education, or mental health services, which are essential components of the rehabilitation process? But an organized society must have rules, Congress says this act is illegal, and this person admits they did the illegal act. Selling drugs while carrying a gun is not allowed; looking at child pornography someone else produced revictimizes an innocent minor every time the image is viewed. All of these issues can be thrown at a judge in one single day. Still, the hearing must end with "the defendant is sentenced to the Bureau of Prisons for _____ months."

However, barring the highly unusual case involving the death penalty (far less than 1% of all cases), death never figures in the equation for sentencing. Almost every defendant will walk out of the BOP. While my "eye for an eye" thought process sometimes makes me want to order something cruel upon an individual who produced pornography of their own child, the much more rational approach is established by our criminal justice system—and that is my job. In all cases I desperately want the defendant to be rehabilitated. I want the addicted drug dealer to go to the BOP, participate in the Residential Drug Addiction Program, come out, and never go back. While it may only be what I tell myself to get through the day, I earnestly believe that everyone in the courtroom—prosecutor, defense counsel, probation officer, family, victim, court reporter, courtroom security officer, and every judge—shares that desire. (*See* ch. 14, Case Study: Sentenced to Healing.)

The process of reading the PSR, reading the sentencing memos, listening to arguments, hearing the allocution statement from the defendant, and sentencing the person to prison plays out time and time again. Dealing with the repetitive sentencing hearings, combined with the corresponding flow of human tragedy, wears on a judge. It's part of the job, but judges must learn to deal with that stress in a healthy way.

III. Resources

There is no doubt that people facing incarceration are under enormous stress. Sitting in judgment of another person is a different kind of stress, and how judges deal with that stress is important. The Federal Judicial Center's *Guide to Judicial Well-Being* succinctly notes that "being a judge can be difficult."

You should expect to encounter tough cases, tough decisions, and tough people that may challenge every aspect of you as a person and a judge. There may be sleepless nights, decisions you struggle over, remarks you regret, and legal issues that seem like the proverbial Gordian knot.[12]

The *Guide* suggests that in challenging times, judges should seek help from senior judges and confer with people they trust. I've been fortunate to be surrounded by other judges who take their jobs seriously and are concerned about mental health. When I first joined the federal bench, Judge Fernando Gaitan offered me this piece of advice: "It's OK to step off the bench to think about it." "It" can be anything, but especially includes stressful sentencings. I've had to follow that advice and should listen to it more.

Counseling

One resource that no one likes to talk about is counseling. Lawyers are especially predisposed to not want to admit to talking to a counselor; we are zealous advocates hired to take on a client's battles. In the Western District of Missouri's reentry court program,[13] we mandate that participants see a counselor. I always tell the reentry court participants that no one wants to go to a counselor, including me, but there is a reason I've been married for 28 years: because I go to a marriage counselor. Our counselor has taught me better ways to deal with stress and how to be a better, more effective communicator. In that same vein, judges are humans tasked with the enormous weight of handing down judgment on our fellow human beings. We need the expertise of mental health professionals, who are skilled in dealing with the craziness of life, to help us manage those pressures in a healthy, productive way.

Healthy Lifestyle

Understanding that stress exists and how your body reacts to certain stressors are important steps in learning how to deal with stress in a

[12] Reiss, *supra* note 1, at 10-11.

[13] The Western District of Missouri's Re-Entry Court is an alternative program for formerly incarcerated individuals on federal supervision who have significant substance abuse treatment needs. The program combines intense supervision, the best practices in addiction treatment, timely court intervention, and innovative case management to improve participant outcomes and reduce recidivism. A key part of this program is regular individualized counseling. For more information, please visit https://www.mow.uscourts.gov/reentry-court.

healthy manner.[14] Lawyers Concerned for Lawyers, an organization out of Pennsylvania, identifies several key areas that should be focused on for judicial overall health:

- The three pillars of good health (sleep, diet, and exercise);
- Substance use and/or mental health issues; and
- A lifestyle appropriate to your (current and long term) needs.[15]

This same organization runs a sister group, Judges Concerned for Judges, which provides support services to judges, including a toll-free hotline.[16] "We know firsthand the price of professional and personal isolation necessary to preserve the appearance of impartiality."[17] Judge Thomas DelRicci, a judge on the Montgomery County Court of Common Pleas in Pennsylvania, is one of the founders of Judges Concerned for Judges. Judge DelRicci told me that in the first 20 years after Lawyers Concerned for Lawyers was founded, only one judge ever took advantage of the free services. He observed:

> Judges don't want to be vulnerable in front of the bar. For judges to seek help they need to know there is a safe and confidential place. In the first several years of Judges Concerned for Judges, almost 200 judges took advantage of the program. We offer help through peer advice and professional mental health providers. The most common issues involve mental health, stress, and depression. When we get judges assistance, it helps the litigants, the justice system, and the judge.[18]

In addition to the national hotline managed by Judges Helping Judges, the American Bar Association (and likely every state bar association) has a program for lawyers and judges to receive confidential and free assistance in dealing with a host of mental health, stress, and addiction issues. The need for these services is significant. In what has been described as the "largest survey of judges in the US on stress and wellness," a 2019 study revealed that the top two sources of stress are the importance/impact of

[14] Lawyers Concerned for Lawyers Pennsylvania, *Judges and Stress* (Nov. 2018), https://www.lclpa.org/wp-content/uploads/2019/05/Judges-and-Stress-2018-Update-2.pdf.

[15] *Judges and Stress*, *supra* n. 14, at 5.

[16] 1-800-219-6474; available at Judges Concerned for Judges Pennsylvania, https://www.jcjpa.org/help-for-a-judge.

[17] Judges Concerned for Judges Pennsylvania.

[18] Judge Thomas DelRicci, in discussion with the author, December 4, 2020.

decisions and heavy dockets.[19] Judges often reported feelings of fatigue, sleep disturbance, lack of concentration, and worry. Additionally, approximately 2.2% of judges reported thoughts of suicide in the last 12 months, while 11.5% of lawyers have had suicidal thoughts during their career and 6% of law students have had suicidal thoughts within the last year.[20] Beyond access to mental health services and support programs, the study also identified some recommended resiliency activities, including exercise, hobbies, better sleep, balanced nutrition, and my personal favorite, "diverse friends outside of the field." The good Lord knows lawyers need some non-lawyer friends. The report also recommended that different judicial entities lead by example in judicial well-being, including publishing programs, sharing relevant studies, and simply acknowledging the stressful nature of the job. As with mental health issues more broadly, having a public discourse about these important issues is a critical step.

Dealing with Stress

One excellent article on judicial stressors, *Five Ways Judges Can Improve Well-Being*, discusses simple ways to "increase resilience (one's ability to bounce back and, ideally, grow from adversity) and healthfully cope with the daily stressors of life on the bench."[21] The article encourages judges to:

- Practice gratitude (noting that a gratitude journal can increase a person's happiness by 25%);
- Practice mindfulness (e.g., breathing exercises, meditation, and mindfulness practices);
- Volunteer to help others (high-stress jobs increase rate of death, while volunteering lowers it);
- Practice self-compassion (i.e., sensitivity to the experience of your own suffering); and
- Cultivate your sense of humor (which leads to reduced stress, improved coping, and better perspective).[22]

---

[19] American Bar Association Commission on Lawyer Assistance Programs, *CoLAP's 2019 National Judicial Stress and Resiliency Survey: The Results Are In!*, September 25, 2019, https://www.americanbar.org/content/dam/aba/events/lawyer_assistance/2019/wedgen2/national-judicial-stress-resilience-survey092319.pdf.

[20] *Id.*

[21] Bree Buchanan, *Five Ways Judges Can Improve Well-Being*, Judicature 101(4) (Winter 2017), at 80.

[22] *Id.*

In addition to the support services provided by various state and national bar associations and groups like Judges Helping Judges, these practices offer accessible and practical methods for judges to manage the stress of their position in a healthy and balanced way.

Empathy

Professors Richard Delgado and Jean Stefancic have written a fantastic article, *Do Judges Cry? An Essay on Empathy and Fellow-Feeling*, that asks: "[c]an judges and other lawmakers understand the full human impact of the decisions they hand down?"[23] This law review article explores the role of empathy in judicial decision making. Professors Delgado and Stefancic advance an assumption that "humanizing narratives … seldom alter judges' behavior, much less engage their emotions."[24] Although the professors set forth a deservedly long list of sins committed by the judiciary that demonstrate a total lack of empathy—child labor, gay marriage, Japanese internment camps, slavery, forced sterilization, etc.—I respectfully, if naïvely, disagree with the assumption that judges do not listen to humanizing narratives, nor engage their emotions.[25] Judges *do* cry. Judges do feel empathy. My peers, regardless of their professional background, struggle with sentencing. I also believe that the 18 U.S.C. § 3553 factors require judges to have empathy by making us examine the characteristics of the defendant and consider their needs in terms of education, training, and care.

Aside from the role it plays during sentencing, empathy is a powerful medicine in the fight against stress. "When we give and receive empathy we produce the near magical neurotransmitter oxytocin, which creates a sense of trust and cooperation—keys to negotiating and resolving conflict, whether between couple, communities, states, or countries."[26] Empathetic listening skills include reflecting on what others say, paying attention to body language, asking open-ended questions, slowing down

---

[23] Delgado & Stefancic, *supra* note 9, at 23.

[24] *Id.* at 40.

[25] Professor Delgado is one of the most prolific and most cited academic writers in America, so I admit I could be wrong. I do agree with Prof. Delgado that "consulting outside texts … may be a useful start" to creating empathy and understanding "what one is doing for a living."

[26] Arthur Ciaramicoli, *How to Fight Stress with Empathy*, MINDFUL, January 11, 2017, https://www.mindful.org/fight-stress-empathy.

and taking a deep breath, avoiding snap judgments, and learning from the past (including being aware of your own biases and not jumping to conclusions). All these skills easily and readily transfer to a sentencing hearing. I often repeat something back to the defendant from the sentencing memorandum or something I heard the defendant tell me during allocution. If you are going to federal prison, you deserve to be heard. And slowing down, breathing deeply, avoiding snap judgments—those are all practices straight out of the Federal Judicial Center's *Mindfulness and Judging* and *Guide to Judicial Well-Being*. I'm not trying to suggest that we turn a felony sentencing hearing into an extended deep-breathing or meditation session. But I do think listening to a defendant and their counsel, affirming what you agree with, explaining calmly why you have reached your decision, and being aware of your own biases make a hearing more productive, and less stress-invoking, for all the participants.

Admittedly, crying on the bench—which I have done—is probably not the best way to handle any proceeding, let alone a sentencing hearing. Judge Jeremy Fogel's work on *Mindfulness and Judging* notes that "[a]t least from the perspective of those with whom he or she interacts, perhaps the most important attributes of a judge are demeanor and temperament."[27] When my emotions are so raw that I feel as if I am on the verge of tears, that is the moment when I need to step back and get off the bench to think and be calm. Whether a judge is furious at a defendant who is being sentenced, upset at the unfairness of the justice system, or has simply had enough of a particular lawyer, a "judge should be patient, dignified, respectful, and courteous to litigants, jurors, witnesses, lawyers, and others with whom the judge deals in an official capacity."[28] At the end of the day, a judge takes off the robe and is back to being a person, with emotions and reactions. Many types of proceedings, but especially sentencing hearings, require a judge to walk a tightrope of empathy and being even-tempered. All humans have to learn how to navigate this difficult balance in life, but the scenario of being a sentencing judge sometimes demands a herculean emotional discipline and humanity.

---

[27] Judge Jeremy D. Fogel, Mindfulness and Judging 4 (Federal Judicial Center, 2016).

[28] Code of Conduct for United States Judges, Canon 3(A)(3).

IV. Conclusion

When defendants die, either by suicide or by the actions of another, the ripple effect is widespread. Judges are not immune from the impact of such losses or the range of emotions that can follow an individual's untimely death. Yet the nature of judges' position within the justice system means that they must balance their empathy with administering justice in a fair, consistent, and equitable manner. In turn, judges, like the rest of society, must find positive ways to deal with the stress of their responsibilities to ensure that the criminal justice system remains fair. However, striking this balance does not mean eliminating empathy or emotion from judicial decision making. Indeed, the fair administration of justice demands that judges develop the empathetic skills and healthy habits necessary to carry out the day-to-day responsibilities that occupy judges' dockets. Section 3553(a) requires a judge to impose a sentence that is sufficient but not greater than necessary. But the defendant being sentenced, like William, has a name, a family, and a story. Empathy with society, victims, and the defendant is required during sentencing; occasionally, that means crying is necessary, too.

• • •

Stephen R. Bough is a United States District Court Judge for the Western District of Missouri. Prior to his appointment to the federal bench in 2014, Judge Bough practiced law as a civil litigator for nearly 20 years. He wishes to thank his two law clerks—Anne Case Halferty and Stephen Ahal—for their considerable efforts to edit this article. Judge Bough can be reached at Stephen_Bough@mow.uscourts.gov.

Complete citations are available from the author upon request.

Chapter

8

Suicide Prevention in the Criminal Justice System: Breaking the Silence

The Honorable Ginger Lerner-Wren

In recent years, judges have stepped out of their traditional roles and presided over problem-solving courts. These courts are not only interdisciplinary in nature, but also call on the judge to be more hands-on—indeed, to engage a defendant in conversation about an array of concerns which are not necessarily legal but which nonetheless impact their criminal case.

Judge Ginger Lerner-Wren, the founder of the Broward County Mental Health Court in Florida, is one of the pioneers of the problem-solving court movement. In this chapter, she describes her growing concern that people in her court were precariously vulnerable to suicide. But she also realized that her court could not simply help prevent suicidal ideations, but instead empower people to become healthy, a state that could better enable them to surmount their criminal case and lead productive, law-abiding lives.

• • •

"What mental health needs is more sunlight, more candor, and unashamed conversation."

—*Glenn Close,* Mental Illness: The Stigma of Silence, *HUFFPOST (Nov. 17, 2011), https://bit.ly/2Z3vOUE*

As pioneer of America's first mental health court, I have witnessed the devastating impact of untreated mental illness, the pain of family members whose adult children revolve in and out of jail, hospital emergency rooms, and the streets. Likewise, I have also witnessed the power of community collaboration, where an interdisciplinary coalition of criminal justice and behavioral health stakeholders assemble to seek solutions to systemic problems, and develop new strategies to fill gaps in local community systems of care which intersect with criminal justice. The lessons learned from Broward County's Mental Health Court speak to the progress of the criminal justice system in promoting diversionary strategies to expand access to community care and services for people arrested with serious mental illnesses and co-occurring disorders.

Several years ago, I realized that there was an urgency to elevate suicide prevention in the mental health court. This determination was based on the alarming rise in the rates of suicide in the United States. *See* Sabrina Tavernise, *U.S. Suicide Rate Surges to a 30-Year High*, N.Y. Times (April 22, 2016), https://nyti.ms/370lczd. For me, it was a wake-up call that I must do more to promote suicide prevention. My first goal was to clearly communicate that suicide prevention is now a court priority. I developed a multi-strategic plan which I will later discuss. For the purposes of introduction, however, I want to emphasize the importance of breaking the silence on suicide. As I launched my plan, I thought about all the lawyers, court staff, and members of the public I have engaged with over 20-plus years on the bench. According to the research, lawyers in America have a high rate of substance use and mental health disorders compared to the general population. *See* Jennifer K. Johnson, *Lawyers and Suicide*, Policy Research Associates (May 5, 2020), https://bit.ly/3p53rVQ. These behavioral health disorders are often linked to the practice of law, which involves work conditions and a culture that includes high expectations of perfectionism, social isolation, and chronic stress. These conditions, inherent in the legal profession, are well-known risk factors for suicide. *See* Jennifer K. Johnson, *Lawyers and Suicide*, Policy Research Associates (May 5, 2020), https://bit.ly/3p53rVQ.

Thankfully, the American Bar Association (ABA) has taken the lead to address the high prevalence of substance use and mental health disorder in the legal profession. The ABA is also responding to the disproportionally high prevalence of suicide. *See* Jennifer K. Johnson, *Lawyers and Suicide*, Policy Research Associates (May 5, 2020), https://bit.ly/3p53rVQ. In its groundbreaking report, "The National Task Force on Lawyer Well-Being: Creating a Movement to Improve Well-Being in the Legal Profession," recommendations include a call to action to its members and partnering organizations to engage in open dialogues on suicide. *See* National Task Force on Lawyer Well-Being, *The Path to Lawyer Well-Being: Practical Recommendations for Positive Change from the National Task Force on Lawyer Well-Being* 20 (Aug. 14, 2017), https://bit.ly/2OeOK5C. There are a multitude of ways that stigma, shame, and culture contribute to suicide. *See* Sarah Keller et al., *A Look at Culture and Stigma of Suicide: Textual Analysis of Community Theatre Performances*, 3 Int'l J. Envtl. Resources Pub. Health 16(3), 352 (2019), https://bit.ly/3aT5qr9. Stigma is a critical problem because it prevents people from seeking help. According to the research, "Every 12 minutes 1 person dies from suicide in the United States." *See* Substance Abuse and Mental Health Services Administration, https://bit.ly/2NcqOiY. (*See* ch. 1, The Price of Empathy: Learning to Cope with Trauma in the Criminal Courtroom.)

On September 30, 2018, state troopers were dispatched to the Interstate 82 bridge north of Yakima County, in Washington State, when concerned citizens reported a man who appeared to be threatening to jump off the bridge. *See* Substance Abuse and Mental Health Services Administration, https://bit.ly/2NcqOiY. According to news reports, the state troopers arrived to see Yakima County Superior Court Judge Doug Federspiel pacing back and forth by the guardrails of the bridge. One of the troopers assigned to the bridge, specifically to intervene with people threatening suicide, encountered Judge Federspiel. He introduced himself and asked "What is going on?" The judge responded that he was "having a bad day." When he admitted that he was deciding whether to live or not, the trooper offered an option for help. *See* Substance Abuse and Mental Health Services Administration, https://bit.ly/2NcqOiY. Thankfully, Judge Federspiel accepted the help. He engaged in treatment and was able to return to the bench. *See* Substance Abuse and Mental Health Services Administration, https://bit.ly/2NcqOiY.

It is important to know that suicide is preventable. According to the National Alliance on Mental Illness, "The elimination of stigma starts by understanding the facts, which include the warning signs of suicide, risk factors, and how to respond." *See* Kristin Fuller, M.D., *5 Common Myths About Suicide Debunked*, NAMI Blog (Sept. 30, 2020), https://bit.ly/3a9H2m5. There needs to be more training and education for judges, law firms, lawyers, and law students on suicide. When I consider the advancements in the collaborative and problem-solving courts, I am encouraged by the transformative shift in America's criminal justice system to focus on "root cause problems," the interdisciplinary knowledge which includes the impact of adverse childhood experiences, domestic violence, trauma, addiction, mental illness, brain injury, and cognitive disorders. *See* Rebecca Vallas, *Disability Behind Bars*, CENTER FOR AMERICAN PROGRESS (July 18, 2016). The intersection of poverty and disparities in health and education all contribute to depression, despair, and hopelessness. Public health inequities are pervasive in the criminal justice system.

Problem-solving courts are largely focused on reducing these disparities for those involved in the justice system. Services of the court include care navigation and recognition that connection to social services and economic benefits is essential. A great deal of time in mental health court is spent on mental health literacy and education, including teaching lawyers and the public about person-first mental health treatment planning, psychiatric rehabilitation, and the benefits of peer support. It is important to dispel myths and stereotypic thinking about mental illness. I have learned that information about community resources is critical, such as where to apply for the certain types of services like Medicaid. The court's focus on education and teaching as we go has provided many young lawyers with a strong foundation in mental health and understanding of how to navigate community systems of care, and the importance of integrating best practices and the science into court processes. *See* Rebecca Vallas, *Disability Behind Bars*, CENTER FOR AMERICAN PROGRESS (July 18, 2016). Yet there remains a vacuum of education and training about suicide for judges and lawyers. I believe this is significant for their own well-being and for that of those they serve, including men and women who are incarcerated.

The Revolution of Problem-Solving Courts and Therapeutic Jurisprudence

Can courts act as therapeutic agents? That is the fundamental concept of Therapeutic Jurisprudence (TJ). Therapeutic Jurisprudence is a law reform science which studies the impact of the court process, and how it can impact behavior and social consequences. It was conceived in the mid-1980s by two law professors, Professors Bruce J. Winick and David B. Wexler. *See* Michael L. Perlin, *What Is Therapeutic Jurisprudence*, 10 N.Y.L.

Sch. J. Hum. Rts. 623-636 (1993), https://bit.ly/2Z0IWPl. They met at the University of Miami College of Law during the emergence of the field of mental health law. Through their scholarship and friendship, they frequently analyzed case law related to mental health law, and studied the role of courts, legal process, and the capacity of courts to act as a therapeutic agent. Through legal scholarship Professors Winick and Wexler examined the possibilities of the law, and how through court process, the law can become a positive force for change: not only for the individual, but for the community, and the world. *See* Bruce J. Winick, *Therapeutic Jurisprudence and Problem Solving Courts*, 30 Fordham Urb. L.J. 1055 (2003), https://bit.ly/3aOHEMW.

The law reform science of TJ, which includes principles of procedural justice, was applied in the first problem-solving drug court established in Miami-Dade County in 1989. Through TJ, judges, prosecutors, defense lawyers, and substance use treatment providers shared a common goal of rehabilitation and relapse prevention for those arrested for possession of cocaine. The decision to establish a diversionary treatment court shifted the focus to address the "root cause" problem of drug addiction and to offer treatment over punishment. The drug court opened the door to a new criminal justice paradigm. In 1989, former U.S. Attorney General Janet Reno had been appointed to serve as the Dade County State Attorney. At the time, Miami was the epicenter for cocaine addiction. According to Dade County State Attorney Katherine Fernandez Rundle (then Chief Assistant State Attorney), "The onslaught of drug arrests, where [there were] as many as 200 new drug violators a night in the county jail, had created a revolving door of drug arrests ... They'd walk out the door, go back on the streets and return to what they were doing." Janet Reno understood that there needed to be a new strategy to address this crisis, which impacted both public health and Dade County's criminal justice system. *See* Michael Isikoff & William Booth, *Miami Drug Court Demonstrates Reno's Unorthodox Approach*, The Washington Post (Feb. 20, 1993), https://wapo.st/3qiWm5v. She believed strongly that drug offenders needed an alternative court process and an offer of treatment rather than punishment.

Hailed as "one of the most extraordinary courtrooms in America," the Dade County Drug Court, through the application of Therapeutic Jurisprudence, forever altered the jurisprudential landscape of criminal justice in America. *See* Michael Isikoff & William Booth, *Miami Drug*

Court Demonstrates Reno's Unorthodox Approach, The Washington Post (Feb. 20, 1993), https://wapo.st/3qiWm5v. For the first time, criminal court judges could step outside the role of a neutral arbiter. Through the application of the science of TJ, judges and lawyers understood their ability to harness the social forces of the court process to promote rehabilitation and relapse prevention. According to the U.S. Department of Justice, there are currently more than 3,000 drug courts in the United States. *See* U.S. Department of Justice, Office of Justice Programs, *Drug Courts* (Nov. 2020), https://bit.ly/3aRb39i. In addition, there are thousands of kinds of public health-oriented problem-solving courts. *See* Center for Court Innovation, https://bit.ly/370ByrL. This includes domestic violence courts, mental health courts, veterans' courts, family drug courts, reentry courts, safe baby courts, community courts, girl's courts, juvenile mental health courts, teen courts, homeless courts, DWI courts, and tribal courts. *See* Center for Court Innovation, https://bit.ly/370ByrL.

We All Have a Role to Play for Suicide Prevention

I will never forget the moment I saw the alarming news that deaths in the United States by suicide have surged. I was preparing to speak at the Executive Forum for the New York Association of Psychiatric Rehabilitation Services, Inc. *See* New York Association of Psychiatric Rehabilitation Services, https://bit.ly/2Oo6D24. It was a Friday afternoon: April 22, 2016. As I waited for my panel to be called, the news came through a media alert on my cell phone. According to a story in *The New York Times*, a newly released national research study by the National Center for Health Statistics showed that "suicide in the United States has surged to the highest levels in nearly 30 years." *See* Sabrina Tavernise, *U.S. Suicide Rate Surges to a 30-Year High*, N.Y. Times (April 22, 2016), https://nyti.ms/370lczd. I recall quietly checking in with several colleagues to see if they shared my concern. They did! When it was my turn to speak, I opened my remarks with the shocking news that for the first time in 30 years, suicide in the United States had "surged to the highest levels across virtually every age group." *See* Sabrina Tavernise, *U.S. Suicide Rate Surges to a 30-Year High*, N.Y. Times (April 22, 2016), https://nyti.ms/370lczd.

On the flight back to Florida, I thought about how I addressed the subject of suicide in the mental health court. I have always taken great pride in the fact that I view the courtroom as a classroom. It was the venue where delegations of criminal justice and mental health stakeholders, psychologists, and students from colleges in law, nursing, psychology, and social work would come to observe the court in action. It was an opportunity for me to teach and model a mental health court which promotes recovery from a dignity and human rights framework. I have been diligent to keep up with the literature on mental health policy as well as research on psychiatric rehabilitation and recovery so I could integrate the science into the court process. This included discussion about the social consequences of adverse childhood experiences, the impact of victimization and trauma, and the cascading consequences of untreated mental illness. It was my intention to humanize the court process. I wanted court participants to feel safe to talk about mental health and share their stories so that I could understand "what happened to an individual" and how the court needed to intervene. To humanize the court process, the culture of the courtroom needed to convey caring and compassion. I understood the impact of trauma and marginalization. The vision of the court is to create a court of refuge through the application of the law reform science of Therapeutic Jurisprudence—yet I never asked about suicide.

Listening Is Where Hope Thrives

I will never forget the look of despair on the man's face as he sat alone in the back of my courtroom. I was between sessions. I preside over both a regular criminal division and mental health court, and expected the courtroom to be empty as I prepared for my next docket in the regular criminal division. I asked the court deputy to please check to see which docket this person was here for. As the deputy spoke to him, I observed that the man appeared upset. I wondered whether he was late for the mental health court. As the deputy returned to the bench, he indicated that Mr. Richards (not his real name) was on the docket for the regular criminal division for the crime of petit theft. The court deputy, who has years of experience working in the mental health court, mentioned to me that Mr. Richards was not doing well.

I immediately left the bench and walked over to where Mr. Richards was sitting. I calmly asked if I could sit down next to him. He agreed. I noticed that Mr. Richards appeared thin and pale. His clothing was disheveled, and he looked as if he had not slept for some time. I introduced myself.

To build a rapport, I explained that I preside over two different court divisions. I briefly described the mental health court to him. I explained that it was a treatment court, and asked him if there was anything wrong. Mr. Richards began to cry. He stated that he had lost his job. I listened and watched as he lowered his head into his hands. Then, Mr. Richards leaned forward and placed his head on the back of the seat in front of where we were sitting and sobbed. He said, "I tried everything to get work. I am afraid I am going to lose my home." As he continued to cry, I sensed that he had lost hope. In a whisper, he stated that he did not know what was going to happen to his family.

I sat silently for a few moments and got up the nerve to ask him if he was thinking about hurting himself. He nodded, "yes."

Based on my experience, I recognized that Mr. Richard's despair was palpable. As a mental health court judge and advocate, I am all too familiar with the stigma, myths, and shame surrounding the subject of mental illness. If Mr. Richards had been experiencing chest pains, or another kind of medical emergency, the court deputy would have called 9-1-1. Not so with a mental health crisis. I reassured Mr. Richards that everything was going to be OK and asked if I could call mental health counselors to come to the courtroom. He agreed. I proceeded to call the mobile crisis team and asked my deputy to stay with him. This specially trained mental health team has responded to court emergencies many times in the past.

Within 30 minutes the team arrived. Two mental health clinicians entered the courtroom. One member of the team approached the side of the bench to get basic information, while the other therapist took a seat by Mr. Richards. As I proceeded to prepare to call the next docket, a team member approached the bench to tell me that Mr. Richards had agreed to go the hospital for mental health treatment. Further, the therapist said that, based on their preliminary screening and assessment, Mr. Richards was at risk for suicide. I recall pausing, as the team member shared the results of their assessment. I reflected on what might have happened had he not gotten access to mental health resources. Several months later, Mr. Richards appeared in court. I did not recognize him; he looked quite different. As he approached the bench, he announced that he was working part time in an accountant's office with hopes of a full-time position. He thanked me for my help.

I realized that I rarely talked about suicide. I thought about the various ways suicide had been addressed in the courtroom up to this time.

The truth was that discussions about suicide were largely delegated to the in-court mental health clinician. I felt it was the clinician's role to privately make inquiries about suicide risk as a part of the psychosocial screenings and assessments.

Raising the Bar for Suicide Prevention

I understood that I needed to raise the bar for suicide prevention in both the mental health court and my regular criminal division. I thought about how I would message and communicate my intention to elevate suicide prevention as a court priority. I looked to the goals and standards of care of the Zero Suicide movement, and publicly declared the mental health court a Zero Suicide Initiative Court. *See* Zero Suicide, https://bit.ly/3d1fkJR. What did that mean? First, it meant that from now on, suicide prevention would be elevated to the number-one priority of the court. To memorialize this objective, I wrote several blog posts about what it meant to declare a court a Zero Suicide Initiative. *See* Ginger Lerner-Wren, *Mental Health Courts: Raising the Bar for Suicide Prevention*, Suicide Prevention Resource Center (Oct. 7, 2016), https://bit.ly/3tQrc7J. My goal was to ensure that I began to talk about suicide from the bench, and not delegate those discussions to the court clinician. Further, every mental health court participant would receive a packet which included a mental health crisis resource information sheet. This included the telephone numbers to First Call For Help, 211 Broward, the National Suicide Prevention Lifeline, the mental health mobile crisis team, Broward County's Centralized Crisis Receiving Center, and local detox programs. I included the instructions that if there is a mental health crisis which requires calling 9-1-1, you should specify that you are calling with regards to a mental health crisis and request a Crisis Intervention Team (CIT) officer, a law enforcement officer specially trained to respond to intervene and respond to mental health crises.

In addition, I provide a set of handouts which includes a brochure from the Broward County Chapter of the National Association on Mental Illness (NAMI). NAMI offers a (free) evidence-based 12-week Family to Family educational program. *See* NAMI, *Family-to-Family Education Added to National Registry of Evidence-Based Mental Health Programs* (May 28, 2013), https://bit.ly/3cYzJ2q. My efforts to raise the bar for suicide prevention and education may seem simple, yet information on how to identify whether a friend or loved one may be at risk of suicide is essential information to save lives.

Suicide Is More than a Mental Health Problem

According to the CDC's *Vital Signs* (June 2018), more than half of all suicides are not related to an underlying mental health condition, but to various social conditions which can cause undue stress. *See* Centers for Disease Control, *Suicide Rising Across the U.S: More than a Mental Health Concern* (June 7, 2018), https://bit.ly/3aPxf3x. Personal problems, such as those experienced by Mr. Richards, include loss of a family member, physical health, divorce, unemployment, legal problems, substance use, and housing stress; all are examples of social factors which can contribute to suicide.

Kevin Wesley grew up in Fort Lauderdale. He had been a stellar athlete, excelling in the 400- and 800-meter races in track and field. He had been arrested for the offense of criminal mischief. According to the arrest affidavit, Kevin allegedly threw a rock through a store window. Kevin had been referred to mental health court by his public defender. Kevin appeared in court accompanied by his mother. Mrs. Wesley explained that Kevin came from a large family that was deeply involved in their church. His mother had raised three other children and worked two jobs. "I do the best I can," she said in her meeting with Janis (the in-court clinician). "Kevin was always a sweet boy and hard-working athlete. But by Kevin's junior year in high school, his attendance started slipping," Mrs. Wesley explained. "It was heartbreaking. He was being considered for a full scholarship to a major university. Then, he got into the wrong crowd and experimented with drugs. After that, he was not himself." Mrs. Wesley noted that he had been "Baker-Acted"[1] several years ago for a serious mental illness, and she worried at times, as he became so withdrawn, that he was contemplating suicide. When she asked him if he was thinking about harming himself, that was when he agreed to seek help, but he did not keep up with his appointments. Mrs. Wesley saw Kevin's behavior as a cry for help.

[1] Provision in Florida law which allows for the involuntary institutionalization and examination of an individual for up to 72 hours. Named after Florida State Representative Maxine Baker.

A Nation in Despair: The Need to Prioritize Suicide Prevention

The young man walked slowly with his head down as he approached the podium in the Broward County Misdemeanor Drug Court. Several years ago, I assumed this division upon the retirement of one of my colleagues. Along with Broward's mental health court and a regular criminal division, I looked forward to continuing to provide the opportunity for people with qualifying charges to earn a dismissal through successful completion of the court program. It was not long before I realized that most individuals in this court were young adults in their late twenties and thirties.

As the first case was called, Mr. Henderson approached the podium. He was 29 years old and had been charged with possession of drug paraphernalia.

"Mr. Henderson" I asked, "how are you doing today?"

He looked up and began to weep. "Judge, I am months behind in my rent and concerned that I will lose my job if I do not report to work on time." He added, "My mother's water is off, and I'm trying to help pay the bill." I asked him to please sit down and motioned for the in-court therapist to speak with him to assess overall needs.

Unfortunately, Mr. Henderson was not alone in his despair. If the court is going to be effective, I understood it must consider social determinants of health (SDOH, e.g., economic stability, employment, housing, education, discrimination, food, community supports) which may be contributing to criminal justice involvement. For those engaged in the juvenile or criminal justice system, the intersection of health care and criminal justice involvement remains a prevailing challenge, as poverty and lack of publicly funded resources, stigma, and cultural barriers fuel a revolving door of incarceration and over-reliance on emergency rooms and crisis response systems. According to the National Alliance to Impact the Social Determinants of Health, "SDOH are conditions in the environments in which people are born, live, learn, work, play, worship and age that affect a wide range of health, functioning, and quality of life outcomes and risks." *See* Joyce Frieden, *Experts Urge More Focus on Social Determinants of Health*, MEDPAGETODAY (Nov. 14, 2018), https://bit.ly/3aR9XKI. The recommendations by the National Alliance urge us to take a holistic approach to problem-solving through community linkages and from a systems level—recognizing that simply asking "what a person and/or family needs" could ultimately lead to a new vision of building healthy communities and social justice.

As stated by Marian Wright Edelman, "The challenge of social justice is to evoke a sense of community that we need to make our nation a better place, just as we make it a safer place." *See* BrainyQuote, *Marian Wright Edelman Quotes*, https://bit.ly/2Z0HH2z. In my search for clarity on how best to serve the young adults in this court, I turned to an issue brief, "Pain in the Nation: Building a National Resilience Strategy—Alcohol and Drug Misuse and the Millennial Generation—A Devastating Impact." *See* Trust for America's Health & Well Being Trust, *Pain in the Nation Update: While Deaths from Alcohol, Drugs, and Suicide Slowed Slightly in 2017, Rates Are Still at Historic Highs* (Mar. 2019), https://bit.ly/2MOHv45. According to this issue brief, "Increases in alcohol, drug and suicide related deaths have affected all age groups and all communities, but the impact on people in their 20's and early 30's has been especially pronounced." *See* Trust for America's Health & Well Being Trust, *Pain in the Nation Update: While Deaths from Alcohol, Drugs, and Suicide Slowed Slightly in 2017, Rates Are Still at Historic Highs* (Mar. 2019), https://bit.ly/2MOHv45. Based on data, the death rates of young adults have increased by 400% over the past two decades due to the opioid crisis. As to alcohol use, the deaths rates have increased 69% between 2007 and 2017 and suicide deaths for young adults went up 35%. *See* Trust for America's Health & Well Being Trust, *Pain in the Nation Update: While Deaths from Alcohol, Drugs, and Suicide Slowed Slightly in 2017, Rates Are Still at Historic Highs* (Mar. 2019), https://bit.ly/2MOHv45. This was a call to action for a national resilience strategy, and provided the impetus for me to make changes to the court. In a simple gesture, in order to inspire hope and opportunity, I realigned the goals of the court to promote quality of life, as well as new pathways to purpose, opportunity, and healthy lifestyles. I also changed its name to Broward County Substance Use and Prevention Court, to emphasize the significance of prevention.

We All Have a Role to Play in Suicide Prevention

As a member of the Executive Committee of The National Action Alliance for Suicide Prevention, I want to emphasize that it is important to know that we all have a role to play in suicide prevention. According to the #BeThe1To campaign, there are five action steps for speaking to someone who may be suicidal, which are supported by the research. *See* #BeThe1To, *How and Why the 5 Steps Can Help*, https://bit.ly/2LzrdeH. These steps are much like what I did with Mr. Richards, when I saw him sitting alone in the courtroom, and went over to him and asked him if he was thinking of harming himself. According to the evidence, asking someone about suicide does not increase the risk of suicide. *See* #BeThe1To, *How and Why the 5 Steps Can Help*, https://bit.ly/2LzrdeH. Additional steps include to "be there," physically or otherwise, to support that person; keeping them safe; trying to find as much information as possible to evaluate risk; connecting them with care; and developing a safety plan. The last step is to follow up.

I appreciate how challenging it could be to break the silence and begin speaking about suicide. Even for me, a mental health court judge, it took many years before I realized that I needed to lead by example, and to help others lawyers, court staff, and members of the public realize that is OK to talk about suicide. Based on my decision to prioritize suicide prevention in mental health court, I made sure that I continually messaged about mental health and suicide prevention in my criminal divisions. This includes reminding people that help is available through the National Suicide Prevention Lifeline, 1-800-273-8255 (TALK). *See* National Suicide Prevention Lifeline, https://bit.ly/3rCL9N5. In July 2020, Congress passed the National Suicide Hotline Designation Act to establish 9-8-8 as the universal hotline for the National Lifeline for Suicide prevention and mental health crisis services. *See* Chuck Morris, *Congress Passes Bill Establishing 988 for Suicide Hotline, Awaits President's Signature*, NEWS4 NASHVILLE (Sept. 22, 2020), https://bit.ly/3a6H5yE. Advocates for the new three-digit crisis number wanted a crisis hotline number similar to the 9-1-1 emergency number to make it easier for people to learn and remember in the event of either a mental health crisis or need for someone to speak to a suicide prevention counselor.

I believe resource information is vital. This could include a mental health handout or resource page posted on your website. This is a simple way of communicating to the public, clients, friends, or colleagues that mental health and suicide prevention is a priority, and must be taken seriously. The resource page can include a list of major publicly funded local mental health organizations, including your local or county NAMI, Mental Health America, First Call for Help 211, as well as publicly funded community mental health/behavioral centers, and substance use treatment centers in your county or court jurisdiction.

The Promotion of Suicide Prevention as a Matter of Social Justice

Professor Bruce J. Winick, co-pioneer of TJ, often spoke about the significance of humanizing law, and the multiple dimensions of the law, as a helping profession. He understood that perhaps judges and lawyers are not the ideal people to address psychosocial problems such as mental health, substance use, and domestic violence. Yet, often, these are the problems and underlying social conditions which we face in the criminal justice system.

Since the establishment of America's first drug court in 1989, the criminal justice system has assumed a unique role in public health. The principles and goals of TJ are now commonly applied in courts of general jurisdiction, as lawyers and judges find great satisfaction in making a difference in the quality of life for the people they serve, and the community and society as a whole. For the judges and lawyers who are doing this work, it is important to appreciate that you are also leading social change: that these efforts to promote hope, dignity, and equality are the essence of the pursuit of justice. Court conversations and dialogues surrounding mental health, trauma, rehabilitation, and suicide prevention are critical to educate and inform the people we serve. In this regard, the evolution of TJ and problem-solving justice is not only about the promotion of health and public safety—it is about saving lives.

• • •

Judge Ginger Lerner-Wren was elected to the County Court, 17th Judicial Circuit, Broward County, Florida, in 1997. Judge Lerner-Wren is a former Director of the Office of Public Guardian for the 17th Judicial Circuit and served as Plaintiff's Monitor in the federal class action, *Sanbourne v. Chiles*, No. 89-6283-CIV-NESBITT. Judge Lerner-Wren pioneered the first problem-solving court in the United States, dedicated to the safe decriminalization of people with mental illness and neurological disorders. Judge Lerner-Wren is an adjunct professor in Nova Southeastern University's College of Psychology and Neuroscience. Judge Lerner-Wren serves on the Board of Trustees of the International Society for Therapeutic Jurisprudence. She can be reached at Jwren@17th.flcourts.org.

Complete citations are available from the author upon request.

Chapter

9

Pretrial, Probation, and Parole

Jack Donson

Judges, prosecutors, and criminal defense lawyers are experts about what goes on inside a courtroom. However, their expertise is often limited regarding jails, prisons, and reentry. This gap is particularly relevant when it pertains to defendant suicide, because these are the points in the criminal justice process where defendants are uniquely vulnerable.

This chapter by federal prison consultant Jack Donson explains the institutional culture of jails and prisons as well as the reentry process. He gives practical advice about how to communicate with clients, families, courts, and correctional officials. His information can be applicable to state or federal defendants. The worlds of jails, prisons, and reentry can be bureaucratic and even incomprehensible, but armed with knowledge and persistence, each can be navigated. All of this may be necessary in order to prevent someone charged, convicted, or exiting confinement from committing suicide.

• • •

The Perils and Challenges of Prison, Correctional Treatment, and Supervision

This chapter was difficult to write from a correctional treatment perspective. Jail operations have little, if any, long-term clinical treatment programs because of the administrative mission and transient nature of the population. In contrast, state and federal prisons primarily focus on substance abuse treatment and broader mental health disorders. Correctional systems treat the multitudes from a general treatment perspective and simply do not have the clinical resources for regular individual psychotherapy. While I will be writing this chapter from a general perspective, I will draw upon examples and protocols based on experiences in the trenches of the federal prison system in a treatment capacity. There is "no one size fits all" given our nation's fragmented network of federal, state, county, and city jails which, according to Peter Wagner of the Prison Policy Initiative, includes 1,833 state prisons, 1,772 juvenile facilities, 3,134 local and county jails, 110 federal prisons, 218 immigration detention facilities, and 80 Indian Country jails.

One would think a controlled and structured prison environment would be conducive to the supervision and treatment of someone at risk for suicide. There are full-time mental health professionals on site and extensive suicide protocols, and most, if not all, staff receive training on suicide prevention. The reality is that despite these systemic procedures, suicides occur at an alarming rate in a prison setting. According to the Department of Justice (DOJ) National Institute of Corrections, the rate of inmate suicides is far higher than the national averages and even higher still for special populations including juvenile and LGBTI inmates. A disturbing DOJ-Inspector General report which I will reference later in this chapter indicated that the rate of suicide had almost doubled from 2014 to 2018. The higher suicide rates are not limited to the incarcerated and transcend the walls, affecting prison workers as well. (*See* ch. 3, Suicide in Prison.)

Correctional systems lack transparency regarding prison operations and more specifically the reporting of suicide. While I was writing this chapter, I received a call from a colleague who informed me about a recent murder and suicide at U.S. Prison (USP) Thompson, which was a controversial purchase made by the government from the State of Illinois and has been repurposed as a Bureau of Prisons (BOP) special management unit (SMU). While I found a brief local media story entitled "Inmate Dies in Thompson Prison after Fight," I could not find any media regarding the suicide. It is not until a high-profile incident like Jeffrey Epstein's suicide or the British Court's refusal to extradite Julian Assange that this issue is brought to the public's attention temporarily. The Epstein case is an example I will refer to throughout this chapter to make certain points and contextualize the difficulties correctional professionals face in combating suicide. In the Assange extradition, the inability of the prison system to prevent his suicide was an element considered by the magistrate judge.

I have been directly and indirectly involved with four suicides over my career plus serious and feigned attempts, most of which occurred within a federal jail operation. One of the suicides was a well-respected and popular high-level administrator. The death had a significant impact on the facility staff and culture given the close working environment. In that case, the signs and signals one hears in training sessions were apparent, but only recognized in hindsight during informal staff conversations. I was not surprised when I heard of the Epstein suicide because controls, policies, and protocols cannot stop someone from harming themselves in a prison setting. Suicide ideation can be temporarily confronted and interrupted in prison, but death is inevitable for a person with a mission and exit strategy.

I often refer to a quote of Justice Anthony Kennedy, who summed it up best before the House Appropriations Committee in 2011 when he stated:

> I think, Mr. Chairman, that the corrections system is one of the most overlooked, misunderstood institutions we have in our entire government. In law school, I never heard about corrections. Lawyers are fascinated with the guilt/innocence adjudication process. Once the adjudication process is over, we have no interest in corrections. Doctors know more about the corrections system and psychiatrists than we do. Nobody looks at it.

This general observation from Justice Kennedy is important because if justice professionals and practitioners are disconnected from the basic understanding of general correctional practices, what kinds of misconceptions exist regarding procedures and treatment for specialized populations like those prone to suicide?

I have been interacting with attorneys, probation officers, and judges on correctional treatment issues for over three decades and there is no better understanding of correctional treatment today than there was in 1986 when I began my career at the state level. The lack of cohesiveness, communication, and synergies among the courts, government agencies, and mental health professionals creates deficiencies and adversely impacts correctional treatment goals, including suicide prevention. Rather than assume that the "system" will take care of a person's needs while in prison, one must be a staunch advocate for a client or family member and understand that these systemic deficiencies are a reality.

Let us take the Jeffrey Epstein suicide as an example of misconception. Based on the correctional pundits and constant media attention at the time, one probably has surmised that he was taken off suicide watch prematurely or that the correctional officers' alleged lack of regular 30-minute checks contributed to his demise. While I will cover specific suicide watch protocols later in the chapter, the reality is that Mr. Epstein was on suicide watch almost *twice* the length of the average similarly situated person. Prior to the termination of the watch, termination was required to have the approval of his clinician followed by everyone up the chain of command all the way to Washington. People with ongoing national media attention receive a "Broad Publicity" designation under a central inmate monitoring program which requires that management at all levels be made aware of, and have input to, case decisions.

The conspiracy theorists and Monday-morning quarterbacks point out that breaches of protocol had insignificant impact on the outcome. Thirty-minute checks are just that. It only takes a person one day in a special housing unit to figure out when or if the officer walks by the door. It is unlikely they will be back for at least 30 minutes, while death from asphyxiation occurs in far less than 10 minutes. That also assumes the officers are making the 30-minute checks, which I can tell you from personal experience was not a reality in many federal prisons pre-Epstein. One of the suicides I was involved with had also been on suicide watch, familiarized himself with the protocols, then methodically executed a successful plan when back in the general population. He said all the right things to the clinician to be removed from watch, manipulated his way into being put in a single cell when back in the population, then hung himself in the cell. Epstein met several of the criteria covered in annual suicide prevention training to identify those who are at risk: namely, that he was a recently received, first-time offender who was abruptly incarcerated in a chaotic jail operation.

It is never easy to manage prisoners with a diagnosed mental health disorder. One must be aware that many people arrested may be undiagnosed. Prison officials at the early stages are relying heavily on self-reporting at intake screening. It is difficult for intake staff to determine if suicidal thoughts have been set in motion by the arrest and abrupt incarceration and the many obstacles inherent in the prison setting and subculture. It is important to educate and prepare clients for the potential realities of prison, especially first-time offenders. The myths and misconceptions about prison in the psyche of the general public are tainted and can create anxiety along with very real triggers for suicidal ideation. Our prison systems have fallen short in emulating community mental health care standards. However, there are usually written policies and protocols in place. It is education and awareness of these policies and protocols which is needed to help protect the welfare of clients to obtain the best outcomes.

Triggers (The Unknown—Make It Known!)

The baseline of understanding from justice professionals regarding prison nuances and culture is abhorrent. What is worse is that often people facing a term of imprisonment are steered to a person who has served time to prepare for the experience. This is a concern to me because a person serving a prison term at one location in one moment of time is extremely limited on systemic issues. I like to use the analogy of someone going into the hospital then coming out and advising people on how to practice medicine. There is some benefit in understanding the subcultural norms and behaviors in a prison setting. But the greater benefit is education about the more technical aspects of the system. Following are five important universal issues all people should be prepared for to lessen the shock of incarceration. The primary consideration for practitioners is to temper the communication by filtering realistic information without further increasing the person's anxiety. This is no easy task.

Intake screening: Intake screening is a demeaning process involving a strip search and the possibility of being placed in a small, crowded cell for hours, sometimes overnight. This is the time when accurate self-reporting is needed regarding medical conditions to get them documented with prison officials. Intake is not the time to be embarrassed or to withhold information. For instance, I have seen people fail to report "shy bladder," a condition which impedes a person from urinating in front of another, only to receive a greatest severity incident report for refusing a urinalysis or not being able later to provide a sample under direct staff supervision. At the federal level, the first thing a lieutenant does when a person claims shy bladder is to call the medical department to see if it is documented. Intake screening disclosure documents the record and sets the follow-up in motion for any applicable protocols.

Vetting: This is how inmates "check out" new arrivals. It is part of the subculture of most prisons whereby new arrivals are asked to show their "papers." This could increase the stress level for new arrivals, especially if they have a sex offense or have cooperated.

Extortion: One of the motivations for vetting, especially in higher security facilities, is extortion. Extortion has many layers and often starts as "friendly" extortion that quickly escalates. The more predatory people assess new arrivals to determine weakness and offer protection which may seem like a good idea at the time. Clients should be warned that most correctional systems have regulations about giving anything of value to other inmates, so the client also may be subject to incident reports.

Sentencing: Prepare for a remand despite the minimal possibility of one. I have worked with many clients who were remanded unexpectedly and were unprepared on what to expect. It is the fear of the unknown which creates an additional stressor.

Isolation: Clients should be made aware that segregation units exist in just about every jail and prison. People can be placed there for a variety of reasons, such as protective custody, security concerns, pending investigation, and (recently) quarantine. Segregation units are where most suicides occur. It is ordinarily 23 hours on lockdown with one hour of recreation and a shower every two or three days. There is minimal access to property, telephone calls, and visiting.

Pretrial Considerations

Remand: Suicides occur at the highest rate in pretrial operations such as detention centers and county jails. The triggers of a jail environment and the abrupt removal from family, substances, and community support networks are traumatic and unpredictable for clients with suicide ideation. Psychiatric medication can be interrupted or changed because of the limitations of the jail's pharmacy, if any, and a lack of clinical mental health documentation.

All correctional systems have an intake screening process which ordinarily involves social, psychological, and mental health assessments. For people with a history of, or who are prone to, self-harm, the best-case scenario is to relay such information to the arresting and transport officers, who can document the information for prison officials upon arrival. It should be noted that suicide-related questions are part of the screening process. However, at such an early stage, the assessment is based on self-reporting in the absence of documentation. A person with prior prison experience understands that being forthcoming may lead to isolation within a restrictive housing unit or, even worse, a formal suicide watch. Statistical outliers mentioned in every suicide prevention training session point to the risk of suicide for young, first-time offenders arriving in a jail operation.

Special attention should be given to a client's medication regimen, because it is not uncommon for medication to be discontinued or substituted depending on what the facility has to offer by way of their formulary. At the federal level, the Federal Bureau of Prisons publishes a two-part formulary of approved drugs dispensed by the institution pharmacist (https://www.bop.gov/resources/pdfs/2019_winter_national_formulary_part_I.pdf and https://www.bop.gov/resources/pdfs/2019_winter_national_formulary_part_II.pdf). If possible, the specific medication, dosage, and diagnosis should be communicated to the arresting officers or facility medical staff as soon as possible. When a person is remanded and is taking a nonformulary medication, an appropriate substitute will be provided unless there is documentation confirming that the formulary substitute is ineffective for that individual. Prison officials may not be aware of the individual's medical profile so as to make the proper determination regarding the efficacy of the substitute. Although there is a process for requesting nonformulary medication, requests are often denied based on the limited historical medical data and costs. In smaller jail operations, the medication regimen may be totally interrupted, thus elevating suicide risk and behaviors that may result in disciplinary infractions.

I once had a client who had been denied gabapentin upon arrival and was given a substitute which the client's community doctor previously prescribed. But the substitute proved ineffective and caused migraines. It took several weeks to finally get nonformulary medication approval because we first needed to obtain the medical records with proof of the adverse side effects. Once received, the gabapentin was provided within days. Every case and medication regimen is unique. Remember: there are established policies and processes to help counsel proactively manage these situations.

There are various pretrial detention operations throughout the country, including federal detention centers, city and county jails, and even private prisons. One should familiarize oneself with any memorandum of understanding (MOU), statement of work (SOW), and other specific contract agreements authorities have with the holding facility regarding medical treatment and suicide prevention protocols. Most jails or transfer holding facilities have specific contractual obligations to the entity for which they are holding the prisoner. Often overlooked is the U.S. Marshal's website, which includes the general policy on prisoner operations including resources on suicide protocols (U.S. Marshals Service, *Suicide Prevention and Recommended Practices*, https://www.usmarshals.gov/business/index.html).

Unfortunately, many times prison practices disregard the actual contractual requirements, so it is important to be aware when a facility is violating an agreement. County jails and private facilities that consider the U.S. Marshals a "cash cow" want to avoid the scrutiny and can quickly comply with requests once they know that you know of their obligations. More diligence is needed when a client is in the custody of private prison providers, who are often cited for deficiencies by audit authorities, particularly when it comes to the delivery of medical treatment.

> ***PRACTICE TIP:** The U.S. Marshals' form USM-129, "Individual Custody/ Detention Report," is provided to the Federal Bureau of Prisons for jail custody credit, but also includes a summary of the medical condition and treatment history while in pretrial detention.*

> ***PRACTICE TIP:** The BOP has a computer case management assignment (CMA) for "PSYC ALERT" which requires a person to be physically interviewed at intake prior to being placed in the general population. Ordinarily, the psychological intake interview is not completed until several days after arrival. There is a psychological intake form completed upon arrival, which is referred to as a "PSIQ," and people who self-report suicidal ideation will be seen at intake.*

The Watch

At the federal level, a suicide watch can be initiated upon arrival or at any time staff perceive that a person may harm themselves. There is a delicate balance in placing someone on formal watch because of the isolation and administrative costs. Moreover, formal watch can be demeaning for the inmate. The decision for a suicide watch can be determined by any staff under exigent circumstances, but ordinarily it is made by a clinician who has the difficult task of determining the sincerity of any gestures, as opposed to a person seeking attention or isolation due to being victimized or other ulterior motives.

In a formal suicide watch, the inmate is given tearaway clothing and is locked in a cell specifically designated for a suicide watch located within the hospital unit of a facility. There is direct, 24-hour supervision by staff, and sometimes inmate supervision. The cell may also include video monitoring. The person initially has no property or any item with which to harm themselves and is provided a specially made suicide blanket. Staff, usually correctional officers, are stationed outside the cell and provide direct supervision while documenting behavior on a periodic basis. Food and a plastic utensil are brought to the cell unless the utensil is considered an item to be used for self-harm. I conducted suicide watch duty throughout my career at the federal level, which does require watches to be done by a correctional officer. We were required to make a notation in a logbook every 15 minutes, such as "*inmate appears to be sleeping*," and document any other observable behaviors. Clinical and administrative staff also signed the logbook, which was archived with the other watch documentation. This all would be a critical discovery request for any prison-related litigation. It should also be noted that if a person were to make a suicide attempt, the incident itself would also be documented on a form referred to as "Form 583-Report of Incident."

Some correctional systems have inmate companions who are trained by clinicians to perform suicide watch to save on administrative costs. Inmate companions are not used on high-profile cases.

A formal suicide watch is a short-term function. After 72 hours, the person is assessed for transfer by a clinician to a federal medical center to be housed in a hospital environment. Practitioners should be aware that all aspects of a watch are documented within the Bureau Electronic Medical Records (BEMR) and Psychology Data Systems (PDS). The governing federal policy includes a considerable amount of C.F.R. material and can be found at https://www.bop.gov/policy/progstat/5324_008.pdf. While researching this chapter, I also came across suicide protocols for the Texas State prison system, which has experienced increased suicide rates: https://www.tdcj.texas.gov/divisions/cmhc/docs/cmhc_policy_manual/G-53.01.pdf.

PRACTICE TIP: Although there are seven Federal Medical Centers (FMCs) throughout the country which are comprehensive in nature, some medical facilities have a unique focus and serve specific populations. For instance, FMC Rochester has always been known for its psychiatric care, mainly due to its relationship with the Mayo Clinic, which serves as the facility's comprehensive medical services contractor.

Post Watch

A person making it through a suicide watch becomes immediately at risk upon returning to the general population if they still have the intention of self-harm. Federal policy requires a clinical interview and assessment prior to removing a person from watch. However, it is not hard for a deceptive person to make it through the clinical interview regardless of their intentions. There is also subtle pressure on clinicians to end watches because of the associated costs. Although one of the goals after removing someone from watch is to get a person back to a general population setting with a cellmate, this is not always possible.

The most common contributor to suicidal ideation in prison is depression, but treatment in the prison setting is difficult. Prison systems do not have the clinical resources for regular, regimented individual psychotherapy. I was always reminded of the inability for individual treatment by psychology services staff when I would forward them a judicial recommendation for such therapy. Judges and justice professionals must know that despite what correctional agencies claim they can provide by way of treatment, the realities of policy application are substandard to what one may receive in the community.

That leads to another misconception and criticism of the Epstein suicide. General population was simply not an option for him. Inmates have the right to request protective custody, which means that they will be housed in the special housing unit. While staff have the ability in some cases to order a person into the general population after a threat assessment is conducted, it is difficult to conclude that a high-profile sex offender with resources is not at risk for exploitation such as extortion and assault. In addition, pretrial (unconvicted) inmates are the responsibility of the U.S. Marshal Service and have more rights while on pretrial status than convicted prisoners.

PRACTICE TIP: ***It is common for a person attempting to injure themselves to receive an incident report for self-mutilation. Incident reports may result in the loss of good time and program privileges like the telephone and visiting, which increases anxiety and frustration. Chapter 3, page 22, of the BOP Inmate Discipline Policy includes a section based on the C.F.R. which discusses when inmates are not responsible for their behavior and/or not competent to participate in the disciplinary process. Too often, inmates receive an incident report and have little understanding of the policy, then regret appealing it later when they are more rational.***

Sentencing Issues

When I prepare federal declarations for sentencing, I search the plethora of available reports from the DOJ, Inspector General, and Government Accounting Office (GAO) to review audits and target issues of noncompliance with protocols for mitigation purposes. While the trend in prison populations is decreasing, one must not forget that they are still overcrowded, lack adequate treatment, and place incapacitation front and center of operations. I often quote the annual DOJ "Top Management and Performance Challenges Facing the Department of Justice" report issued by the Inspector General, which reveals the many deficiencies related to staffing, medical care challenges, contraband, etc. The recently released 2020 report is every bit as critical as in previous years (https://oig.justice.gov/reports/top-management-and-performance-challenges-facing-department-justice-2020).

The 2019 report referenced earlier in the chapter (https://oig.justice.gov/reports/top-management-and-performance-challenges-facing-department-justice-2019) includes this telling quote about suicides at the federal level:

> From FY 2015 through July 2019, the BOP has experienced 46 inmate deaths by homicide and 107 inmate deaths by suicide, including the deaths of high-profile inmates, James "Whitey" Bulger and Jeffrey Epstein. Inmate deaths by suicide in BOP facilities have increased from 8.1 per 100,000 federal inmates in FY 2016 to 14.7 per 100,000 inmates in FY 2018.

From a correctional treatment perspective, it is important to be as comprehensive as possible in the sentencing memorandum, but it is every bit as important to include as much information as possible about a client's mental health history in the presentence report. The BOP does not ordinarily have the sentencing memorandum when processing the initial designation, as it is not a document typically uploaded into the E-DES system, which is the centralized database for designation processing that relies heavily on PSR data. I recommend counsel ask probation and the court to upload any additional relevant psychological reports into E-DES to make it part of the record so it is considered when processing the designation. Any mental health information not uploaded into the E-DES system can be mailed to the facility, to the attention of the chief psychologist. State prisons and local jails will be similarly structured. The goal is to make sure prison official mental health assessments for treatment are based on the complete medical record and not just what they receive within the judicial process.

As stated previously, it is equally important to provide a specific list of medications, dosage units, and the diagnosis relative to each medication for inclusion in the PSR. I have spoken with several BOP clinical directors who have informed me that knowing the diagnosis for each medication assists them when making the decision to continue it upon incarceration and/or consider supporting a nonformulary medication request.

Designation and Classification

Every case has unique characteristics from both the classification and treatment perspectives. Depending on the size of the correctional system, psychiatric services and treatment will most likely be limited. Federal, state, and local governments ordinarily have good policy and protocols in writing which they proudly show the courts. But counsel should dig deeper into what those policies and protocols really look like in practice. Correctional systems lack transparency, and in many cases, accountability. They often fall short of the claims made by administrators who draw treatment comparisons to "community standards."

Although there are treatment programs in most correctional systems, it is helpful to independently research rather than rely on the correctional entity to place a client in the most conducive setting. Be cognizant of classification issues and other program criteria restrictions. I sometimes get involved with cases post-conviction which have impractical judicial recommendations based on the classification and/or program requirements.

At the federal level, there is a perception that the BOP does not comply with judicial designation recommendations; however, I find that often it is due to an ineligibility issue rather than indifference.

There is no "one size fits all" when it comes to a designation of a person with a history of depression or suicidal behavior. For instance, if a federal inmate's classification is likely to be minimum security (camp), paramount to designation may be proximity to the family. Federal prison camps are benign environments with minimal exploitation. However, satellite camps have no on-site clinicians and minimal staffing, programs, or activities. Clients with mental health disorders who are minimum security and camp eligible would be better served in a larger, independent camp or a specialized program even if it were to mean placement in a low-security setting.

It is crucial to conduct facility research in advance of sentencing regardless of whether the court accommodates recommendations. The BOP tracks judicial recommendation compliance at 75%, and in my experience, recommendations are not followed when the recommended facility is not commensurate with the individual's classification and program needs.

If the circumstances of the case dictate a higher classification due to the offense severity, violence, criminal history, or other criminogenic factors, one should seriously consider a specialized program to avoid predation, especially for people with a mental health disorder. Some of the federal specialized programs, like STAGES and Life Connections, may be an option for a client seeking a healthier and more supportive prison environment. While STAGES would be appropriate for someone with a more serious clinical diagnosis for a mental health disorder and prior suicide attempts, Life Connections is a faith-based program open to all faiths that fosters a support system and includes interactive journaling; it was listed on the Substance Abuse and Mental Health Services Administration's (SAMHSA's) national registry of evidence-based programs. These programs are included in the BOP's "Directory of National Programs," which is periodically updated and includes a description of the eligibility criteria of several national programs offered at select facilities. Most state systems have detailed program resources on their websites. As a comparison, I accessed the Texas Department of Criminal Justice (TDCJ) site to search for intensive mental health programs. I did not find any significant programs, but I did find a statewide map directory of substance abuse programs.

In many states, inmates are initially transferred to prisons designated as classification centers, sometimes referred to as *reception centers*, for an indeterminate amount of time. During this period, they receive a risk assessment, are evaluated for programs, and then are transferred to a permanent facility. During this initial evaluation, it is important for the correctional administrators to have all pertinent information. Never assume that a bureaucracy will have all the records relative to a client's diagnosis.

One issue I cannot emphasize enough is to pick up the telephone and reach out to correctional administrators. When I am reminded of the unresponsiveness and bureaucratic walls when calling most agencies, my comeback is "you need to at least try." It is sometimes a frustrating experience, but having persistence and reaching a responsive person along the chain of command can move mountains.

When it comes to the unique circumstances of a mental health disorder, it is learning how to navigate the bureaucracy via the chain of command which can be productive. Calling facilities directly can also be a dead end, so it may be equally important to cultivate regional contacts and resources at the federal level and the Department of Corrections (DOC) headquarters at the state level.

I am only belaboring this point because of its importance. My experience indicates attorneys are apprehensive in even trying and not knowing whom to call depending on the particular bureaucracy.

GENERAL PRACTICE TIP: ***Have one or more consent forms signed and on file prior to contacting prison administration officials and/or treatment staff. Consent forms can be executed prior to incarceration, during a legal visit, or by institution staff at your request.***

FEDERAL PRACTICE TIP: ***Any psychological reports submitted for sentencing should be forwarded to the BOP Designations and Sentence Computations Center separately or uploaded into the E-DES system by the probation office, if allowed.***

Reentry and Community Supervision

Every person must have short-term and long-term program goals for release, with a focus on the eventual release plan. That includes community aftercare, which may or may not be facilitated through a halfway house. Most inmates view the halfway house as a panacea and become fixated on getting out of prison as soon as possible. While that may be a practical thought and desire, clients should be reminded that halfway houses are usually private at the federal, state, and local levels. They have minimal treatment resources. A person on a regimen which includes medication will find themselves transitioning without structure and routine. A myth at the federal level is that people can obtain government-subsidized medical and psychological services free of charge. Federal inmates are transferred to the halfway house so the financial responsibility rests with the government. A more important point about transitional reentry is that people become comfortable in a tolerable prison routine. Transfer or release to a halfway house may mean entering an even more stressful, chaotic environment devoid of services to meet their needs. It is practical for people with family and resources to research the available community programs prior to release rather than relying on the government to coordinate them.

What is overlooked at this stage is the assistance that may be available from probation and parole officials who will eventually be conducting the release supervision. Supervising officers want people to succeed, even if due to a self-serving interest of less work for processing violations and more intensive supervision of others. Supervising officers also know the local lay of the land as far as resources far better than the prison officials. They can identify any effective local programs, resources, free clinics, etc. In larger federal districts, probation agencies even have separate contracts for services independent of the prison system.

Probation and parole officials are more likely to approve release plans which include an area with immediate family support and potential employment opportunities and will often deny a plan to an area void of such support. Probation and parole officers are sometimes assigned by geographic location, while other officers are assigned by specialization such as mental illness disorders and are trained accordingly. Most agencies use risk assessment tools to determine the required level of supervision and consider formal mental health diagnoses when determining if the case should be supervised by a mental health specialist. Supervised-release officials will make sure treatment services are also in place for people with a mental health disorder because their primary responsibility is protecting the community. New releasees are given intake screening and any special health-related aftercare conditions are communicated.

I spoke to several federal supervision officers while writing this chapter, and the common themes expressed were not much different from the prison system issues. Suicide rates are high, mental health resources are thin, and the overall transparency of people committing suicide while on supervision is lacking. Most districts have very few supervision officers that specialize in mental health caseloads. For instance, I spoke to an officer in one of the largest districts in the country that had only two mental health experts but five drug treatment specialists. Also similar is the upward trend of suicide rates for people on supervision, and it is particularly high for people on pretrial supervision and when they are first released from prison. I did a cursory Google search and found very little data on suicide rates for people on supervision in the United States. There were several studies done in the United Kingdom which seems to have recognized this trend. (See ch. 4 Recognizing and Addressing the Problem of Suicide Following Incarceration.)

According to *The Guardian*, the number of people who took their own lives after leaving prison since 2010 increased six-fold. The suicide rate among people leaving prison in 2018-2019 was 212 per 100,000, while for people serving community orders and suspended sentence orders (who are under supervision but have not been jailed), the rate falls to 132 per 100,000, Inquest said. The rate for prisoners is about 83 per 100,000 and among the general population it is about 14 per 100,000.

Many people leaving prison have undiagnosed disorders like depression and bipolar disorder. Often there is no formal clinical diagnosis prior to confinement. This makes it difficult to assign a person to a mental health caseload given agency resources. In recent years, drug and mental health courts have been used for diversionary purposes, but once again, drug courts take the limelight and the lion's share of the limited resources. One mental health expert I spoke with reported there is little consistency across federal mental health courts because the procedures are governed by the specific district. Earlier in the chapter I discussed how it is impossible to prevent suicide even in a controlled prison setting. It is even more challenging to prevent suicide for people on supervision. (*See* ch. 11, Suicide Risk Assessment for Individuals Involved in the Legal System.)

I suggest practitioners begin at the front end by documenting prior suicidal thoughts or behaviors in the presentence report and obtaining a formal clinical evaluation and diagnosis, if applicable. This also allows the court, or, eventually parole officers, to mandate mental health treatment as a condition of parole or supervised release. Equally important is the need for prison clinicians to have current and comprehensive mental health records so they can be electronically documented and used in an appropriate correctional treatment plan.

The risk for self-harm is most prevalent upon the initial arrest, initial incarceration, and shortly after release from a prison term. Attorneys ordinarily disengage from a client after sentencing, so it is incumbent upon the individual and family to check if prison officials have properly provided adequate reentry planning for aftercare treatment. Release is usually not a seamless transition, so it is important to have contact with supervision officials prior to release to discuss release planning. This is best accomplished when the supervision officers call or visit the release residence to determine if it is a satisfactory environment for the person to be released.

While suicide is one of the most challenging issues at any stage of our criminal justice system, there are ways to prevent it. The justice system in this country is fragmented at all levels, so communication, education, and support for clients and their family members are vital.

• • •

Jack T. Donson is a consultant, advocate, and educator with over 32 years of experience in federal prison issues. He is retired from the Federal Bureau of Prisons where he held positions within the Correctional Programs Division (case management related) working directly with diverse populations of all security levels as well as pretrial and the Witness Security Program.

From an administrative perspective, he assisted in facility audits, participated in national policy-writing workgroups, drafted institution policy, and trained counselors and case managers in classification and programs issues. During his career, he received three national awards and over 30 other meritorious performance awards.

Mr. Donson serves on several nonprofits including FedCURE, Out4Good, and Choosing Integrity. He is a member of the American Bar Association and National Association of Criminal Defense Lawyers Corrections Committees and has testified on federal prison issues throughout the United States and the United Kingdom. He provides training to federal defenders, judges, and the Criminal Justice Act Panel through a company called "Prisonology" which he co-founded.

Mr. Donson's passion is federal prison reform, which he believes can be accomplished under the existing statutory framework by broadening policy application and improving transparency, accountability, and oversight. He can be reached at jack@mfpcllc.com and his website is http://www.mfpcllc.com.

Complete citations are available from the author upon request.

Chapter

10

Suicide in the Criminal Justice System

Cindy Arends Elsberry

The following three chapters deal with the complicated issue of what an attorney should or can do when dealing with a client who is likely suicidal. The first chapter, by attorney Cindy Arends Elsberry, is written from the practical perspective of someone who was a King County, Washington Public Defender and now serves as the Felony Resource Attorney for the Washington Defender Association. The second chapter, by Dr. Ryan C. Hall, is written from the perspective of a medical doctor who through his practice as a forensic psychiatrist has a good deal of familiarity with the realities of the criminal justice system. The third chapter, by Professor Lissa Griffin, is written from the perspective of an ethics professor at Pace University School of Law who understands that a criminal defense lawyer's goals and medical exigencies don't always harmonize with legal ethics.

• • •

In our role as criminal defense attorneys, we provide much more than legal advice to our clients. We tell the story that humanizes our clients in the eyes of prosecutors, the courts, and the public. We guide our clients on the path through the court system and we provide hope to our clients for a positive outcome: gaining or maintaining their freedom, obtaining a reduction in the charge(s) or lighter sentence consequences, finding a path to redemption, or exonerating the wrongfully accused.

We come into the lives of our criminal clients at one of the most difficult times in their lives. Many live with mental illness, intellectual disability, substance use disorders, or a combination of these. Most criminal clients have suffered trauma at some point in their lives and for many, becoming embroiled in the criminal justice system traumatized them further. Being criminally prosecuted can trigger a high degree of shame, fear, loss of reputation, loss of significant or close personal relationships, and wider social isolation. Social, professional, and financial consequences may be dire.

A number of the well-documented suicide risk factors are present when a person is charged with a crime and facing the possibility of punishment. This is not just a concern for individuals incarcerated in local jails. The risk is significant for those who are accused and released on bail, bond, or personal recognizance as well (Flood and Kelley, Criminal Justice Magazine, Summer 2019). Criminal defense attorneys, investigators, and other defense team members need to be aware of this potential risk for their clients and possible warning signs. Defense team members must have the skills, tools, and resources to respond to a client who is thinking about suicide.

For criminal defense attorneys, representing a client with suicidal ideation brings up both legal and ethical issues, as well as practical challenges. This chapter provides an overview of the risk of suicide in individuals who are criminal justice involved, practical tips for effective communication around suicide, and some concrete steps the criminal defense attorney can use to address the important personal, legal, and ethical issues that may arise.

Our client, "Jerry," is facing a felony assault charge with serious consequences after he got into a bar fight and broke the nose and eye socket of his opponent. Jerry is a veteran who served two tours in Iraq. Jerry hasn't adjusted well since his discharge from the military; he has not returned to work and his wife just started divorce proceedings. She won't let him see their two young kids, claiming his drinking makes it unsafe. Jerry was injured during combat and as a result lives with chronic pain. If Jerry is convicted, he will face a prison term and loss of his firearm rights. Jerry's case is set for trial in a month. Lately, Jerry has been pretty down when we talk, and I am starting to worry. Before his wife filed for divorce, Jerry was very engaged and helpful to me. He was eager to go to trial. Now he says he doesn't care what happens to him anymore.

Risk Factors and Warning Signs

Risk Factors with Criminal Defense Clients

There are a number of risk factors and potential warning signs for suicide. *Risk factors* are characteristics that make it more likely that someone will consider, attempt, or die by suicide; they do not cause suicide. *Warning signs* are current or recent behaviors indicating that a person may be contemplating suicide. This is especially true when the behavior is new, has recently increased in intensity, or seems related to a recent loss or tragedy.

A number of the suicide risk factors are common in individuals who are criminal justice involved. These include:

- A previous suicide attempt
- A family history of abuse or child maltreatment. Suicide is higher among people who have experienced violence, including child abuse, bullying, and sexual violence
- Living with a mental illness or disability, particularly clinical depression
- A history of substance use disorders or intoxication. Alcohol and drug use can create mental highs and lows that worsen suicidal thoughts
- Feelings of hopelessness
- Impulsive or aggressive tendencies
- Experiencing prolonged stress
- Isolation, a feeling of being cut off from other people
- Barriers to accessing mental health treatment
- Suffering a recent tragedy or loss (relationships, social, work, or financial)
- Unwillingness to seek help because of the stigma attached to mental health and substance abuse disorders or to suicidal thoughts (*see also* ch. 11, Suicide Risk Assessment for Individuals Involved in the Legal System)

Our client, Jerry, has several of these risk factors showing up in his case: he may have a mental illness or disability or substance use disorder (or a combination), he is likely feeling isolated, he has experienced prolonged stress with his deployments, and he has suffered a recent loss. An additional stressor (and it may be prolonged) is his pending criminal case.

In addition to individual risk factors for suicide, certain groups are more at risk of suicide. Our client Jerry has two important group risk factors:

- Men are at higher risk than women. Although more women attempt suicide than men, men are four times more likely to die by suicide than women
- Veterans and active military personnel are at higher risk than civilians

Additionally, there are protective factors that buffer individuals from suicidal thoughts and behaviors and increase individual resiliency when facing hardship and stress. These factors are often absent (or insufficient) for individuals who become involved in the criminal justice system:

- Access to effective physical and mental health care
- Access to substance use disorder treatment
- Family and community support
- Skills in problem solving, conflict resolution, and nonviolent ways of solving problems

Jerry, as a veteran, can access treatment services through the Veterans Administration. He may be lacking support from extended family and community and the nature of the charge suggests he is struggling with problem-solving skills.

Warning Signs

Your client's words and actions matter more than what group or individual risk factors are present. Knowing the warning signs may help you determine if a person is currently having suicidal thoughts. Warning signs range from subtle to obvious. These signs may appear when an attorney is meeting with a client in person, by video, or by phone. They may appear when a family member or friend of the client appears in court or reaches out to the defense attorney. Warning signs may be obvious in the factual summary of events contained in the police report, in statements by witnesses that the accused has a mental health condition, or in discovery the defense attorney receives later in the case. Jail screeners who gather information about the individual at booking may flag them as a person with a mental health condition. Jails may place an individual on suicide watch.

Warning signs may not appear at the beginning of the representation. Rather, they may emerge later in the legal process. Litigation stressors may push a person to new levels of despair, as the tension that builds as a trial approaches may increase the client's stress. Proceeding through trial can be overwhelming, especially when the outcome looks unfavorable to the client.

A red flag went up when Jerry stopped engaging in his case. It's a good idea to check in with clients by talking about more than the case to take a pulse on their mental well-being. Other warning signs that a criminal client is thinking about suicide include:

- Talking about wanting to die or to kill themselves
- Looking for a way to kill themselves, like searching online or buying a gun
- Talking about feeling hopeless or having no reason to live
- Talking about feeling trapped or in unbearable pain
- Talking about being a burden to others
- Increasing the use of alcohol or drugs
- Acting anxious or agitated
- Behaving recklessly
- Giving away valued personal possessions
- Sleeping too little or too much
- Withdrawing or isolating themselves
- Showing rage or talking about seeking revenge
- Extreme mood swings (*see* ch. 6, Death Suggested, Cause Abated)

Talking with Clients About Suicide

Most criminal defense attorneys have little formal education or work experience in counseling or evaluating individuals with mental health or behavioral health conditions. While attorneys are taught to counsel their clients, this usually involves developing the skills to discuss the legal matter and to provide legal advice. Little time is spent teaching law students or training lawyers in how to talk with clients about living with the symptoms or a diagnosis of a mental illness, having an intellectual or developmental disability, or use or abuse of alcohol and/or drugs, despite the reality that a large percentage of criminal defense clients have some type of mental health, cognitive, or behavioral health condition, and many have co-occurring disorders.

Be Honest, Open, and Direct

Don't be afraid you will cause suicide by bringing it up with your client. Talking about suicide will not cause suicide. It is okay to be very direct. You can ask if your client if they are thinking of hurting themselves or thinking about suicide. One way to phrase a question is: "Sometimes when people are in a hard situation and *[feeling overwhelmed and hopeless, withdrawing/isolating, or other warning sign you see]*, they are thinking about suicide. Are you thinking about suicide?"

If a client shares with you that they are struggling, but don't tell you they are thinking about suicide, follow up with another question or two. You could ask, "How worried should I be?" or "Are you thinking of killing yourself?" Reassure them that you are listening and want to know more, with statements such as "I am so glad you told me" or "Tell me more, I am listening" or "It's OK to be honest with me, I am here to help." It may be a welcome relief for the client that someone is willing to make the time and hold the space for them to safely share their thoughts. The client may not feel that they have anyone else with whom they can share their feelings.

Listen More, Talk Less

Just listen—this is sometimes very hard to do. As attorneys, we are trained to receive information and analyze it, fit it into a rule or structure, and reach an outcome. Set that aside when talking with a client about their deep, dark feelings around suicide. When a client shares that they are feeling despair or hopelessness, or your client tells you they are having suicidal thoughts, don't judge them. Don't tell the client that you can or will fix the problem.

Do convey that you are engaged in their case, that you care about what happens to them and you will do your best for them in their criminal case. This may alleviate the hopelessness. Be thoughtful and stay honest. Don't overpromise or set unrealistic expectations. Help the client to see that there can be meaning in their future life, even though it may be very different from the life that they had before the criminal charge.

Take It Seriously, No Matter What

When you learn that your client is contemplating suicide or you see the warning signs, take it seriously, every time. Trust your gut if you are concerned, even if a client is reluctant to talk about it or says they don't really mean it. Your client may feel ashamed or embarrassed, because mental disabilities and suicide are both stigmatized in our society. Your client may not be comfortable with you yet.

Breathe and Stay Calm

While talking about suicide might be very uncomfortable, it is important to stay calm. Don't discuss the value of life, or debate whether suicide is right or wrong. Don't argue, threaten, or raise your voice. If you are nervous, try not to fidget or pace. Remember that in this moment of crisis, your client is sharing their darkest feelings: feelings that are not generally accepted in our society, feelings they may have not shared with anyone before you. If you remain calm, your client will be more comfortable opening up to you.

Action Steps to Take with a Suicidal Client[1]

If there is imminent danger, call 9-1-1, connect the client with a local or national crisis line, or recommend that the client get to (or be taken to) the emergency room for evaluation and treatment.

Remove Access to Lethal Means

Recommend removal or remove access to lethal items or locations. If the client has support, encourage loved ones to do this for them. Putting time and distance between the lethal means of suicide and an individual at risk is an important step in the prevention of suicide. Take inventory and discuss what access a client has to lethal means. Do they have guns in their home? Do they have access to alcohol, drugs, or large quantities of prescription drugs or over-the-counter medicines? Do they have poisons, ropes, or access to high places? Is there anything else that might be used by the client to effectuate suicide?

- If they have access to guns, have a friend or family member take them temporarily for safekeeping.

[1] Forefront Suicide Prevention, University of Washington. https://intheforefront.org.

- If they have prescription drugs or over-the-counter medications, reduce the amount they have access to at one time. This includes common pain medications such as ibuprofen and acetaminophen.
- If your client is detained, consider whether to alert the jail health or psychiatric staff to remove access to items used to attempt suicide in the jail.

Help Them Connect with Others

If your client is thinking about suicide, they need prompt, professional help from a mental health treatment provider. If your client is out of custody and not currently receiving mental health services in the community, you can help them find those resources.

- The website www.psychologytoday.com is a great resource for finding mental health providers by type (licensed counselor, psychologist, psychiatrist), location, and willingness to bill insurance providers (and if so which ones).
- If your client has health insurance, check with the insurer. The websites of many health insurance companies have searchable databases that allow you to find a participating practitioner in your area.
- A primary care physician can screen for mental health needs and refer.
- For uninsured, low-, or no-income clients, the website for your state or local county government may have information about health services in your area.
- The National Alliance for Mental Illness (NAMI) provides resources to individuals with mental illness, including information to consider and steps to follow to find a treatment provider who will be a good fit (https://www.nami.org/Your-Journey/Individuals-with-Mental-Illness/Finding-a-Mental-Health-Professional).

If your client is alone with no support and you have the time to help your client find a mental health provider or set up an initial appointment, then do that. People experiencing severe depression have a very difficult time "initiating" or starting a task.

Establishing or maintaining connections beyond the mental health profession are also important for a person having suicidal thoughts. Encourage your client to have regular contact with a friend, loved one, or spiritual advisor for ongoing support and assistance during this difficult time.

Do Not Leave Them Alone

If your client is in custody, there is not a lot you can do about their circumstances of confinement, other than alerting the jail to their situation and waiting for the jail to respond.

If your client is not detained, do what you can to ensure that the client is not left alone. Does the client have someone with them at home? If not, is there a friend or family member who can help? Can you look beyond the client's immediate circle to a health or mental health care provider, clergy, or other spiritual advisor?

Ask to Share Information

At some point in the representation, you may want to share your concerns about a client's suicide risk. Before worrying about the attorney ethics regarding sharing confidential client or case information, start by asking the client if you can share the information with others, including jail staff if the client is confined, friends and family, or another trusted support person. Give the client a sense of control. You might be surprised at how many individuals will authorize you to disclose this information. This can go a long way toward preventing any ethical issues while accomplishing the goal of protecting the client.

If the client does not consent, attorney ethics rules come into play and must be reviewed and carefully considered. If after review and consideration, you decide to share the information without client consent, tell the client what you are doing, why, and what they can expect to happen as a result. The jail may move a detainee to a different area of the jail or to a different cell stripped of bedding and basics. The jail may place them on "suicide watch," resulting in constant supervision or visual checks every 15 minutes by corrections staff. A local mental health professional may visit an individual and evaluate them for possible civil commitment, triggering another legal process that may result in involuntary psychiatric hospitalization and loss of firearm rights. (*See* ch. 12, Suicide in the Criminal Justice System: Ethical Considerations.)

Give the Client Resources

An attorney should compile and have a list of resources available for a client at risk for suicide. The resources may include the following:

- The Crisis Text Line—text "help" to 741741.

- Go to the website for the National Suicide Prevention Lifeline (https://suicidepreventionlifeline.org/) or call 1-800-273-8255. There is a portal for an online "chat" option as well from the website (https://suicidepreventionlifeline.org/chat).
- The local state, county, or city suicide hotline. For example, in Washington State, there is a statewide resource that also has local resource information by county. Washington State Suicide Hotline: 1-800-784-2433 (1-800-SUICIDE) or 1-800-273-8255 (1-800-273-TALK) (http://suicidehotlines.com/washington.html).
- Veterans in crisis and their loved ones can call, text, or chat with a caring VA responder on the free and confidential Veterans Crisis Line. Call 1-800-273-8255 (1-800-273-TALK), chat online at the Veteran's Crisis Chat (https://www.veteranscrisisline.net/get-help/chat), or send a text to 838255.

There are also targeted resources you may find; examples include crisis resources for teens and the LGBTQ+ community.

Make a Safety Plan for Future Crisis

Does the client have a safety plan in place for the future? Individuals who have had previous suicide interventions do. A safety plan includes identifying things that may trigger suicidal thoughts. A plan includes the names and numbers of who to call if/when suicidal thoughts return. Does the safety plan include the anticipated increased stress of going to court or an approaching trial date? If not, help the client plan for a future time when they may become overwhelmed by their criminal case and feel suicidal again.

Follow Up After an Event

After a crisis, follow up with the client. Don't pretend it didn't happen. Visit your client who is in isolation or on suicide watch in the jail regularly to monitor how they are doing and the care they are receiving. This could be weekly or more often, whatever your schedule allows. Talk with your client about what services or medications the jail is providing. Advocate for your client if the jail is not responding appropriately. If you don't have the time to follow up, engage other defense team members who can visit the client, such as a social worker, investigator, or mitigation specialist.

If your client is out of custody, follow up regularly by phone, video, or in person to check in. You don't have to have new information about the case to relay; it's just helpful to check in on the client's well-being. Studies show that follow-up contact by mental health responders after a suicide attempt can reduce future suicidality. Follow-up contact from the client's attorney may be beneficial as well.

Legal Issues in Criminal Cases

Competency

If the client is very depressed, thinking about, or at risk for suicide, the client may not be competent to proceed with the case. *Dusky v. United States* established the test for competency in criminal cases. The well-known *Dusky* standard provides that a person must meet this test for competency: "the test must be whether he has sufficient present ability to consult with his lawyer with a reasonable degree of rational understanding—and whether he has a rational as well as factual understanding of the proceedings against him." 362 U.S. 402 (1960).

- Is the client willing and able to meet with the attorney and discuss the case?
- Can the client rationally set the goals of representation?
- Can the client assist the attorney by providing information needed to plan the investigation or to develop the theory of the case?
- Can the client rationally consider a plea bargain and weigh the risks of forgoing a plea offer and proceeding to trial?
- Is the client able to attend and participate in trial?
- Can the client make a reasoned decision to testify or not?
- Has the client attempted suicide leading up to or during the trial?

A client who is severely depressed, feeling hopeless, or thinking about suicide may not be making *rational* decisions about how to proceed with the case. The defense attorney must carefully weigh the client's ability to assist and to proceed. At any point in the representation when the client's competency is uncertain, a defense expert evaluation of competency is warranted.

Attorney-Client Confidences

At some point in the representation, you may be in a position where you feel you must share information about your client's current mental status, and you may not have permission to do so. In general, attorneys are bound by strict ethics rules that require them to maintain client confidences and to protect, and keep private, information learned in the course of representation. The ethics rules provide two main caveats that allow the attorney to share client or case information: an attorney can share information if the client gives "informed consent," or an attorney may share information if the disclosure is "impliedly authorized to carry out the representation."

In a situation where the client has not given informed consent and sharing information is not authorized to carry out the representation, it may seem that the attorney's hands are tied. There may be an exception for a situation of life or death, such as a client's statements or behaviors indicating suicidality. Check the Rules of Professional Conduct in your jurisdiction and check to see if your state's Bar Association has an advisory opinion on this topic. Both the American Bar Association (ABA) Model Rules of Professional Conduct (RPCs) and the Washington State Rules of Professional Conduct permit confidential information sharing "to prevent death or substantial bodily harm." ABA Model RPC 1.6(b)(1) says "A lawyer *may* reveal information relating to the representation of a client to the extent the lawyer reasonably believes necessary: (1) to prevent reasonably certain death or substantial bodily harm." In Washington State, the Rules of Professional Conduct provide similar language but compel the attorney to act: "A lawyer to the extent the lawyer reasonably believes necessary: (1) *shall* reveal information relating to the representation of a client to prevent reasonably certain death or substantial bodily harm." Washington RPC 1.6(b)(1). (*See* ch. 12, Suicide in the Criminal Justice System: Ethical Considerations.)

Mental Defenses or Reduced Culpability

Developing the defense theory of the case should include investigation and consideration of all possible defenses. A criminal defense client who has experienced a mental health crisis at or near the time of the charged incident, or who contemplated or attempted suicide during or shortly thereafter, may have available mental defenses or relevant psychological evidence to rebut the charge(s). Investigation may reveal a diminished capacity defense, or an argument to support voluntary or involuntary intoxication if the client attempted suicide by taking poison, or excessive amounts of medications, alcohol, or drugs.

A client's mental state may be relevant to the degree of culpability. Perhaps the client, due to their mental status, is not guilty of the charged offense, but instead is only guilty of a lesser degree or lesser included offense.

As you would gather information about the factual circumstances leading up to and including the incident, you can gather information about your client's mental state and consult with an expert. Typically, the defense expert evaluation for this work is done by a forensic psychologist, neuropsychologist, or psychiatrist. The right expert depends on the client's circumstances and must be determined individually in each case.

Mitigation and Sentencing

Even if your client's mental health status at the time of an offense isn't relevant to a mental defense or to the reduced culpability of your client, it may be relevant to determining an appropriate and fair sentence following conviction. A recommendation for a sentence that best serves the client may include participation in mental health evaluation and treatment as recommended, instead of other types of punishment such as incarceration, fines, or community service. Always get the client's permission to share mental health information before providing it to the court or the prosecutor.

Mental Health Courts and Other Problem-Solving Courts

Some jurisdictions have Mental Health Courts or mental health dockets. The goal of these courts and special dockets is to identify the cases where the individual and community will be better served by an approach that focuses on rehabilitation rather than punishment. Mental Health Courts are staffed differently and operate differently than traditional courts. Attorneys and judges have, or gain, more experience and knowledge of mental disabilities. These courts seek to address the underlying problems that contribute to criminal behavior and may have resources to get the client connected to services, housing, and other supports. For a client who has contemplated or attempted suicide, this may be an appropriate and beneficial alternative to the mainstream traditional court experience.

Other problem-solving courts may be worth considering, such as Drug Courts, Community Courts, or Veterans Courts. For Jerry, a Veterans Court would be a good option to consider. Veterans Courts are supported by an interdisciplinary team that understands the unique experiences and issues of veterans. A Veterans Court judge will be more familiar with treatment resources at the Veterans Administration, and financial benefits available through the Veterans Benefit Association or State Department of Veterans Affairs, and how community resources for veterans can benefit the individual. (*See* ch. 8, Suicide Prevention in the Criminal Justice System: Breaking the Silence.)

After a Loss

A death by suicide is usually unexpected, often sudden, and may be violent. A criminal defense attorney who loses a client by suicide can feel a wide range of emotions, among them shock, sadness, guilt, or regret. The attorney may wonder if they missed something, or could have done something more for the client, or could have prevented the suicide. There may be intrusive images of the client or the death that linger. Moreover, an attorney may be alone or may feel isolated as they deal with the loss. A death by suicide makes many people uncomfortable and unsure how to react.

Criminal defense attorneys are accustomed to intense, high-pressure work that is stressful, but this type of stress is extraordinary. Recognize that it will take some time to process the loss. It is important to take care of yourself. This can mean taking some personal time off from work, or lessening the workload for a short period of time. Consider postponing upcoming hearings or trials, and even meetings with other clients. This may be a good time to seek support from office colleagues, other attorneys who have been through something similar in the past, or the local Bar Association Lawyer's Assistance Program (LAP). Many people have found it helpful to talk with a counselor or therapist who understands grief and loss. Counselors experienced in suicide-specific grief are helpful, because this type of loss is unique.

Conclusion

Suicide is a serious risk for individuals who are embroiled in the criminal justice system. Criminal defense attorneys serve in a key role to participate in suicide awareness and prevention. By knowing the risk factors and warning signs, criminal attorneys can screen clients for both individual and group risk factors and can pay attention to client behaviors that may be the warning signs a client is considering or planning suicide.

More support is needed in this area, including professional training on suicide awareness and prevention for criminal lawyers and defense team members. Large offices should have a plan for debriefing difficult cases or hard things that happen, including client suicide. State and local bar associations should provide resources to attorneys in solo practice or in small firms.

As a community, we need to do more than provide support. We need to collectively talk and shed light on mental health and suicide. It needs to be easier and more acceptable for individuals in crisis to come forward and get the help that is available. These issues have been stigmatized and hiding in the shadows for too long.

• • •

Cindy Arends Elsberry is the Felony Resource Attorney for the Washington Defender Association (WDA) in Seattle, Washington. She has worked in public defense for more than 25 years and has a diverse background, having worked on all types of criminal cases, from low-level crimes to aggravated murder. She has experience with problem-solving courts and mental competency hearings, and is death penalty certified. Before joining WDA in 2009, she worked as a staff attorney providing representation to indigent defense clients at the Associated Counsel for the Accused in Seattle for over 15 years. In her role as a Resource Attorney at WDA, Attorney Elsberry provides technical assistance to attorneys and develops resources for public defenders across the state. She is a frequent speaker at continuing legal education (CLE) presentations and has a special interest in the issues involved with representing youth in adult courts, in representing clients living with mental illness, and in promoting defender well-being. She received her J.D. from the University of Washington School of Law. In her spare time she enjoys getting outdoors, spending time with anyone who makes her laugh, walking her dogs, and tending to her garden. Attorney Elsberry can be reached at cindy@defensenet.org.
Complete citations are available from the author upon request.

Chapter

11

Suicide Risk Assessment for Individuals Involved in the Legal System

Ryan C. Hall

Introduction

From an actuarial perspective, being involved as a defendant in criminal legal proceedings increases one's risk of suicide (Kellogg et al., 2014). Therefore, this is a topic that many attorneys, as well as probation/parole officers, will be exposed to at some point during their careers. It is not the goal of this chapter to turn the readers into experts in suicide risk assessment since that takes many years of training and staying current with ongoing research. Rather, the goal is to help individuals involved with the criminal justice system better understand what to look for when dealing with individuals who may be contemplating suicide. The hope is that, by understanding what the risk factors and signs for suicide are, this chapter will better allow people to understand why they may have a gut feeling of unease related to an individual they are working with, qualify their concerns, and be better able to encourage the individual to get treatment or to communicate with mental health providers.

As a point of clarification, this chapter focuses primarily on *suicide*, which is generally defined as engaging in an action with the intention of taking one's own life (Jacobs et al., 2010). There can be actions of self-harm that are not necessarily suicide attempts (Fagan et al., 2010).

Table 11.1 Additional Resources Related to Suicide

American Foundation of Suicide Prevention	www.afsp.org
National Institute of Mental Health	www.nimh.nih.gov
Suicide Prevention Resource Center	www.sprc.org
American Psychiatric Association	https://www.psychiatry.org/patients-families/suicide-prevention
American Psychological Association	https://www.apa.org/topics/suicide/index.html
National Suicide Prevention Lifeline (1-800-273-8255)	https://suicidepreventionlifeline.org
The Columbia Lighthouse Project: Identify risk, prevent suicide	https://cssrs.columbia.edu/the-columbia-scale-c-ssrs/about-the-scale
National Institute of Corrections: Suicide in Corrections	https://nicic.gov/suicide-in-corrections

Self-harm behaviors can occur for a multitude of reasons, such as pathological mental health behaviors like Munchausen syndrome (also known as factitious disorder, where one fakes or induces medical problems in order to be treated for psychological gains more than traditional secondary gain), manipulative behavior or malingering (e.g., actions are primarily for secondary gains, such as trying to get a change of housing), or as a poor coping mechanism to deal with the stress and boredom of their current situation or incarceration (e.g., someone who cuts in order to feel something other than anxiety or boredom). However, it needs to be noted that it may be difficult at times to distinguish between a self-harm action versus a suicidal action. In addition, self-harm, no matter the motivation, is also a risk factor for suicide (Knoll 2010; Pompili et al., 2009).

As noted, suicide risk assessment is an ongoing and growing field, so although this chapter may provide a good foundation, you may need to consult additional resources (Table 11.1).

General Information Regarding Suicide

Suicide, fortunately, is a relatively rare occurrence, but, unfortunately, is an event that is hard to predict. Suicide is the tenth leading cause of death in the United States and the second leading cause of death after accidents for those aged 10 to 34 years old (Parekh, 2018). It is estimated that roughly 1.3 million adults will attempt suicide each year. Women attempt suicide at a much higher rate than men, but males actually die by means of suicide at a higher rate than females. Current theories regarding suicide highlight that it is not caused by a single factor, but occurs due to multiple factors with varying weights of significance for each unique individual (Jacobs et al., 2010) (*see* Table 11.2).

It also needs to be noted that many individuals can have potential risk factors and never attempt suicide. Therefore, the presence of a risk factor is best thought of as a way to address the probability that someone will commit suicide, but no risk factor is 100% indicative that someone is going to engage in the act of suicide. In addition, some individuals may have protective factors or are likely to be more resilient to situational stressors (Table 11.3). However, just like with risk factors, there are no definitive resilience attributes that 100% rule out suicide risk.

Given the number of potential factors, it is not possible for mental health professionals, let alone lawyers or parole officers, to consider or weigh all potential factors (Jacobs et al., 2010; Knoll, 2010). Unfortunately, some factors only come to light after a suicide attempt occurs (e.g., information found in a suicide note). In addition, it may not even be easy to determine if a death was a suicide, because many suicides occur impulsively without a note or clear indication of what occurred (e.g., single-vehicle accident could just be an accident or an intentional attempt to take one's life). Although access to a firearm may increase the risk of an individual following through with a suicide attempt, it is almost impossible to limit the ways for someone determined to take their life from doing so. For example, many over-the-counter medications, such as Tylenol, can be fatal in overdose and relatively easy to obtain; minimum resources are needed to hang oneself; most people have access to kitchen knives or shaving razors if they want to cut their wrists; and if someone is determined they can likely gain access to a structure tall enough to jump off, such as a parking garage.

Although there are several potential screening instruments for suicidality, some of which require little training and can be used by lay individuals (e.g., Columbia Suicide Severity Rating Scale), screens alone are not enough to prevent suicide (Knoll, 2010). What most screening instruments do is help determine the risk level, help ensure that important questions are asked, and provide a means for a more detailed discussion

Table 11.2 General Suicide Risk Factors as Broad Categories in Alphabetical Order

(Pompili et al., 2009; Jacobs et al., 2010; Favril et al.,2017; Winters et al., 2017; Parekh 2018)

1. Abnormal thoughts or fixation (tunnel vision on problems, not able to see improved future, nihilistic)
2. Active mental illness symptoms (e.g., depression, bipolar disorder, schizophrenia, anxiety disorder, substance use disorder)
3. Agitation
4. Chronic physical pain (e.g., back injury, nerve injury, terminal illness with difficult death)
5. Chronic psychological pain (e.g., regret, shame, rumination on past actions)
6. Easy access to lethal means (e.g., firearms)
7. Expressed statements of not wanting to be alive (e.g., frequent jokes, serious but vague statements, stated plan)
8. Family history (e.g., mental illness, suicide of close relative)
9. History of adverse childhood events (physical abuse, sexual abuse, verbal abuse, neglect)
10. History of impulsivity, medically based (e.g., head injury, multiple sclerosis, stroke)
11. History of impulsivity, personality based (e.g., gambling, speeding tickets, risk-taking behavior)
12. History of violence to strangers and/or people close in their life
13. Hopelessness/helplessness/diminished self-esteem
14. Lack of therapeutic relationship with medical professional and/or mental health professional
15. Lack or degeneration of social supports (e.g., divorce, single, bankruptcy, ostracized from spiritual community)
16. Loss of purpose (e.g., loss of family, loss of job, loss of title or position)
17. Past history of mental health treatment, especially psychiatric hospitalization
18. Past history of suicidal ideation or attempts
19. Personality disorders, especially cluster B (e.g., extreme narcissism, antisocial, borderline personality)
20. Recent stressful life event (e.g., death of child, divorce, legal troubles, bankruptcy)
21. Seeing suicide as noble action ("don't want to be a burden"; "people better off and will move on")
22. Substance use (acute intoxication even if no past history of substance use disorder)
23. Sudden change in behavior (e.g., no longer cares about something previously worried about, giving away possessions)

to occur. It is often the intervention done after a screening and an assessment that has the biggest impact on whether a suicide will occur or not (e.g., placed on suicide precautions, placed on direct observation status, hospitalization).

Table 11.3 Factors Which Suggest Resilience or Reduce Risk of Engaging in Suicide Attempt (listed in alphabetical order)

(Jacobs et al., 2010; Fagan et al., 2010, Knoll, 2010; Perry et al., 2010)

1. Belief in ability to overcome current situation/stressors (e.g., problem solving, conflict resolution)
2. General sense of life satisfaction
3. If history of mental illness, receiving stable mental health care and physical health care
4. Positive social support (family, friends, community)
5. Sense of future
6. Sense of obligation or positive relationship with children or grandchildren
7. Sense of personal value or accomplishment (e.g., learned skills, education, productive output)
8. Sense of spirituality (e.g., most religions forbid suicide; teach redemption, forgiveness; and provide purpose or sense of meaning)

General Statistics Related to Suicidality in the Criminal Justice System

It has been estimated that the suicide rate for incarcerated individuals is about two to nine times higher than for the general population (Kellogg et al., 2014). International studies found that roughly 25% of male inmates and 40% of female inmates have reported having at least one suicide attempt at some point in their lives (Favril et al., 2017; Shaw et al., 2017). International studies looking at suicidal ideation noted that roughly 25% of prison inmates had suicidal ideation within the last year of their incarceration (Favril et al., 2017). Since 2000, suicide has been the leading cause of death in jails (about one-third) and is the fourth leading cause of death in prisons (about 5%; Cramer et al., 2017). The numbers of people who died in local jails and prisons in 2016, which is the last year that official Department of Justice data was available at the time this chapter was written, were 333 and 255 respectively (Carson & Cowhig, 2020; Carson & Cowhig, 2020b). Numbers for the average rate of completed suicides from 2001 to 2016 found the per capita rate to be about 45 out of 100,000 for male jail inmates and about 17 out of 100,000 for male state prison inmates. Female populations had a rate of about 29 out of 100,000 for jails and about 13 out of 100,000 for prisons. Federal prison suicide rates were slightly better at about 10 out of 100,000. In comparison, some international studies have reported a rate of about 100 out of 100,000 for prisons (Marzano et al.. 2011).

There are some unique situational and population factors that apply based on where one is held (Perry et al., 2010). For example, frequency of suicide in jails is roughly four times that seen in prisons (Carson & Cowhig, 2020; Carson & Cowhig, 2020b). Some population and demographic factors also affect the risk: Caucasians involved in the criminal justice system are six times more likely than African Americans and three times more likely than Hispanics to commit suicide while incarcerated (Perry et al., 2010; Kellogg et al., 2014). Although some experts caution that there may be a racial bias that affects the reported numbers, others believe that this is a real difference that needs to be appreciated. In addition, the age range, at least in jails, that is most likely to attempt suicide is 25 to 34 years old, followed by 35 to 44 years of age (Carson & Cowhig, 2020). This is slightly different from the general population, where historically it was middle-aged males (45 to 55 years old) who were felt to be at highest risk (Jacobs et al., 2010).

Suicide is always a potential concern when an individual expresses suicidal ideation; however, simply because someone identifies as being suicidal, it is not always a thought they will act on. It is estimated that only one out of five incarcerated individuals who report suicidal ideations will actually attempt suicide, with fewer actually being successful (Pompili et al., 2009). Although not everyone who expresses suicide ideation will attempt, it is advisable, especially for someone outside the mental health field, not to see these statements as just manipulative statements, just a "cry for help," or a way to obtain attention. Even if someone is making empty statements or nonlethal gestures, there is the risk that one time it will not be an empty statement, or that there could be a miscalculation in the "gesture" which could result in an actual fatality. (*See* ch. 6, Death Suggested, Cause Abated.)

In general, the time periods for which an incarcerated individual is at the greatest risk to commit suicide are often early in their incarceration, the time period leading up to trial, or after a transition (e.g., moved to special population) (Daniel 2006; Marzano et al., 2011; Kellogg et al., 2014; Kucmanic & Gilson, 2016; Favril et al., 2017; Winters et al., 2017; Carson & Cowhig, 2020). For example, some studies found the first 48 hours of incarceration in a local jail or lockup to be a high-risk period of time. Other studies have found the transition from a lockup to a jail or jail to a prison to be a period of time when an individual is at an increased risk. When looking at local jail incarcerations, the average number of days served at the time a suicide occurs is nine days, but the highest-risk timeframe is actually the first two to four months as a whole. Similar numbers were found for prisons as well.

In summary, lawyers need to appreciate that individuals in jails or prisons have a higher rate of committing suicide than the general population, a higher likelihood of having had a past suicide attempt prior to their current incarceration, and are at the greatest risk around times of transition (just incarcerated, post-trial, moved to new facility).

General Concepts for Suicide Risk Assessment for Individuals Involved in Criminal Legal Proceedings

Much of the research on jail and prison suicides started in the 1980s; however, most of the studies on this topic are small (less than 1,000 participants), primarily focused on male populations, had limited variables assessed, are lacking in replication, and at times have found conflicting results (e.g., Does length of prison sentence increase risk or not? Does nature of initial offense increase risk or not? Does history of prior incarceration increase risk or not?) (Pratt et al., 2010; Kellogg et al., 2014; Marzano et al., 2016; Favril et al., 2017; Cramer et al., 2017). In addition, it is sometimes difficult to determine why a factor may be correlated with a suicide attempt (e.g., someone who commits a violent crime may feel shame and regret, and therefore is at higher risk; somebody who commits a violent act may have a lower threshold for committing violence against themselves, and therefore is at a higher risk; people charged with violent crimes may be facing a longer period of incarceration, and therefore are at a higher risk; or all of the above to varying degrees).

Considering that each individual is unique and that at times there can be conflicting studies, the factors identified in this chapter must be seen as general factors that should be assessed and weighed for each individual (Table 11.4). Additionally, as noted earlier, it is a fool's errand to try to identify and weigh all factors, since rarely does anyone have that much knowledge, insight, or understanding of another human being. This

Table 11.4 General Risk Factors for Incarcerated Individuals (in alphabetical order)

(Marzano et al., 2011; Kellogg et al., 2014; Kucmanic & Gilson, 2016; Favril et al., 2017)

- Catastrophic view of the future
- Childhood abuse or other significant adversity in youth
- Extreme personality traits
- Lack of mental health treatment, if needed
- Lack of purposeful activity
- Lack of social supports (inside institution and outside)
- Medical history (e.g., brain injury)
- Mental health history (e.g., depression, past psychiatric hospitalization)
- Negative personal view of self
- Overcrowding
- Past suicidal ideation/attempts
- Psychosocial stressors (family member's death, divorce, injured child)
- Severe loss of perceived autonomy (more than just incarcerated)
- Social isolation
- Substance use
- Times around court hearings
- Times of transition
- Victimization/bullying
- Violence history (violent offending against others = greater potential to self-harm)
- Younger age (less than 40 years old)

is especially true in a legal situation where the individual may be hesitant to be fully open or honest out of concerns of a potential negative legal outcome or loss of opportunity to act on a suicide plan. Also, there can be causative factors (e.g., I did it because ...) rather than a triggering event, which may be an innocuous or not-so-innocuous occurrence that leads to a change in mind state. One often thinks of a triggering event as something that brings all the stresses and pre-existing factors together, but in and of itself is not necessarily "the direct causation." For example, an inmate may have a good family visit while awaiting trial, which then results in the individual believing his family would be better off without him, which then leads to a suicide attempt even though the family visit by all reports was positive.

Like other forms of risk assessment, people in the mental health field often view suicide factors as either *static*, meaning historical and unchanging (e.g., participant in past crime), or *dynamic*, something that develops at the time or applies to the moment in which a suicide attempt occurred (e.g., current age, current state or level of intoxication). Although most, if not all, correctional institutions in America will screen for suicidality, many of the instruments used may result in either false positives or false negatives (Knoll, 2010; Perry et al., 2010; Simlot et al., 2013; Kucmanic & Gilson, 2016). Screening instruments often just categorize people into a degree of risk, but in-person one-on-one interviews and interactions are still needed to truly understand somebody's mental state. Although screening does occur in correctional facilities, it does not necessarily occur on a continuing basis unless there is a reason to believe the level of risk has changed or screening should be ongoing.

There are some gender differences, as noted earlier. Male prisoners often suffer from mood disorders (e.g., depression, bipolar), schizophrenia, anxiety conditions, or substance use disorders, with mood disorders and schizophrenia being the most likely diagnoses for an individual who commits suicide in prison (Friedman et al., 2013; Kellogg et al., 2014; Kucmanic & Gilson, 2016; Marzano et al., 2016; Sorrentino et al., 2016; Friedman et al., 2016). However, for females, post-traumatic stress disorder is a much more common mental illness to be diagnosed with, as well as mood disorders, anxiety, and substance abuse. Although not all mental health issues need to be addressed with medications, many inmates, especially those with severe mental illnesses, will likely be prescribed some form of psychotropic medication. As a general rule of thumb, psychotropic medication often takes four to eight weeks to become fully effective. In addition, if someone stops taking their medication, it may also take up to four to eight weeks to determine their potential baseline off medication. This means that there is often an increased risk around the time people either start medication (e.g., may not have been taking at time of arrest) or stop it. Furthermore, some inmates may stockpile medication with the intent to use it as a means to commit suicide.

An additional factor that must be remembered with incarcerated populations is that they have higher rates of personality disorders than the general population (Daniel, 2006; Pompili et al., 2009; Friedman et al., 2016). Individuals with certain personality disorders, such as antisocial personality or narcissistic personality disorder, which are frequently found in incarcerated male populations, often lack empathy for others. Their rationale for committing suicide tends to be more related to their own perception of their potential suffering (e.g., time will be hard for me, unfair prosecution brought undeserved shame, I am being targeted and singled out even though others do the same thing). Individuals with borderline personality, common in incarcerated female populations, often engage in manipulative behavior and self-harm behaviors (cutting), and experience frequent suicidal urges with a diminished sense of self. Even if somebody is manipulating or "just acting out," they are at an increased risk since, if they misjudge the suicidal manipulation action (e.g., try to hang self in front of others, likely leading to rescue), they may actually be successful. In addition, if manipulation does not work, they may be more likely to engage in a real attempt due to not being successful with their usual coping techniques and not knowing how to control their emotions or the situation.

One of the largest markers for potential suicidality in either the legal population or the general population is substance abuse (Jacobs et al., 2010; Marzano et al., 2011; Kucmanic & Gilson, 2016; Parekh, 2018). Substance use, especially acute intoxication (e.g., impaired judgment, labile mood state, precipitant of a crisis) or withdrawal, can be a triggering/causative factor, especially when people are first detained. In addition, frequent substance use can be a marker for impulsivity, risk-taking behavior, dual diagnosis (e.g., both substance use disorder and additional mental health concerns), social withdrawal, poor pre-existing coping skills, and presence of other stressors, such as poor relationship or work functioning, prior to arrest. Even if someone is incarcerated, they may still have access to alcohol or contraband substances that had been smuggled in, diverted, or produced in jail (Marzano et al., 2011; Hall & Meyers, 2016). Individuals on detoxification or maintenance protocols may be targeted or bullied for the detox medications being prescribed.

As mentioned earlier, the nature of the crime (e.g., violent, sexual) does look to be a factor at times, but other research indicates that it is not. Again, it may come down to the individual, as well as the length of time already incarcerated. For prisoners who have been incarcerated for years, the charge seems less significant, but for people who are just entering the criminal justice system or potentially just leaving on parole, it may be more of a concern since there may be more stigma for certain charges (Rivlin et al., 2013).

The location where one is held may also affect suicide risk. Several studies have found that being held in a special population or a special unit (medical, protective) may increase the risk of a suicide occurring (Knoll, 2010; Marzano et al., 2011; Cramer et al., 2017; Favril et al., 2017). In addition, if one is in a single-occupant cell, there is increased likelihood of committing suicide since there is less chance of being interrupted or rescued by a cellmate. Other factors, such as isolation and boredom, may also be a factor. However, it still needs to be remembered that those in the general population can still commit suicide, with 47% of jail suicides occurring in individuals in the general population (Carson & Cowhig, 2020). A study of postmortem jail suicides by Kucmanic and Gilson (2016) did not find the presence of another inmate in the same cell to have an independent deterrent effect.

Times of transition, especially into special housing units, are often times for increased risk of suicide. Transfers often occur due to a specific event, which may be a marker for how stable the individual is; the inmate is less of a known entity in the new housing situation; someone who had been suicidal may potentially find an opportunity to act in the new environment; and change of routine/physical transfer can potentially interrupt surveillance and protective measures.

In a very global sense, one of the greatest risk factors in jails or prisons is a sense of hopelessness; however, not everyone who is suicidal or hopeless will announce it (Daniel, 2006; Knoll, 2010; Kellogg et al., 2014; Winters et al., 2017). For that reason, changes in an individual's behavior are often the only outwardly noticeable indication that they may be having suicidal thoughts. Noticeable changes can be decrease in grooming, increasing anxiety/panic attacks, loss of appetite/weight loss, or people not engaging in behavior they used to have energy for, such as yard recreation, reading, or going to the legal library to work on their case. In addition, people may start talking in what seems to be code to family members or, possibly, their legal team (e.g., talking about their release coming soon or they are "getting out"). Many of these behaviors can also be seen with depression or other mental health problems, which is why, if noticed, encouraging an individual involved with a legal issue to seek evaluation and treatment is important.

In a correctional facility, there may be varying ways in which someone attempts suicide. Historically, hanging has been a common approach (Kellogg et al., 2014, Kucmanic & Gilson, 2016; Marzano et al., 2016). For example, most bars can serve as an anchor point for a noose, and most cells will have some sort of cloth which can be used to hang oneself (bedsheet, pants legs, shirt arms, or even socks). Many correctional facilities, especially short-term facilities such as jails or lockups, have made great strides in making it more challenging to commit suicide (e.g. "safe cells," breakaway fire sprinklers, removal of ligature points such as pipes, other alternatives to bars when possible, removal of exposed bedframes); however, as mentioned earlier, determined individuals will often find a way. Other common means in correctional environments include jumping from heights (top of the cell block), medication hoarding resulting in overdose, lacerations to one's wrists with a "shank," obstruction of the airway with a foreign body, and ingestion of toxic items (e.g., cleaner, razor blades). Although reducing access to easy means is important, additional steps such as increasing observational status, good general surveillance/monitoring, good communication among staff, and access to mental health treatment are often the best way to deter or interrupt a suicide attempt in a corrections environment over the long term. (*See* ch. 16, Case Study: An Insider's View of Suicide in Prison.)

In summary, lawyers need to remember to pay attention to dynamic factors such as an individual becoming hopeless, using substances, experiencing a change in demeanor, having a change in situation (new housing), or either recently starting back on psychotropic medications (takes time to become effective) or just stopping medication (potential for deteriorating mental health). In terms of static factors, being aware of an existing diagnosis of mental illness or personality disorder, past violent actions, and past suicide attempts is relevant. Even though correctional facilities often screen for suicidality, take precautions to limit access to lethal means, and provide psychiatric help to inmates, suicides can still occur. If you have concerns that your client is actively suicidal, from a medical standpoint, you should encourage them to get help (e.g., seek medical assistance, be compliant with medication) or voice concern to the appropriate level of correctional administration to ensure that reassessment, access to treatment, and appropriate level of precautions are occurring.

Individuals Awaiting Trial Either in Jail or on Release

As noted earlier, there are some unique factors for people who are awaiting trial. For some, this may be their first arrest, so there is more uncertainty about their situation, environment, what to expect, and what the outcome will be. If one is intoxicated at the time of arrest or going through withdrawal, their emotions may be more extreme and result in them thinking the situation is worse than it is. Additional concepts to potentially keep in mind when looking at people new to the criminal justice system are aspects of the Kübler-Ross stages of grief (Lester & Smith, 1989). Although these stages are usually attributed to people suffering from a death or terminal illness, many who are facing new and/or uncertain legal charges may also qualify (e.g., "my life is over," "I am going to die in prison"). Traditional stages are denial, bargaining, anger, depression, and acceptance. Although this belief is based mostly on anecdotal evidence, potentially the greatest risks for suicide would occur during the anger and depression stages. Aspects may also apply to individuals with a history of multiple incarcerations, especially if there is a concern that "my life is not going to change," "it is not going to get better," or "there is nothing to live for."

For jail inmates, times/events when somebody may be at the most risk of harming themselves are around family visits; time of court hearings; transitioning within the facility, such as being sent to isolation or returning to general population; revocation of bond status/remand; and coping with the release of friends (Pompili et al., 2009; Perry et al., 2010; Marzano et al., 2011; Shaw et al., 2017). In addition, the most frequent time of the day for suicide is often nighttime, when other inmates may be asleep, staffing levels may be lower, and there is less visibility due to lights being off.

Jails also have unique stressors due to their constantly changing population. You get a more volatile mix of people being incarcerated, and there is some literature indicating that there is a greater risk of substances being brought into jail due to the rapid turnover. Many also report poor sleep in a jail environment due to unfamiliar surroundings and constantly changing population. For people who have never been incarcerated before, the environment can be perceived as chaotic and "traumatizing," with them having little control over exposure to events such as violence, intimidation, bullying, or forced sexual encounters (Pompili et al., 2009; Knoll, 2010; Marzano et al., 2011; Rivlin et al., 2013; Marzano et al., 2016).

The location of where one is incarcerated can also have an impact. There has been some literature suggesting that risks for suicide may actually be higher in some smaller or rural facilities due to decreased staffing, less surveillance, and lower inmate population density, resulting in more opportunity to attempt suicide, less chance of rescue, and less access to mental health services (Daniel, 2006; Fagan et al., 2010). However, other literature notes that larger facilities can lead to more stress, bullying, or victimization, especially of younger inmates (Marzano et al., 2011; Rivlin et al., 2013; Favril et al., 2017).

Jail incarceration will often have a more profound acute effect on social supports, relationships, and family than prison incarceration (Marzano et al., 2011; Rivlin et al., 2013). By the time someone has been sentenced to prison, there may be more stability in what the new dynamic is. The inmate and the social supports have had more time to adjust and accept what is and what has happened. Someone awaiting trial or sentencing, however, is still facing many unknowns, such as if they will make bond, if a plea deal will be offered, what the actual evidence is against them, and how employers, friends, and family will respond to them being charged and incarcerated. Social or family supports may need time to understand what occurred, decide whether they are going to stay involved with the incarcerated individual, and determine how to deal with their own stress while someone in their life is incarcerated.

Another concern is the potential for less positive interactions with jail staff or for activities for the inmate to engage in. Given the amount of turnover, inmates may not have as many supportive/respectful relationships with staff, as can occur in prison. Although we are not trying to romanticize the guard/prisoner relationship, at least in the prison environment inmates and staff can potentially know each other for years and some form of stable dynamic can develop (Cramer et al., 2017). In addition, while one is incarcerated in jail and awaiting trial or serving a short-term sentence, there may be less opportunity for purposeful activity, such as work in the system or trying to pursue academic goals (GED, trade classes, or possibly even college), which can occur in a prison environment (Rivlin et al., 2013).

From a medical perspective, many people in jail may have a discontinuation or interruption of their medications, especially psychiatric medications. While lockups and jails do screen for suicidality, it may take time before somebody is placed back on their medications. In addition, the jail formulary may not have the medications, or the jail physicians may not continue some medications, such as bupropion (antidepressant with potential for abuse in an incarcerated environment) or quetiapine (antipsychotic/mood stabilizer with potential for abuse in an incarcerated environment) (Hall & Meyers, 2016; AAPL Resources for Prescribing in Corrections, 2018; Friedman et al., 2019). In addition, certain controlled classes of medications, such as benzodiazepines, opiates, and stimulants, may be tapered off or just stopped due to general safety and abuse concerns. The risk of experiencing benzodiazepine withdrawal or opiate withdrawal for people with chronic anxiety or pain conditions may be higher. Some studies have specifically identified either opiate abuse or prescribed opiate use as an increased risk factor for suicidal ideation while incarcerated, especially if they have a comorbid psychiatric condition (Daniel, 2006).

For individuals who may be on bond or on release pending their court dates, their daily life is often disrupted (e.g., meeting with lawyers, urine tox screening, ankle monitoring). In addition, there may be an increased risk of partner or family strife, especially if children are involved. The stress of being pretrial may result in developing/relapse with substance use or worsening of existing substance use issues, as well as there being greater access to means by which a suicide can be attempted, such as firearms. Often, potential reminders, such as having an ankle bracelet, make it hard to relax or temporarily distract oneself from one's situation. In addition, released pretrial individuals may be unwilling to open up or work with their mental health providers out of concerns that records or notes could be used against them in court. Often mental health providers, as well as release supervision officers of the court, may need to educate the individual about which interactions are confidential and which interactions may not be.

In general, the more exposure one has had to the criminal justice system, the less risk that may potentially occur in a jail setting, since there may be an idea of what to expect. However, there have been some studies indicating that people who have violated release or probation do have an elevated risk once placed back into the jail setting (Marzano et al., 2011). This is thought to be related to new uncertainty related to a case that the individual thought was progressing, anger at oneself for being violated, and/or less hope for lenience from a judge when legal issues are heard.

In summary, attorneys need to pay special attention for substance issues (prescription medications or recreational drugs), changes in emotional support network (sense of isolation, loss of support), how their client is adapting to the environment (sleep, changes in world view, overwhelmed), and if there are any issues of fear or apprehension for their physical safety (e.g., victim of violence, bullying, sexual abuse) around being in the jail environment.

Post-Trial

For individuals who are placed in prison, transitions are, again, the riskiest period of time. The first four weeks of moving to a new facility are of particular concern, with risks generally decreasing over a one- to two-year period of time (Marzano et al., 2011). Length of incarceration is more of a factor at the beginning of an individual's sentence (Rivlin et al., 2013). Other factors for suicide in the prison population include chronic health concerns and receiving bad news (e.g., denied parole hearing, denied appeal, death of a family member) (Pompili et al., 2009; Knoll, 2010; Winters et al., 2017). Family visits, although generally more positive in a prison situation, could lead to feelings that life is continuing without them. Those who are in higher-risk populations, whether it is segregation, disciplinary confinement, security-risk offenders, or specialty floor, such as mental health, tend to be at higher risk as well (Kellogg et al., 2014; Eck et al., 2019). Certain types of specialty confinement, such as isolation, may increase risk. However, other units, like sexual offender units, may actually decrease risk due to people feeling a little more protected, less risk of victimization, and ability to find support or peer group similar to themselves (Daniel 2006).

For individuals who are released from prison or are on parole, there is an eightfold greater risk for suicide compared to a general population for the first year of release (Perry et al., 2010; Pratt et al., 2010; Shaw et al., 2017). Some studies that focused on female inmates found the risk of suicide to be roughly 35 times higher after release compared to the general population. The risk for suicide, again, was highest within the first four weeks of release (20%), with the first four months being identified as a significantly higher window of risk (50% of suicides occurred within four months). It is important that individuals with a mental illness or past suicide attempts establish a relationship with a mental health treatment provider in close proximity to release from incarceration.

Oftentimes, people may have had hopes or fantasies that kept them going through incarcerations (e.g., job, family life, housing, community). However, when they try to live out those dreams, the person can become disillusioned or develop anxiety upon return to general life. In addition, they may have to face the nature of their crime from a new or fresh perspective or realize how much the time away cost. Prior to release, they had been in an environment where their crime or activity was known and potentially more accepted, but interacting in a non-incarceration environment results in questions and reactions that are likely different. For some, the social supports they had built up in a controlled environment are not available and past pre-incarceration social supports may not be available anymore. There is also the stress of either intentionally or unintentionally violating probation or other terms of release. In addition, certain temptations that may have been less available in a correctional environment, such as drugs and alcohol, are now easier to obtain. Overdose risk is a concern even if not an intentional suicide attempt, especially during the first two weeks of release, because the individual's tolerance to drugs has decreased (Shaw et al., 2017).

In summary, specific concerns for attorneys and parole officers are periods of transition where individuals' coping/support mechanisms may be disrupted, situations where the new reality does not match up to one's expectations, and potential for self-destructive behavior, such as substance abuse.

Conclusion

In conclusion, there is no one specific set of factors that identify someone who is at risk for suicide. Many times, the factors must be assessed based on each individual's temperament, life experience, and current situation. The more of a relationship somebody has with their lawyer or probation/parole officer, the easier it may be to identify risks. From a medical perspective, one of the greatest services the lawyer or probation officer can do if they have concern over a client's safety is to help ensure that they get professional mental health treatment, either by encouraging the individual to seek treatment or encouraging compliance with existing treatment.

Dr. Ryan C. W. Hall graduated Phi Beta Kappa with honors with a double major in biology and psychology from Johns Hopkins University. He completed his medical training at Georgetown University School of Medicine and did an internal medicine internship at Johns Hopkins University. He completed his psychiatric residency in the Department of Psychiatry and Behavioral Sciences at Johns Hopkins and a forensic psychiatry fellowship at the Case Western Reserve School of Medicine. Dr. Hall has been practicing psychiatry in Central Florida since 2008.

Dr. Hall has served as President for the Florida Psychiatric Society, Southern Psychiatric Association, and the Physicians Society of Central Florida. In 2019, he was selected to be part of the Florida Medical Association Delegation at the American Medical Association's House of Delegates, which is responsible for determining national policies for the organization. Dr. Hall has written numerous peer-reviewed journal publications and multiple textbook chapters on topics varying from psychopharmacology, psychotherapy, forensic issues, and societal concerns. He has also served on the American Academy of Psychiatry and the Law's newsletter Editorial Board.

Dr. Hall serves as an Affiliate Associate Professor for the University of South Florida's Department of Psychiatry in Tampa, Florida, as well as an Associate Professor of Psychiatry for the Department of Medical Education at the University of Central Florida College of Medicine in Orlando, Florida. Dr. Hall is also an Adjunct Faculty Member at the Barry University Dwayne O. Andreas School of Law in Orlando, Florida. Dr. Hall can be reached at Dr.rcwhall@live.com and his website is http://www.DRRYANHALL.com.

Complete citations are available from the author upon request.

Chapter

12

Suicide in the Criminal Justice System: Ethical Considerations

Lissa Griffin

This chapter by Professor Lissa Griffin helps navigate the "thicket of ethical rules governing lawyer decision making" when a client expresses a desire to end their own life. Some of the issues Professor Griffin deals with are the duty to consult with a client (Model Rule 1.4), the duty to exercise independent judgment (Model Rule 2.1), the duty of confidentiality (Model Rule 1.6), and the duty of competence (Model Rule 1.1). She also discusses how the issues of competency to proceed and the option of withdrawing from the case may impact the lawyer's representation. Amongst all these ethical concerns is the very human concern for the welfare of the client and what may be a well-founded fear that the client may be serious about attempting suicide—with tragic consequences.

• • •

Helping a person who shares an intent to commit suicide is not an issue unique to lawyers. Friends, family members, co-workers, classmates, doctors, nurses, and others all face the difficult decision about what to do when someone expresses an intention to take their own life. For many people this issue is not complicated: confronted with someone who seriously threatens suicide, you feel the impulse to stop it—call family or friends, call the police, take the person to a hospital. For lawyers it is not that simple. A lawyer's response is bound by a thicket of ethical rules governing lawyer decision making, including the duty to maintain client confidences, the duty of loyalty to the client, the right of the client to make her own decisions, the duty to counsel and advise the client, and the duty of candor to the court. In addition, in our adversarial legal system, the criminal defense lawyer has a unique constitutional and ethical role as the protector of the individual against the state and possesses a fierce desire to protect the client's autonomy at all costs. At the same time, lawyers, as empathetic human beings, feel an equally strong responsibility to keep a client alive; the social concern for the preservation of human life may be paramount. Often, against their clients' wishes, such loyal, zealous advocates may need to seek help from the client's family, medical professionals, the police, or even the court. Revealing a client's intent to commit suicide, however, can have devastating legal consequences for the client, including loss of liberty, loss of control of major life and legal decisions, disruption or loss of family relationships, loss of custody and visitation, and the prosecution's use of information about the defendant's mental state to prove its case. With so much at stake, how does a criminal defense lawyer, wholly committed to client-centered zealous advocacy, resolve conflicts between her ethical duties and the deeply felt moral responsibility to keep a client alive?

Consider this. Jane Jones is a married mother of two school-aged children who has been indicted for embezzling funds from her corporate employer. Jack Morris has been assigned by the court as her attorney. Jones is free on bail pending trial, but she has lost her job and has no income. The crime she is charged with carries a potential sentence of five years, and the prosecutor has offered her a promise of no more than 18 months if she pleads guilty. Her husband has moved out with the children, is seeking full custody, and is living nearby but is limiting her visitation with the children. Morris has met with Jones several times at his office to discuss the plea offer. At each meeting, Jane seemed distracted and disoriented. She was generally able to listen to Morris, but did not seem to understand the reality of her situation. She insisted "I never did anything wrong" and "someone is out to get me" even though, to Morris, the proof is clear that she stole the funds. She was mostly concerned about her children: according to her, her husband "wants to get me out of their lives entirely," and "thinks I'm crazy." She cannot plead guilty because that would allow her husband to have sole custody. Jane believed that "if I go to trial I will be acquitted and everything will go back to normal. My husband will come back and the four of us will be fine." The last two times Morris met with her she said that she could not live without seeing her children, that she was terrified they would be taken away if she were convicted, and that she couldn't live with the possibility of being imprisoned. She said, "I can't take this anymore, I want to end my life. I just can't go on." After the last meeting, Morris is alarmed that she may commit suicide.

What are Morris's ethical obligations and options? What, if anything, must Morris do? What can Morris do? What should Morris do?

To begin with, the sources of a lawyer's ethical duties are found in the law governing legal fiduciaries, who are bound by the duty of utmost loyalty (*Milbank, Tweed, Hadley & McCloy v. Boon*, 13 F.3d 537 (2d Cir. 1994); *In re Cooperman*, 633 N.E.2d 1069 (N.Y. 1994)), and the ethical rules enacted by the courts in the state in which the lawyer is admitted to practice. While there are some differences among the states' ethics rules, most of them are similar to the ABA's *Model Rules of Professional Conduct* (American Bar Association 2019) (Model Rules or MR). The Model Rules address the ethical requirements in all aspects of the lawyer-client relationship, from the duty to be competent and diligent to the allocation of decision making between lawyer and client. There are very strict rules to maintain client confidences, to avoid conflicts of interest, and to promote the duty of candor to the court. Many ethical considerations are implicated when a client shares with her lawyer an intent to commit suicide: the duties of competence, confidentiality, loyalty, and candor; the duties to investigate and counsel the client; special duties that arise if a client is operating under "diminished capacity"; and duties of candor to the court. The rules also reflect and recognize society's concern for the preservation of human life and the professional duties of a lawyer to protect those values.

1. Maintain Confidentiality; Investigate, Counsel, and Advise

Like most lawyers, Morris will view his role as one of unwavering loyalty that requires him to act immediately to save Jane's life. In most states, a person who threatens suicide can be temporarily committed on an involuntary basis, and Morris's initial instinct may be to reach out immediately to a mental health professional, hospital, or the police to have her treated as her condition demands. After all, criminal defense lawyers are also human beings and members of a society that values human life and dignity. The Preamble to the Model Rules reminds lawyers that they should be "guided by personal conscience and the approbation of professional peers," and many of the ethical rules exist to protect the public's confidence in the legal profession. Morris should treat Jane with compassion. But, without her permission or more information, Morris cannot ethically share Jane's suicidal threat with anyone, even to save her life.

Morris's first duty is to counsel Jane. The better part of zealous representation is effective client counseling. Morris should spend some time with Jane attempting to convince her that suicide is a poor option. He must also determine the seriousness of the danger to her and both counsel her on the law relating to suicide and dissuade her from suicide or encourage her to seek help herself. Under Model Rule 1.4, a lawyer must "reasonably consult with the client about the means by which the client's objectives are to be accomplished" and "consult with the client about any relevant limitation on the lawyer's conduct when the lawyer knows that the client expects assistance" that is not permitted by ethics rules or law. If suicide or assisting suicide is a crime, Morris may not assist Jane to commit suicide and he must tell her so. Suicide has been decriminalized, though, largely because of the belief that most suicidal individuals are mentally ill. In most jurisdictions, assisting suicide is still a crime.[1] But dissuading a client from taking her life is not assisting suicide. Morris may suggest that she talk to a mental health professional or family member or friend, and help her to arrange to do so. Morris has a moral as well as ethical duty to counsel her and try to dissuade Jane from taking her life or to convince her to get help. (*See* ch. 10, Suicide in the Criminal Justice System.)

Morris can and should go beyond the law and legal consequences and address the morality, personal and family consequences, and other relevant dimensions of Jane's intent to commit suicide. With respect to the role of advisor, Model Rule 2.1 requires a lawyer to "exercise independent professional judgment and render candid advice." Beyond the law, that advice may include advice as to "other considerations such as moral, economic, social and political factors that may be relevant to the client's situation." Morris should directly address Jane's desperation: where is it coming from, what can be done to relieve it, how the client will be hurt, and how it will hurt others? If the concern is her children, he should discuss ways to protect her right to custody or visitation; if the concern is going to prison, he

[1] Assisted suicide is a crime in every state, except California, Colorado, District of Columbia, Hawaii, Maine, Montana, New Jersey, Oregon, Vermont, and Washington.

should discuss the plea offer and the possibility of seeking a better offer or a reduced sentence. Maybe Morris can offer to reach out to the prosecutor, who may be willing to talk about a lesser plea or a different sentence, or even about terms of confinement. If her concern is financial, he can brainstorm about possible sources of temporary assistance, suggest that she seek outside help, and, if she agrees, assist her in seeking it. He can talk about the impact of her death on her children, other family and friends, and the morality of suicide. While this advice may seem well beyond the legal advice required to defend against Jane's criminal charge, Morris can and should try to dissuade Jane from taking her own life (MR 2.1 cmt. 2). If she is willing to seek help of any kind, counsel should help her arrange it (MR 2.1 cmt. 3) and if she wants, arrange to meet with them. This is what lawyers often call "remonstrating" with a client. Because Jane is obviously upset, Morris must be patient, compassionate, and clear. In many cases, counseling by a compassionate, patient, and well-prepared attorney will convince the client not to take her own life.

At this point, Morris may not reveal any information he has learned from Jane, including her intent to commit suicide. At the core of the attorney-client relationship is the duty of confidentiality. Lawyers cannot effectively assist clients unless they know the facts, and clients will not be forthcoming and candid unless they know that what they tell their lawyers is secret. One of the strictest, and most rigorously enforced, duties of a lawyer is to keep information about a client confidential. Under Model Rule 1.6, a lawyer may not reveal information relating to the representation of a client "unless the client gives informed consent, the disclosure is impliedly authorized, or the disclosure is permitted by one of the rule's exceptions." Confidentiality protects all information related to the representation. For that reason, Morris must keep Jane's intent to commit suicide confidential.

But after unsuccessful attempts to remonstrate with and talk Jane out of her suicidal intention, Morris may truly fear for Jane's safety. While all jurisdictions recognize the importance of confidentiality, all jurisdictions also have exceptions that recognize the overriding importance of preventing death or physical harm to the client or others. Thus, a lawyer may disclose confidential information if the lawyer concludes that disclosure is "reasonably necessary to prevent reasonably certain death or substantial bodily harm" (MR 1.6(b)(1)). In 42 states and the District of Columbia, this is permissive: the lawyer *may* reveal a client confidence for this purpose; in only eight states is disclosure mandatory.[2] Under this exception, however, the lawyer's disclosure must be "reasonably necessary"; it will not be deemed reasonably necessary if Morris can convince Jane to disclose it herself. In many cases, careful counseling by a well-prepared, compassionate lawyer will convince the client to stay alive.

At the same time, Morris must assess the danger to his client. Since he, like other lawyers, is not a psychologist or psychiatrist, he must educate himself about what to look for and the meaning of Jane's conduct and statements. As set forth in MR 1.1, the ethical duty of competence requires that a lawyer have "the legal knowledge, skill, thoroughness and preparation reasonably necessary for the representation." To satisfy this ethical duty, Morris must preliminarily understand how to assess the risk of a suicidal client. A client's suicide threat may be a cry for help from an overwhelmed defendant, a sign of a larger depression, or an actual signal that the client's death is imminent. Morris cannot properly evaluate the danger to Jane without understanding the literature and consulting a mental health professional (maybe an experienced attorney), or otherwise educating himself about how to assess the danger to his client. He can reach out to Jane's treating doctor, if there is one, or it may be best to reach out to a mental health professional who is not familiar with her case. If Morris does seek help of any kind, Model Rule 1.6(c) requires that a lawyer make "reasonable efforts to prevent the inadvertent or unauthorized disclosure of, or unauthorized access to" confidential information. For that reason, Morris should try to avoid identifying the client either by name or by identifying information, in order to protect Jane's confidentiality (MR 1.6 cmt. 18). In addition, some mental health professionals are permitted or even required to report when it is "necessary to prevent or lessen a serious and imminent threat to the health or safety of a person or the public."[3] The duties of competence and to advise also require that he know the law relating to suicide in his jurisdiction and counsel Jane accordingly.

---

[2] The states that do not have any duty-to-warn or disclosure laws are Arkansas, Georgia, Kansas, Maine, Nevada, North Carolina, Pennsylvania, and Vermont.

[3] Specifically, 30 states mandate disclosure and 14 states leave disclosure to the discretion of the mental health professional. The states that mandate disclosure are: Alabama, Arizona, California, Colorado, Connecticut, Idaho, Indiana, Kentucky, Louisiana, Maryland, Massachusetts, Michigan, Minnesota, Montana, Nebraska, New Hampshire, New Jersey, New Mexico, New York, Ohio, Oklahoma, Rhode Island, South Carolina, Tennessee, Utah, Virginia, Washington, West Virginia, Wisconsin, and Wyoming. The states that make disclosure discretionary are: Alaska, Delaware, District of Columbia, Florida, Hawaii, Illinois, Iowa, Mississippi, Missouri, North Dakota, Oregon, South Dakota, and Texas.

2. Whose Decision Is It? The Duty of Loyalty and Zealous Representation Versus Client Autonomy

Like any other compassionate human being, Morris will want to call a hospital, doctor, or other agency to secure Jane's safety and get her psychological help. But Morris must recognize that ethically the decision whether to commit suicide belongs to Jane. A lawyer has a duty to zealously represent a client's interests within the bounds of the law (MR, Preamble, paras. 2, 8, 9), but what that means is not always clear. Because Jane wants to end her life, must Morris respect that? In jurisdictions with laws permitting aid in dying, can he even help her do so? Or can he substitute his judgment about her best interests and thwart her plan? Zealously representing Jane's interests may mean defending her right to make a decision with which Morris disagrees. On the other hand, like other lawyers, Morris does not have to do whatever his client says she wants.

The criminal defendant clearly has the right to make all fundamental decisions about the case (*McCoy v. Louisiana*, 584 U.S. __ , 138 S. Ct. 1500 (2018)). The dimensions of this duty are also defined in Model Rule 1.2, which allocates decision making between lawyer and client: a lawyer must "abide by a client's decisions concerning the objectives of representation," and, in a criminal case, the lawyer must specifically "abide by the client's decision, after consultation with the lawyer, as to a plea to be entered, whether to waive jury trial and whether the client will testify." Because of the risks both to his relationship with Jane and to Jane herself, Morris must do everything he can to dissuade Jane from taking her own life. It should be her decision. Morris might decide, as a last-ditch effort, to tell Jane he is going to reveal her condition and get her help. This might convince Jane to do so herself. Of course, if Morris thinks that will increase the danger to Jane, he should not reveal his plan.

3. To Disclose or Not to Disclose

Assume that Morris cannot persuade Jane to seek help or abandon her suicidal plan. If, based on what he has learned from her and from consultation with mental health authorities, he believes it is reasonably necessary to intervene to prevent her reasonably certain death, he may reveal her condition to ensure her safety. The state ethics opinions that have addressed the question, as well as the ABA and the *Restatement*, all permit him to do so.[4] Morris need not have absolute certainty that she will commit suicide. While the rule reflects a fairly high threshold, Morris will be considered to be reasonably certain that death will occur if "it will be suffered imminently or if there is a present and substantial threat that a person will suffer such harm at a later date if the lawyer fails to take action necessary to eliminate the threat" (MR 1.6 cmt. 6). Again, the duty of competence requires that Morris consult his state's ethics rules and determine whether he is required to disclose Jane's plan. If his state's rules require disclosure, he must disclose; if disclosure is permissive, he will have to decide whether he should disclose against his client's wishes. Assuming Morris is in a permissive jurisdiction, the decision whether to disclose will be up to him. Importantly, Rule 1.6(b)(4) permits him to share client confidences for the purpose of complying with his ethical obligations, so he may reach out to other lawyers and ethics resources about how to fulfill his ethical duty (MR 1.6(b)(4) and cmt. 9).

In deciding whether to disclose, Morris should consider the following factors: 1) the seriousness of the risk to Jane; 2) the likelihood that the harm will occur and its imminence; 3) whether there is any other realistic way to prevent it; 4) the fact that he learned the information in confidence and that it is protected; and 5) any other aggravating or mitigating circumstances, as he sees them. This last factor gives Morris a tremendous amount of discretion, but he will find little helpful guidance about how to exercise it from the ethics rules, opinions, or other legal ethics authorities.

If Morris concludes that Jane has made a rational decision to take her own life, he has the option—out of a sense of loyalty, to protect her autonomy, confidentiality, and the dignity of controlling her own decisions—not to disclose her intent to commit suicide. He might decide not to reveal. This is not the course most criminal defense attorneys would take, even given their zealous loyalty to the client's autonomy. Such a decision might well, of course, result in Jane's death, something he will have to live with forever. Of lesser concern, Morris might be sued for legal malpractice by

[4] Alaska Ethics Op. 2005-1; South Carolina Ethics Op. 99-12; New York City Judicial Ethics Op. 1997-2; Utah Ethics Op. 95; Alabama Ethics Op. RO-95-06; Pennsylvania Ethics Op. 93-43; Arizona Ethics Op. 91-18; Virginia Ethics Op. 560; ABA Informal Op. 83-1500 (permitting disclosure); Massachusetts Ethics Op. 79-61; New York Ethics Op. 486; Restatement § 66. *But see* New Mexico Ethics Op. 1987-1 (prohibiting disclosure of a client's intent to commit suicide if suicide is not a crime). *See also* Pennsylvania Ethics Op. 93-43 ("When disclosure is mandated or permitted, the lawyer must disclose no more information than is required to meet the requirements or accomplish the purposes of this rule.").

her survivors, although it is highly unlikely that he would be held liable. A lawyer does not have a duty to prevent a client suicide, so the failure to do so is not actionable. Similarly, he is unlikely to be subject to discipline for making a decision that was ethically permissible, especially one that was based on competent investigation and counseling.

Most lawyers would probably not take that route. Knowing that the decision is his, Morris will likely feel compelled to save Jane's life by calling a doctor, hospital, or the police; the result may be that she is temporarily committed to a mental institution or otherwise receives treatment. If he does so, his disclosure must be limited to the information reasonably necessary to assist Jane. But disclosure has serious consequences for Jane. She may well be involuntarily committed, restricting her liberty and causing financial, personal, and family suffering. Her bail may be revoked. She may lose custody of her children and her ability to visit them, unsupervised, may be taken away. It may delay her case and make it more difficult for Morris to meet with her to continue representing her on her case. If Morris discloses against Jane's wishes, their relationship of trust and confidence will be damaged and he will have difficulty helping her with her case. Jane has an important decision to make—whether to plead guilty or go to trial—and it will be difficult for Morris to help her if she no longer trusts him or feels betrayed. If the relationship is reparable, it will take time and attention to repair it. If it is not, Jane may ask the court to appoint a new lawyer, or Morris may do so. Time will go by, and the request might in any event be denied, further exacerbating the damage to their relationship. If she is appointed a new lawyer, she may have difficulty forming a new trusting relationship. The obvious stigma of involuntary commitment will be difficult to avoid and it may well come to the attention of the prosecution and the court. Any public entitlements might be taken away. In addition, if the prosecution learns of Jane's suicidal threats, the court may allow this to be used as evidence of consciousness of guilt at her trial, if there is one, or at sentencing.

4. Counsel Again: Get Assistance for Defendant's Decision Making

Whether or not Morris decides to disclose under Rule 1.6, he still has another concern: whether, given her state of mind, Jane is capable of making rational decisions. And here he also has another way to help her.

A client who insists on committing suicide may still be able to make rational decisions, of course, or the decision to commit suicide may itself reveal an inability to understand alternatives or decision making hampered by emotional distress or mental illness. And even if Morris convinces Jane not to take her own life, she still has to decide whether to plead guilty or go to trial. Morris may be rightly concerned that she is unable to understand or process the advice and information she needs to make the decision. She may also be paralyzed and unable to make any decision at all.

If Morris reasonably believes Jane is not capable of making a rational decision in her own interests, Morris's ethical obligations increase. Without her permission, should he nevertheless help her get advice from people she trusts? Should he simply make the decisions she cannot make that he truly believes are in her best interests? Simply, neither course of action is an option. Under MR 1.14, lawyers are directed that when a client's capacity to make adequately considered decisions in connection with a representation is diminished, they first must "as far as reasonably possible, maintain a normal client-lawyer relationship with the client." That is not so easy. It means that Morris must work harder to competently and effectively counsel a cognitively or emotionally challenged client, such as Jane, and, importantly, respect her decision-making authority (MR. 1.14 cmt. 2). As he assesses her capacity for decision making, Morris will probably feel that Jane cannot act in her own best interests; that would be a logical conclusion. He will decide to act to keep her safe. But Rule 1.14 makes clear that, at this point, that is not an option.

Unfortunately, again, there is little guidance about the definition of "diminished capacity." The Model Rules leave this evaluation to the lawyer and present a serious dilemma. Comment 6 to MR 1.14 advises the lawyer to consider "the client's ability to articulate reasoning leading to a decision, variability of state of mind and ability to appreciate consequences of a decision; the substantive fairness of a decision; and the consistency of a decision with the known long-term commitments and values of the client." Thus, under Model Rule 1.14(b), if Morris reasonably believes that Jane has a diminished ability to make a rational decision AND "is at risk of substantial physical, financial or other harm unless action is taken and the client cannot adequately act in her own interests," he may but is not required to "take reasonably necessary protective action, including consulting with others who can take action to protect the client or seeking appointment of a legal guardian," even without Jane's consent.

Again, Morris may not take protective action simply because he reasonably believes Jane is operating under diminished capacity. He may only do so if there is the added risk to her.

While the rule provides a framework for the exercise of the lawyer's discretion, it provides no meaningful guidance. What should Morris do? Morris should begin by taking the kind of protective action that least intrudes on Jane's autonomy and dignity. If he considers what he is facing a life-threatening emergency, MR 1.14 comment 9 suggests that he may act to maintain the status quo, even if he cannot communicate effectively with Jane. If it is not an emergency, his duty to maintain as normal a relationship as possible means he must act in accordance with a reasonable view of Jane's values and wishes as he may know them, as well as what he understands to be her best interests (MR 1.14 cmt. 5; Restatement § 66 cmt. b and c). The danger of paternalism, even though exercised to help the client, is real. Morris may consult trusted members of Jane's circle to determine what she really wants. If Morris does seek help from others, he should do so in a way that least intrudes on client confidentiality. Morris is impliedly authorized to reveal confidential information but only to the extent necessary to protect Jane's interests (MR 1.14 cmt. 8). His duty to take reasonable measures to protect against the inadvertent or unauthorized disclosure of client confidences and the duty of competence require that he know whether anyone whose assistance he seeks has a duty to disclose Jane's suicidal threats (MR 1.1; MR 1.6(c)). While Morris risks being sued for legal malpractice or being charged with an ethical violation by breaching confidentiality, it is unlikely any such action would succeed. Once protective action is taken and Jane is safe, Morris should continue to assist Jane in defending the ongoing criminal case.

5. Consider Seeking a Professional Evaluation of the Defendant's Competence

If seeking outside help does not succeed, the more drastic step is to have the client examined by a mental health professional to determine whether the client is competent. The legal competency standard contains two elements: a defendant must be able to "consult with his lawyer with a reasonable degree of rational understanding ... and ... a rational as well as faculty understanding of the proceedings against him" (*Dusky v. United States*, 362 U.S. 402 (1960)). Among other things, a defendant must understand the charges, possible penalties, and likely outcomes; the roles of the judge, prosecutor, defense counsel, jury, and witnesses; the factual basis for the charges and available plea options; and must be able make rational choices among them in evaluating the evidence. She must be able to control behavior in order to avoid disrupting the proceedings and, if relevant, be able to testify coherently in her own defense. If Jane is incompetent and unable to make decisions on her own behalf, she will be hospitalized until she is deemed competent. Unlike in civil cases, where a guardian or conservator may be appointed to make decisions for the client, a defendant in a criminal case has a constitutional right to make certain decisions personally, to be present and to participate in her own defense. If Jane cannot do so, she may not be subjected to criminal process and no one can make these decisions in her place.

Again, because lawyers are not mental health experts, it is difficult to determine whether a distraught client is likely to be found incompetent, and thus to weigh the importance of protecting the client's decision-making autonomy against fairness and institutional concerns. From a competency perspective, mental illness is not a static state; its intensity and impact on a defendant's ability to make decisions can vary over time (*Indiana v. Edwards*, 554 U.S. 164 (2008)). Clearly, the duty of competence requires that counsel investigate the competency issue if the defendant's conduct raises questions of incompetence. At the same time, raising competency issues can result in serious risks for Jane. These risks should be explained to her and Morris should seek her permission for an examination. Competency examinations are usually done on an in-patient basis, in a secure facility, so even if Jane is found competent, her liberty will be taken away. It is very likely that her bail will be revoked. Jane has already lost her job, but she might lose custody of her children. Certainly, she will be unable to see them temporarily. Sometimes, if the client is charged with a relatively minor crime, raising competency issues may actually extend loss of liberty beyond what he would experience if he were found or pleaded guilty. Here, if Jane pleads guilty, she will likely be sentenced to 18 months in prison. If she is found competent, this will be delayed; if she is found incompetent, she could be involuntarily detained well beyond that time period. (*See* ch. 11, Suicide Risk Assessment for Individuals Involved in the Legal System.)

Aside from the severe personal consequences, Jane will be interviewed by a mental health professional who, in addition to a possible duty to report her suicide threats, will necessarily inquire into her personal, family, education, and medical background and ask questions about the client's understanding of the current proceedings and the underlying offense. If Jane is found to be incompetent, these responses will be recorded and shared with the prosecution and the court. The prosecution will thus have information to use at trial to rebut a defense, to advise against a reduced plea or sentence, or even to use as evidence of guilt. While in some cases there may be strategic advantages to raising competency—such as delay, getting treatment for the client, gathering support for an insanity claim, or getting help in securing a dismissal—in most cases the disadvantages will outweigh the advantages of committing a defendant for an examination that will cause her to distrust her own attorney and that will reveal personal and possibly incriminating information to the prosecution.

Because seeking a determination of Jane's competence is fraught with dangers, the question of whether to have the client examined must be discussed with Jane. If she agrees to an examination, the retained lawyer can arrange for the examination or the assigned lawyer can move the court, *ex parte*, for permission to have the client examined at state expense. If the client is found to be competent, none of the findings need be disclosed to the court or the prosecution. If, however, the client is found to be incompetent, the lawyer will be required to move the court to have the client declared incompetent and the expert's report will be revealed to the court and the prosecution.

6. Have the Client Examined for Competency to Proceed

If Jane refuses to be examined, Morris has a difficult decision to make. Should he reveal his good-faith doubts about Jane's competency to the court? Some jurisdictions require a lawyer to raise the issue of a client's competency (*see, e.g., State v. Haskins*, 407 N.W.2d 309 (Wis. Sup. Ct. App. 1987)), but most leave the decision to the lawyer's discretion. (*See, e.g., Enriquez v. Procunier*, 752 F.2d 111 (5th Cir. 1984) (noting that the decision not to raise competency may be a tactical decision within the lawyer's discretion)). The lawyer's duty of candor to the court prevents a lawyer from knowingly making false statements or presenting false evidence (MR 3.3(a)(1), (a)(3)), and deciding not to reveal that a client may not be competent to engage in judicial proceedings may be considered a violation of that duty or even ineffectiveness of counsel (*see, e.g., State v. Johnson*, 374 N.W.2d 637 (Wis. 1985)). A lawyer also has a duty to the administration of justice that would prevent representation of a client who may not be competent to understand the proceedings. Allowing an incompetent person to be convicted and sentenced would violate due process and the Sixth Amendment.

On the other hand, acting precipitously can have serious consequences for the client. Those negative consequences will convince most lawyers to forego this opinion unless they truly believe their client is incompetent to proceed. Certainly, the relationship between Morris and Jones will be destroyed; Jones will be hospitalized indefinitely, until she is found competent to proceed; her ability to see her children will be limited and she might lose her parental rights. The court and prosecution will get access to potentially damaging information that will hurt her case. As a practical matter, raising the issue of a client's competency with the court should be a last resort.

If Morris decides to seek an evaluation of Jane's competency, he should only reveal such information as he reasonably believes necessary to keep her safe. Even here, the attorney has discretion about whether, and if so, how much to disclose.

7. Withdraw from Representation

Representing Jane has been and likely will continue to be time-consuming, emotionally draining, and professionally demanding. The ethical dilemmas are near excruciating. Can Morris avoid all of this by withdrawing from the representation? Is that an ethical alternative?

Under Model Rule 1.16, a lawyer must terminate representation if continuing will result in an ethical or legal violation, if the lawyer is mentally or physically impaired, or if the lawyer is discharged. In Jane's case, Morris's efforts to convince Jane to get help, the threat to disclose her confidences, and even the disclosure of confidences, may have so destroyed their attorney-client relationship that Jane will want him fired. If an attorney is fired, he must withdraw; but because Morris has been assigned by the court he can only do so with the court's approval. The court may decline to do so. Extensive time has been spent representing Jane, the case is already at the plea stage, and the court may not be willing to allow the time and expense that replacing Morris would require. Morris himself can try to terminate the relationship if he can establish that the withdrawal can be accomplished without harming Jane's interests, if he finds Jane's determination to commit suicide repugnant, or if Jane's state of mind and conduct create an unreasonable burden for him. Again, of course, the court's permission is required. Despite the frustration of representing Jane, a client who continually refuses to follow his advice, the rules will not permit Morris to withdraw unless he can establish that it will not harm her and has become an unreasonable, unanticipated burden.

Even assuming that he can withdraw, should Morris do so? Morris will know that withdrawal seldom helps a client and may not help Jane. To be sure, if the relationship has been damaged, a new attorney may be able to get through to her and dissuade her from suicide or assist the client in rational decision making. More often than not, however, the new lawyer simply inherits the same problems as the withdrawing lawyer and the client is in the same position again. If Morris believes Jane is operating with diminished capacity, withdrawal is particularly disfavored. (*See, e.g.*, Vermont Ethics Op. 2006-1 (2006); District of Columbia Ethics Op. 353 (2015). *Cf.* Michigan Informal Ethics Op. CI-882 (1983) (the likelihood that the client will have the same problems with a new lawyer does not prevent withdrawal if the client has made representation unreasonably difficult).) Jane may feel abandoned and her condition may suffer; the work undertaken to help her will have gone to waste and will have to be repeated by a new lawyer.

Withdrawal will, however, provide some protection to Morris, both personal and professional. If he withdraws before disclosing Jane's condition, he would avoid being subject to discipline for breach of the duty of confidentiality and the fiduciary duty of loyalty. As discussed earlier, if Jane does commit suicide, his withdrawal will protect him against a civil suit for negligent failure to prevent a suicide. If he withdraws before deciding whether to raise the question of Jane's competency, he will avoid the possibility of being labeled constitutionally ineffective by a court for failing to raise the issue. And, of course, withdrawing may protect him against the personal and professional consequences of Jane's death.

Conclusion

What a lawyer may or should do when a client threatens suicide is not as clear or simple as it may be for other professionals. Few jurisdictions require a lawyer to take steps to prevent client suicide. Most permit a lawyer to intervene when attempts to counsel the client have failed, but there is almost no guidance about whether or when or how to do so. While most criminal defense lawyers would no doubt feel compelled to intervene to save a client's life at all costs, ultimately, as a matter of ethics, if the client is competent, the life or death decision is up to the client. Most lawyers will want to try to save a client's life and may ethically do so. First, however, the criminal defense lawyer must be prepared and informed to counsel the client to convince the client to reveal her intent and seek professional help. If after efforts to persuade the client have failed, the lawyer reasonably believes that revealing the client's intent is necessary to prevent her death or serious harm, the lawyer may do so, reaching out to medical or other professionals to save the client's life. If the lawyer reasonably believes the client is operating under diminished capacity and is in danger of substantial personal, financial, or other harm, the lawyer may seek help for the client, observing confidentiality where possible. The lawyer with reasonable doubt as to the client's competency can have the client examined to determine whether she is competent to proceed, but this should be a last resort. Each of these actions, against the client's interests, has serious legal and personal consequences to the client that must be considered even when intervening to save the client's life feels like the only responsible choice.

• • •

Lissa Griffin is a Professor of Law and the Director of the Criminal Practice Concentration at the Elisabeth Haub School of Law at Pace University in White Plains, New York. She has written extensively on criminal procedure issues, including issues of professional role in the criminal process, both from a comparative perspective and in the context of wrongful convictions. Prior to coming to Pace, Professor Griffin practiced criminal and civil appellate litigation privately and with The Legal Aid Society. She is the author of *Federal Criminal Appeals* and is the co-author of *Multi-defendant Criminal Cases: Federal Law and Procedure* and *New York Evidence with Objections.* Professor Griffin teaches professional responsibility, evidence, criminal procedure, and comparative criminal procedure. Professor Griffin can be reached at lgriffin@law.pace.edu.
Complete citations are available from the author upon request.

Chapter

13

Case Study: The Logistics of Suicide

Jeffrey Grant[1]

The following four chapters are each case studies about people who were convicted of crimes and contemplated suicide. Two are men convicted of federal white-collar crimes. Two are women who were convicted of crimes of violence in state court. Three actively contemplated suicide; the other witnessed a suicide while in jail, and at that moment committed to living as fully as possible. All four have gained a huge amount of self-awareness after doing a deep dive into those emotions and circumstances which ensnared them in the criminal justice system. All four are passionately devoted to helping others in similar circumstances.

The first case study is by Jeffery Grant, formerly a high-powered, hard-charging lawyer in New York City. His story reads like a movie script and illustrates the saying "the bigger they come, the harder they fall." Of particular note are the demands of the legal profession and how his dealing with those demands fed his emotional decline and precipitated the crime that led to his incarceration.

• • •

It's taken me years to unravel what happened on the night of my suicide attempt in July 2002. Even now I'm sure I don't have all of it exactly right.

[1] This is an edited excerpt from a chapter titled "The Logistics of Suicide," in Jeffrey Grant, Last Stop Babylon (Progressive Prison Ministries, 2020).

All I really remember about that evening is sitting down in my favorite chair in the den—it was an oversized wicker chair that we purchased at the Ralph Lauren Country Store in Southampton about a decade earlier. It was big, massive really, but horribly uncomfortable. Now there's an apt metaphor for my life if I ever heard one. It played its part perfectly in the corner of our den—an all-glass room I had taken as payment from a former client of mine in the greenhouse business. There had been a lot of days that I had to drive down to English Greenhouses' headquarters to beg for a check, in the absolutely most depressing area of Camden, New Jersey. In the end, I wound up with this greenhouse in the last days of their business before they filed Chapter 11. That's the way it always was in running a law firm—first I had to get the work, then I had to do the work, then I had to send the bill, then I had to lower the bill, then I had to take whatever I could get before the client went out of business. No wonder I was depressed.

In this case, I guess the deal worked out pretty well, as our whole family basically lived in this glass den almost every day and night. The very best days were snow days when the girls were little. We would all lie on the sofa together and watch the snow pile up over our heads, and guess when the snow would slide off the glass roof. We pretty much raised our daughters in this room. If there were anything I missed about our old house in Rye, I'd have to say that the greenhouse would be it. I guess that's what made it an ironic—and tragic—place to attempt suicide.

I settled down into my usual late-night position, alone as usual after the family had gone to sleep. The big Sony XBR was blaring, as always. I had my usual cup of Diet Coke and ice perched precariously in my left hand, and the channel changer in my right. I insisted that we use plastic cups, despite my wife Laurie's insistence that the kids were old enough for real glasses. It wasn't because of the kids. Night after night it was a sick game to see which would hit the floor first and rouse me from my drug stupor, the channel changer or the glass of Diet Coke. On rare occasions it would be a tie. It was usually a major mess. I just wrote off to the cost of being a drug addict. Not too bad a cost really … a little Diet Coke to clean up here and there. (*See* ch. 1, The Price of Empathy: Learning to Cope with Trauma in the Criminal Courtroom.)

• • •

I had been fighting for my professional life for over three years at that point, the subject of disciplinary proceedings before the New York State Lawyer's Grievance Committee. Simply, I borrowed some of my clients' escrow funds without their permission. I'm not certain why. The amount I borrowed was small compared to the very large law practice I had grown. I offer no excuse. I can only conclude now that I was desperate, confused, frightened, alone—and very stoned. My judgment was just so impaired. I did things I would never let a client think of doing. Yet, it was like I was on automatic pilot, being fed by my muse—Demerol had taken hold of me and refused to let go.

We lived this wonderful, successful life, at least on the surface. Underneath I was confused and tortured, and had never come to terms with any of my issues. As I became more successful, I became more manic, more unable to stand the look of disappointment in my wife or children's eyes. So I gave them everything. Or at least I tried to. It was not healthy. I worked incredible amounts of hours, and had my business swirling all around us.

My law firm was located in Mamaroneck, just over the border about a mile from our center-hall colonial in Rye. I opened a local bistro about a half-mile from our house as a place to schmooze and drink at night. But in reality, I didn't do too much drinking because I was far more interested in painkillers, and had two or three in my pocket at all times. A drink in my hand, and the low-level smell of liquor on my breath was a handy disguise so as to not let on to anybody that I was, and always had been, using prescription painkillers as long as most people there had known me. I was elected to the local school board, and served two terms in public office. It was a source of some local fun, but never personal embarrassment, that I was a school board trustee who wore sunglasses in the evening on televised school board meetings. In truth, I was usually in no position to be seen in public at that late hour. I was perceived as a happy, fun-loving guy, and I guess was for the most part. I backslapped all the guys, kissed all the women, and loved all their kids.

My family was regarded as the one of the chosen, the lucky. My kids thought they were on a magic train ride that would never end. We traveled five or six times a year, and never spent one holiday at home. Most of our vacations were girls' shopping trips. There were no backpacking or hiking trips—not for us. We'd fly into LAX, for example; check into the Chateau

Marmont; and see what stars were in the house for us to rub elbows with. In retrospect, I guess it sounds more trailer-park than it seemed then.

• • •

Once, right after the movie *Titanic* came out, Leonardo DeCaprio was staying at the Chateau Marmont—right across the hall from us. Hearing this, my younger daughter, Amber, camped out in the hall waiting for a glimpse of him for hours. Of course, Leo was on a very different schedule than were we lightweights. Another time, Amber and I were playing ping-pong by the pool: she would intentionally miss the ball so that it would bounce over to Keanu Reeves. He would just keep returning it to her and smiling. Now, if these didn't count as cheap thrills, nothing did. But mostly, L.A. was about shopping. That's big-time shopping. We would divide the city up into a grid: Santa Monica Fred Segal & Montana Avenue, Melrose Avenue & Melrose Fred Segal, Sunset, Beverly Hills, and then a drive down to Newport Beach. Five full shopping days, five nights of restaurants and movies. We were off.

It was pretty much the same in every store we went into. We'd walk in and the girls would spread out sniffing out clothes. I would find the daddy chair that was always strategically placed close, but not too close, to the dressing rooms so that the girls could put on a fashion show, over and over again seeking my approval for this or that. We developed shorthand, spoke in code, got it down to subtle hand and head gestures. I became an expert picker: I knew my family's sizes and shapes, what would look good on them right from the rack, and passed things in to them so they didn't even have to leave the dressing rooms. It became a source of pride for me when something I picked worked out, as if I designed it, or I knew them that well. To this day, women ask me to go shopping with them because I'd developed such a good eye (maybe it'll come in handy in my next life). Mostly I sat on the daddy chair, and the girls who worked in these clothing stores were experts in working us. Mostly in working me. They were young, beautiful, cool music was blaring, and they knew that if I felt good I'd be more likely to whip out my American Express Black Card and get lost in it all. They were right, and I did it time and again. I think the Demerol had a lot to do with it, too. I sat there most days almost comatose and as the girls finished trying on item after item, they just stacked them up on my lap. I could barely see over the top.

After a particularly aggressive day of shopping at Fred Segal Melrose, we decided we wanted to purchase one last thing we had seen the day before. As we walked in the next morning, one salesgirl shouted to another, "Look, it's Jeff and Laurie. They're back again." For some, that would have been a signal that we were a little overinvested in the process. Not for us—we managed to be proud of our small brush with Fred Segal notoriety.

• • •

This all wasn't my first brush with the rich and famous. Growing up on the South Shore of Long Island, we all thought we were all so privileged—and in retrospect I guess in most ways we were. Our house looked pretty much like the Stevens' house on *Bewitched*—my mom looked like Elizabeth Montgomery, my dad was in advertising like Darren Stevens (even if he looked and behaved a lot more like Larry Tate). It was a perfect sitcom life. For a few moments, even I can get caught up in the rapture of this image before it melts away with the reality of absentee parents, incessant fighting, divorce, alcohol, barbiturates, and amphetamines. We never knew anybody from any real places of affluence—places like Westchester County or Greenwich, Connecticut—so we had no basis of comparison. But after my parents split up in the early 1970s, my dad starting dating a woman named Lydia Dirks from Greenwich who changed all that in a hurry.

Lydia was the widow of the late financier James Dirks, who died young. James made his first million while he was still a student at Boston University, or so the story goes, and then became a multimillionaire in bull sperm futures. He certainly made enough money to purchase the biggest house in Greenwich, a palace on Round Hill Road called Dunellen Hall that later became famous as the residence of Leona Helmsley. It had a ballroom large enough to accommodate parties for 200 people. It had enough property for a stable and a full ranch with full-time ranch hands. James was a tough guy, and even tougher on his kids. His son Jimmy was not made of the stuff that James was, and was born with some sort of congenital defect for which he had several operations. James had little sympathy for Jimmy's condition and would do spot checks. One day, while out riding with the hands, James tried to make Jimmy pull down his pants to see if he had soiled them. Embarrassed, Jimmy told his father that he wished that he were dead. That night, James Dirks died.

My great aunt Shirley, who had been the president of the great Jewish charity Hadassah, was friendly with Lydia's mother, Anna Terkel, who had been the president of B'nai Brith, another great Jewish charity. I guess these two women smelled a l merger in the making. My dad needed a home and Lydia needed a majordomo, so it was a perfect match. They never quite married, but my dad lived with Lydia at her place on Central Park West in Manhattan for the next 10 years or so. He stayed through the good years and cared for Lydia through her lung cancer and death. He then stayed another five years and took care of Anna—until he himself got sick and was unceremoniously evicted from the premises. But when the good times were good, they were very good.

• • •

Once when I was in law school, I received a call from my father asking me to throw on a sports James jacket and meet him at the Steer Palace in Madison Square Garden. I was living in Queens at the time, already pretty stoned and in no mood for my dad and Lydia. But something sounded interesting about this invitation. So I hopped on the E train and an hour later was on Seventh Avenue staring up at the big sign in front of the Garden. I found the Steer Palace, which I'd never been in but knew was an expensive steak joint. It was not on a law student's budget. Once inside, I was shown to Dad and Lydia's table and was introduced to a few other people, including the tennis player Jimmy Connors and his girlfriend Patti McGuire. Patti was a former Playboy centerfold who had been the subject of a considerable amount of my teenage fantasies. We had dinner and Jimmy told wonderful tennis stories about Wimbledon and all his travels around the world. I kept an eye on Patti.

After dinner we all made our way into the Garden where we had a center court box to watch the Volvo Masters tournament. To me this was going to be a complete snooze. I was not a tennis fan. And I learned quickly that when you are sitting in a center court box, your head has to keep going from side to side to follow the ball. This was not agreeing with the drinks from dinner and the particular cocktail of drugs I had ingested about two hours earlier. Sitting next to me was Lydia, in her usually get-up of turban, gold caftan, and jewels that were dripping from every visible finger, wrist, lobe, and other appendage. Her makeup artist, who came to the Central Park West apartment at five o'clock every evening, had applied her makeup. She carried an 18-karat gold, jewel-studded elephant handbag that hinged open at the top to reveal her goodies inside. Lydia was a wonderful sight to witness—and on occasion partner in crime.

While everyone in Madison Square Garden was watching what I thought was just another banal tennis match, I was trying to stop the rising tide of vomit from coming up into my throat. I had to leave. Just then, Lydia nudged me and asked me if I wanted to take a walk. We walked out into the hallway that rings the lower level of the garden, just talking and strolling, a young man and his Egyptian Queen. Just then, Lydia spotted a sign for a Chase Bank Hospitality Room, and she sensed some fun. She grabbed my arm and pulled me toward the entrance. We breezed past the security guard—security guards meant nothing to Lydia—and into the main room of the party.

Surveying the situation, Lydia looked at me, threw her arms up in the air and yelled to me, "Freebies, let's eat!" As we helped ourselves to the buffet and then sat down at the bar, a nicely dressed man with a Chase Bank badge came over to us and asked if we had a Chase card for this room. Lydia smiled at him obligingly, opened up her gold elephant, and pulled out a long string of credit cards in a long plastic sleeve. With her very long painted fingernails, she slipped a Chase credit card out and showed it to him, pooh-poohed him away, and dug back into her chicken wings. Undeterred, he protested that he didn't mean a Chase credit card—what he meant was a Chase Bank invitation. With that, Lydia's expression changed into a look that was icy cold. Then, softening into the kind of smile the rich have when they intend to have their way, she calmly told him that she had never before needed an invitation to one of David's parties. And that was that. It was the first inkling that by David she meant David Rockefeller—the chairman of Chase Bank—and that she wasn't kidding. We finished our chicken wings without further interruption.

• • •

July 2002 wasn't my first drug overdose. In 1986, my whole world was collapsing. My father-in-law, Greg Lipshitz, was like a second father to me. He was essentially the only father I ever had; we spent a lot of time together. He was the captain and I was the first mate on a succession of ever-larger boats that he docked in the back yard of the family home in Bellmore, Long Island. The last of these boats, a 55-foot Chris Craft, seemed like it was bigger than the house. He loved his boats, probably more than his family as it turned out, and scheduled his entire life around them. Laurie and I even had to schedule our wedding so as not to interfere with one of his boating weekends.

Greg offered to throw Laurie and me a combined 30th birthday party in the back yard of the house. Of course, with Greg it really meant an opportunity to show off his newest boat. We invited all our friends and the party was off to a roaring start. Soon, people were pairing off on the boat, doing drugs on it—it was pretty much like most Saturday nights, but with Greg picking up the tab. The next day was Father's Day, and the entire extended family was to meet at Judson's Grill on the Upper East Side of Manhattan to celebrate. But Greg was unusually vacant: he got up from the table a lot, he made a lot of phone calls. It was very noticeable—at least to me.

That night, after Greg and my mother-in-law Micki drove back to Bellmore, he drove his Mercedes SL out to Mattituck Marina out on the eastern end of Long Island where he often took his boats in the summer. He left his car out there and took a limo back home. Arriving home after midnight, he kissed my mother-in-law goodnight and they went to bed. At about five o'clock in the morning, Greg woke up, went down to the Chris Craft, fired up the engines and pushed off the dock forever. He left a note behind saying that he had left Micki for his business partner, a woman named Fern. About two hours later, the proverbial s— hit the fan.

Greg soon started pressure tactics on Micki, and tried to get all of their friends and family on his side. But of course, many of Greg's so-called friends came forward with tales of his mistresses and how he used his various boats as floating brothels. Laurie stopped talking to him, a situation that remained for over 18 years. I tried to walk the narrow line between being Laurie's husband and Greg's son-in-law, but ultimately it was just too narrow a line.

A few days later, locked in my office on 42nd Street between Park and Madison Avenues, on my desk was a bag of Quaaludes, a bag of coke, and a bottle of vodka to wash it all down.

• • •

My first law office in the Lincoln Building was on the fifth floor, right next to the big "L" in the Lincoln sign. Some days I would get stoned and just gaze out the window at the throng of people below exiting and entering Grand Central Station on the corner of Vanderbilt Avenue. Sometimes I'd get a craving for oyster stew and run down to the Oyster Bar on the Concourse level. But not on that day. I had already swallowed about 10 Quaaludes and snorted over an eighth of an ounce of coke. I was hazy, and starting to have misgivings. I was not sure if I had enough drugs to kill myself. I snorted another line and then remembered a therapist who was living in an apartment I owned down in Tribeca.

Cal was a therapist of some sort, and he rented this apartment from me that I had bought during the co-op boom. It was a really nice apartment, in a converted pickle factory on Jane Street right next to the High Line. It was a three-bedroom duplex with private roof rights to build a garden. But the neighborhood hadn't yet gentrified; that would take another few years. There were transvestite prostitutes on the corner who would approach my car if I drove down to visit. Laurie and I just weren't adventurous enough to move down to that part of town, so I rented it out to Cal. Cal ran his psychotherapy practice out of the place. He told me that I was the worst landlord he'd ever met; he would call me up with completely reasonable issues, and I would tell him to have it fixed and send me the bill. I guess we both knew that I was the kind of landlord who was too stoned, or too damaged, to get things fixed. Every time we spoke, he would put in a plug for me to get some therapeutic help. "When you are ready, call me," he would say.

Shaking, I pulled Cal's phone number out of my wallet and dialed. He answered. Cal knew my voice and knew that I was in trouble. I tried to explain where I was and what I was doing. He asked me if I was trying to kill myself. I told him that I didn't know. Cal then gave me very explicit instructions: he told me to get up, put all the drugs in a bag, go to the bathroom and flush them down the toilet. Then he told me to go down to the street, hail a cab, and take it to directly to the Jane Street apartment. He said that he would meet me at the curb and pay for the cab.

And that's what I did. I went to Cal's psychotherapy office, in my apartment, and went into session with him for the next 15 years.

• • •

By 1992 I had moved my law practice up to Mamaroneck in Westchester County, and was really flying high. I was representing interesting clients, making lots of money, and was clean and sober for about five years. Everything was going great—great that until one afternoon when I was playing basketball with my biggest client and I ruptured my Achilles tendon. Now that was a shot heard round the world … at least for my family. I called an orthopedist friend and he agreed to meet me at the hospital and to give me a prescription for 40 tabs of Demerol. I got through the surgery in one piece and went home after a day or two. But I wanted—I *needed*—more Demerol.

Chuck Martini was a former college roommate of mine who had moved into Mamaroneck after he went back to school to become a dentist. I was reticent about him and his family moving into town, mostly because I knew that I could manipulate him into writing prescriptions for me. Of course, that's what happened. At first, it was pain control for my ruptured Achilles tendon. But soon Chuck was writing me prescriptions on demand, just because we were friends. And I guess because I was doing legal work for him, he figured he wouldn't have to pay the bill if he just kept writing me prescriptions for Demerol. A month's worth of Demerol would last me about three days, then Chuck would write me another.

Let me explain what Demerol is used for. It's a powerful narcotic in the morphine family, but stronger. A doctor would prescribe it to someone if they, say, ripped open their leg in a motorcycle accident, or were undergoing major surgery. It's the drug that Winona Ryder was caught with when she was shoplifting in Beverly Hills. It's frightening now to think that I got prescriptions from Chuck for Demerol for almost 10 years even though I had nothing physically wrong with me. In retrospect, I have to accept complete responsibility for it. To blame Chuck, or anybody else, would be the same as an alcoholic blaming the bartender for getting drunk.

As my drug use increased, my judgment became more and more impaired. That's when I started making mistakes, and then the mistake that broke the camel's back. One day we couldn't make payroll, so I "borrowed" money from my client escrow fund. The deal with the devil was done—there was no turning back and I did it several more times. An investigation by the Grievance Committee followed pretty quickly.

My Demerol use increased as I sought to avoid the reality of what I had done. Then came 9/11 and, in my stupor, I was hit hard. When I saw the plane hit that second building, I ran to the bank and took out every cent we had. I ran to the beverage store and bought a pallet of water and had it delivered to our garage. We stocked up on food for a month. I went into battle mentality, went crazy. My drug use doubled and my business halved. For the first time in almost 20 years of business, there was no business. There I was, facing possible disbarment, and I was reeling and searching for answers. I called up my accountant, who suggested that I take out one of the SBA 9/11 loans that were being advertised nonstop on the radio. I called up the SBA, explained my situation and—because my business was in Westchester County and was economically impacted—they said I qualified. I'm not sure if it was poor judgment caused by 10 years of drugs, mania, desperation, or just exhaustion, but I just couldn't stop myself from embellishing my application.

So, I lied and said I had an office about a block from ground zero. I committed SBA loan fraud and soon had an SBA 9/11 loan meant to restore my law firm. I was now a white-collar criminal waiting to get caught.

• • •

By July 2002, my grievance proceedings had lasted almost three years. I thought that they had been going reasonably well until they suddenly turned ugly. Mike Tischman, a former business partner of mine, turned whistleblower. Mike had been the chairman of a New York-based nursing home chain. He and I started developing nursing homes and doing real estate deals together when, of course, we had our own falling-out. I have to accept responsibility for that, too. I'm certain that I behaved badly. I don't blame or resent Mike for the letter he sent to the Grievance Committee that sealed my fate. It is only with years of sobriety and perspective I have learned how grateful I truly am to Mike for the letter he sent that saved my life. But I certainly did not have this clarity at the time.

Exhausted and ravaged by 10 years of daily Demerol abuse, I called my ethics attorney and asked him to contact the Grievance Committee to resign my law license. I called Chuck and asked him for my usual prescription of Demerol. He told me to come over and pick up the prescription at his office a couple of blocks from mine. He gave me his usual admonition to be careful, and of course I told him that I would. I took my usual drive to Trotta's West Street Pharmacy in Harrison, where I filled most of my prescriptions. While I was there, I ordered a history of my prescriptions to be mailed to my home, I'm still not sure why. The wait for my Demerol prescription to be filled felt like it was forever.

I went home, had dinner with Laurie and the girls, and waited for everyone to fall asleep. Settling into my wicker easy chair—the one we had bought at Ralph Lauren—I popped the top off the vial of pills, pressed the vial to my lips, and tilted it to my mouth. The pills slid easily down my throat without any need for the Diet Coke I held in my other hand. I set the vial down, picked up the channel changer, put the television on, and surfed for something to watch until I felt the familiar wave of euphoria roll over me that made everything all right.

• • •

Jeffrey Grant, J.D., M.Div., is co-founder of Progressive Prison Ministries, Inc., the world's first ministry serving the white-collar justice community. The ministry hosts an online White Collar Support Group every Monday night. After an addiction to prescription opioids, a suicide attempt, and serving almost 14 months in a federal prison for a white-collar crime he committed when he was a lawyer, Jeff started his own reentry: earning a Master of Divinity from Union Theological Seminary in the City of New York with a focus in Social Ethics.

Jeff is an ordained minister with more than three decades of experience in crisis management, business, law, reentry, recovery (clean and sober 18+ years), ministry, public speaking, and corporate training. Sometimes referred to in the press as "The Minister to Hedge Funders," he uses his experience and background to guide individuals, families, and organizations forward in their lives, relationships, careers, and business opportunities, and to help them stop making the kinds of decisions that previously resulted in loss, suffering, and shame. Jeff can be reached at prisonist.org, jgrant@prisonist.org.

Complete citations are available from the author upon request.

Chapter 14

Case Study: Sentenced to Healing

This chapter is by a gentleman who wishes to remain anonymous. That in itself is hugely revealing because it underscores the stigma of a criminal conviction. One of the many takeaways from this chapter is that an insightful attorney and a wise judge can make a huge difference. This man was fortunate to have an attorney who recognized that his client had significant emotional issues and suggested that he seek counseling. This man was also fortunate to have a judge who studied the case, listened to the attorney's advocacy, and upon careful reflection fashioned a sentence which was appropriate and, indeed, helpful.

• • •

I ask to remain anonymous. This should not be interpreted as an attempt to avoid full responsibility for the actions being described and the life history that may have contributed to the events described in this chapter. Rather, it reflects the opposite. However, my story is very personal and I prefer this route. In addition, the events described herein include people who are either not alive or may prefer to remain anonymous. I am, however, willing to get in contact with interested readers via the editors of this book to engage in any conversation as seems appropriate.

This story starts on a beautiful fall day afternoon on a street corner in Manhattan. I walked home after work and realized, when thinking about my life, that my career seemed to have reached a peak. Highly successful, respected by my peers, being fulfilled by my mission to contribute in major ways to bring hope to people with mental illness, I realized that I was living the dream and was very grateful to those who joined me on this journey. And still, there was an atmosphere of something unknown that seemed to weigh on my mind. I pushed it away.

The crime I committed presented a paradox. I was accused of misappropriation of funds, specifically having used public and private monies for personal reasons. The academic institution I had been affiliated with had initially interviewed me about these allegations and I had acknowledged that some funds were used for purposes other than described in the award. They chose to refer the case to the Southern District Court in New York City for reasons unknown to me. I have always been described as a highly intelligent, refined, and cultured man. I have had a sterling scientific career, not only marked by academic achievement and peer recognition, but motivated by a genuine passion—and unique skill—for alleviating suffering. By all appearances, my life, both professional and personal, has been a great success. But beneath the surface, as I realized only during the months of therapy after being accused of a crime, there is a man who carries tremendous guilt and shame, and who, in an inexplicable manner approaching compulsion, took repeated actions to sabotage my own success and breach the mores of society for little personal gain. This was the shadow that I was unable to describe at the time. A flawed person, whose all-too-human frailties overtook me during critical periods of my life, and have already acted to devastate my career, reputation, and family. When I came before the court, my life up to that point had been shattered by my actions. I have accepted responsibility and have started the process of rebuilding my life. Without any doubt I will continue to punish myself long after the sentencing in this case.

To begin to understand my actions, a full account of my life is necessary. In particular, the seeds of my dysfunction took root during adolescence, which was defined by a passionate love for my best friend, who, despite my best efforts to keep him safe, committed suicide after a prolonged battle with mental illness. The trauma of that loss has had a profound impact on my life: simultaneously launching my career in the neurosciences and also introducing me to my wife and mother to my beloved children, while arresting my emotional development and leading to a pattern of toxic codependent relationships with men. In my relationships with men,

I repeatedly suspended the sound judgment and probity that characterized the rest of my life, and misused funds that compromised my positions at a major academic institution. Yet—not in an attempt to look for excuses—these poor decisions and criminal conduct should not be viewed outside the context of the rest of my life, which I have dedicated to gain of scientific knowledge and the alleviation of suffering for those suffering from mental illnesses.

I was born in a European country into an established family deeply rooted in conservative views and lifestyles. My father was an academic veterinarian scientist, focused on his work, and my relationship with him was cold and distant. My mother stayed home with me and my siblings. Our childhood was very protected; for me it felt like "growing up in an old, conservative family in an old, conservative environment." I attended the local public school in a setting that was intensely rigorous and competitive. I thrived in school and excelled in academics. It turned out that I was especially gifted in music, studied piano starting at age six at the university, and later in addition with private teachers, and my parents strongly encouraged the development of this talent on the piano. From a young age, I practiced obsessively, often for five or six hours a day. Ultimately, I looked forward to a life dedicated to the study and appreciation of music.

But when I was 17, our father died of a brain aneurysm. His sudden death was "a shock to the family system." Our cloistered, safe family life was shattered. As the eldest son, I became the *de facto* head of the household. I was forced to grow up in an instant and had little space to process my own grief—grief around the realization that I had missed out on the opportunity to learn who our father really was. I also was consumed by guilt over not having tried harder to overcome my own arrogance and intentional distance I kept toward him.

Around the same time, I developed a close friendship with a boy in my high school class. He came from a family like mine: conservative and repressive, with an intense focus on academic success. He was, like myself, a brilliant, star student. Our companionship was both intellectual and emotional, and as it became closer, in my memory, we fell in love. We never spoke about our relationship in such terms, and while we were physically intimate, our relationship was never sexual. But I can describe this relationship as "homoerotic." Especially after the trauma of my father's death, the emotional catharsis offered by this intimate relationship with this boy was like the discovery of a whole new way to live. At that time,

I quit playing the piano seriously so that he and I could devote time to being together.

After high school graduation, however, my friend developed odd behaviors and delusions that I later came to understand were symptoms of schizophrenia, a mental disorder that often develops in later adolescence or early adulthood. In several instances when we were together in public, he would act out, becoming belligerent and causing embarrassing scenes. I was shocked and ashamed by my friend's behavior, but, even as all of his as well as our mutual friends pulled away, I made a conscious decision to stick by him—against my mother's approval, who was concerned about the intimacy of our relationship. I became more closely involved with his family as these symptoms worsened. As my friend's illness progressed and his functions declined, his clinicians turned to new medications to alleviate his mental illness. It was through his treatment that I met Dr. Roland Kuhn, a Swiss psychiatrist who pioneered the first antidepressant drug. Kuhn treated my friend and also took me under his wing. He became a mentor and a role model, encouraging me to read Shakespeare and the German-Swiss psychiatrist and existentialist philosopher Karl Jaspers to deepen my understanding of human psychology. Even after his treatment of my friend ended, Kuhn remained an important figure in my life, initiating my interest in neurosciences and encouraging my career.

In the summer of 1989, my beloved friend's condition worsened and he was repeatedly hospitalized. The events took a tragic turn while I was on a family vacation in the countryside during one such hospitalization. Despite the distance and his hospitalization, we spoke regularly on the phone. He appeared to improve at the hospital and was to be discharged. That was when we planned to have him come to the country to stay with me and my family. I hoped that a vacation in natural surroundings and spending time together would help his recovery. He was set to arrive in mid-August.

On a mid-August evening, I received a phone call from him. He told me in slurred speech that he had tried to take his own life the day before at his parents' house by swallowing pills. His mother had found him and taken him immediately to the hospital. He was admitted to a neurology unit in a hospital that had no psychiatric ward. He was calling me from there, complaining about how much he hated that hospital and hospitals in general. I tried to calm him down, telling him how relieved I was that nothing had happened and his suicide attempt was unsuccessful, and that he would hopefully only be at that hospital a short time. I assured him that our plan to spend the end of the summer together would still go forward. I asked him if I had to worry about him and he said no. He added, however, that he would never again agree to inpatient treatment in a psychiatric hospital. This is how we ended the phone call. I was feeling relief that my friend was under the care of medical professionals at a hospital, and was looking forward to arranging his trip to our summer vacation spot.

The next day, he committed suicide. He, who joined a nurse during her tour through the hospital, had found an open window on the ninth floor of the hospital and jumped. Days later I was informed by his family about what had happened. I felt not only the shock and grief of losing my beloved friend, but also powerful feelings of guilt that a flip comment I had made during our phone call—"You can't kill yourself with medications"—may have led him to leap from the window. This thought and the idea that I was unable to provide a safe environment for him would haunt me for years after, and I eventually repressed the guilt, even as I dedicated my life to understanding mental illness and trying to help people suffering as he had in the last years of his short life.

Following my friend's death, and with Dr. Kuhn's encouragement, I, who was enrolled in medical school, considered specialization in the neurosciences. I excelled in medical school and ultimately decided to focus on psychiatry and neurology, starting a five-year residency in that subject. Already, during my residency years, I was heavily involved in research and spent a year doing research at the National Institutes of Health (NIH) in Bethesda, Maryland. On a break for the Easter holiday, while visiting my family, I spent time with my friend's family, with whom I had remained close after his suicide. His mother took it upon herself to set me up, reasoning that if I had a girlfriend, I would return to my hometown in Europe rather than permanently decamping to the United States (neither my nor my friends' families were aware that the intimate bond between us two boys went beyond friendship, nor had I at that point self-identified as gay). She set me up on a date with my friend's cousin, who would eventually become my wife.

While our relationship has followed a nontraditional path, we very much fell in love when we met. We had an instant emotional and intellectual bond and the early years of our relationship were the best and most stable time in my life. Very quickly, we had children and we were both dedicated parents and in love with each other.

At 30 years of age, I was already a professor with a wife and children. Outwardly, my life appeared to be on a meteoric trajectory to success. The focus of my research at that time was dedicated to understanding the biological basis of suicidal behaviors, and while I was not consciously looking for the answer to the question of why my friend killed himself, one cannot miss the parallels between this formative experience and my work at the beginning of my career. My academic work became more sophisticated over the years, guided by the best teachers one can imagine.

On a personal level, my marriage was strong in the early years. We worked well together as co-parents, building a nourishing, safe environment for our children. And we had a genuine friendship, enjoying each other's company and supporting each other's pursuits. Yet, over the years, I had a few casual sexual encounters with men. I felt emotionally bonded to my wife, but could not and over time did not want to suppress this part of my identity completely. Needless to say, I felt enormously guilty about these transgressions and initially hid them from my wife and family.

After a couple of years working in the academic sciences, I began to lead my own research projects. I began to experience a great deal of success getting these projects funded. In addition to being a highly skilled scientist, it turned out that I had a knack for translating these research ideas into plain English and making scientific concepts compelling, while focusing on questions that had great potential for both successful studies and treatment development. I was suddenly a hot commodity and envied by colleagues competing for the same pools of funds. I enjoyed a period of the greatest success of my career, but then began to develop a relationship with a man outside my marriage. In an effort to hide this double life, and perhaps as a result of my deep-seated internal conflicts about these relationships, I charged expenses related to this boyfriend to research funds.

At the same time, I confessed to my wife that I had had several affairs with men. This was obviously a profoundly difficult time for our marriage, and we were estranged for a time when I first moved out of the household, though I remained involved in the children's lives and schooling. Over time, we reconciled and despite our nontraditional relationship, continued to see ourselves as companions and as life partners working together to raise children and support each other.

Around that time, I met a young man who was in his early twenties, roughly the same age my teenage friend had been at the time he died. This new acquaintance had a history of trauma and I was attracted to him in the same caretaker role I had adopted with my high school friend. Soon after we had met, we started a relationship, and only then I gradually learned about his past. This man had been the offspring of an aristocratic Caribbean family. He grew up in the midst of political chaos, with his family's fortune and security rising and falling with each shift in power. This young man's family ultimately sent him and his brothers to live with a relative in the United States when he was a teenager. There, without any guiding parental figure, the young man fell into a predatory party culture, taking drugs and having sex with men who supported his lifestyle and habits financially. I was taken with and sympathetic to the profound trauma and chaos that this young man had experienced, and was determined to try to take care of him.

Although we were in a relationship, we realized quickly that we were sexually incompatible. Instead, we developed an intimate—certainly an erotic—companionship primarily centered around me as a caregiver, with me attempting to show this man that someone could care for him without his having to exchange sex for support. Notably, much like the relationship with my teenage friend, I was conscious of a deliberate choice to stick by this man in this relationship and help him, whatever the obstacles. This was not easy; the relationship became all-consuming, and his whirlwind lifestyle and constant neediness were the dominant forces that drove it. I thought at the time that I was the one in control: the adult with a serious job, financial security, and emotional maturity. But in fact, the relationship was filling a deep need for me, one that I was not consciously aware of and that had become an unconscious fixation since my stunted relationship with my teenage friend.

It was in the context of this toxic relationship that I misappropriated my own research funds to travel to see my boyfriend and to pay for his travel to stay in touch with me, in addition to stays at various hotels and several meals, among other things. To justify the travel, I began to develop justifications that only served the purpose to allow me to act on my "responsibility" toward him to protect him within this relationship.

This relationship was more than simply that of an older man taking a young lover; it had deep reverberations in my psyche. It played out in some respect the dynamic between me and my teenage friend: me trying to "save" a young, troubled man with whom I had a romantic intimacy. In this regard, this all-consuming relationship enhanced my self-destructive behaviors and appeared to manifest in a disconnect between my highly functional outward life and my internal personal pain and conflict of which I was not even aware at the time.

To be clear, I do not try to contend that any of this excuses the misappropriation of funds. I have always fully accepted responsibility for spending money on personal expenses, which was without justification. However, I provide this background to demonstrate the unique conditions that explain this misappropriation of the money. Even a cursory psychological analysis makes clear that my relationships with men are informed by the traumatic history with my friend during my teenage/early adulthood years, and it appears that my inability to move beyond that history produces seemingly inexplicable self-destructive behaviors, including the misappropriation of funds and the failure to be honest about that conduct when initially confronted. It was the clear instruction of my attorneys, at the time when I discussed the complaint that had been filed in a court of law, to seek professional psychotherapeutic help—not only to cope with the intense anxiety facing the collapse of my life, and to avoid the intense self-directed aggressions which included suicidal thoughts as being the only exit strategy that seemed to be available to me at that time—that offered me an opportunity to face events that had happened more than 20 years ago. This intervention being strongly recommended by the attorneys was a critical early step in the right direction. Unable at the time to function properly because of the events that were unfolding, it was tremendously helpful that they referred me to a therapist whom they personally knew and trusted. I must emphasize one additional step they took, which was to ensure that I really attended the first therapy session. This is of critical importance in such situations, given that many clients, including me, may not have the strength during such challenging times to follow through. From that point on it was the therapist-client relationship that defined the setting of therapy, but the attorney's follow-up on whether a first session occurred or not seems critical at this point. (*See* ch. 10, Suicide in the Criminal Justice System.)

The abrupt halt that was put to my life at the time I faced these allegations was almost unbearable at the time. However, now in retrospect, they were an important interruption in my life path, which would otherwise have led me toward full destruction. Therapy offered me an opportunity to face the realities of my life in a safe and protected environment. To work myself through the tremendous emotional pain that was present but hidden behind a wall of professional functioning, being responsible toward my family and at the same time displaying behaviors that cannot be explained when unaware of the forces that were driving them and are in sharp contrast to my personal moral compass, felt like diving into an unreal script.

Besides the intense anxiety that was unearthed by the unfolding events, it was the social isolation that contributed to massive suicidal episodes during the weeks and months to come. The idea that a suicidal act would provide relief from the emotional pain and shame that filled my life at the time became almost an obsession during those days. When asked if I would accept help from medication, I refused, because I was not convinced that any medication could change the realities of my life at the time. In retrospect, I think it was the isolation—my withdrawing from the world in an attempt to cope with my inner life, the shame and inability to find anything acceptable about myself—that drove my mental state at the time. It was the presence of my immediate family, the relationship to the therapist, and in a very important way the relationship to my attorneys that saved my life. If I find two words that allowed me to continue my life, those were "respect" and "hope." These built a bridge into a future that I had no idea at the time what it could look like, but over time became an idea that started to replace overwhelming suicidal thoughts.

I was asked how it was possible that an expert, a clinician, and person whom anyone would tend to seek when needing help and mental health support had not been aware of these psychological forces that directed aspects of my life at the time. While there is no definitive answer to that question, I have asked myself many times; it seems that this pause in my life pathway has forced me to face these demons of my past. The people I am most grateful for at this time, having worked through my past, are my immediate family, the few friends who stayed with me, the therapist who patiently and cautiously allowed me to self-direct myself out of this crisis, and my attorneys who were clear and direct when seeing my internal conflicts at a time when I was unable to see them. The one thing I did right at that time was following their advice to seek professional therapeutic support despite my initial internal resistance.

A final section of this chapter should concern the judge who, as an initial review of the sentence may make people believe, was too lenient. This judge issued a complex and wise sentence of probation and community service. This sentence was in agreement with a proposed sentence coming from pre-sentencing probation services, and was in sharp contrast to what the prosecutors had requested. It was obvious that the judge had reviewed very carefully the information that was provided, including a quite detailed analysis of the psychological contributions to my wrongdoing. Attending the court proceedings is a difficult and scary experience for anybody, and certainly was for me, but the respect and polite approach that the judge took toward me as a person made these proceedings manageable. At no point was the judge judgmental. This was a critical positive experience that had a major impact on me personally. What was stunning to me while receiving the sentence and then acting on what the judge had required of me while on probation was to realize that this sentence allowed me to connect back to critical situations in my personal life. The sentence at no point appeared retaliatory to me, but instead was therapeutic and had a positive impact on my life. It certainly was a very unusual sentence, as I felt and got confirmed by my attorneys, a "first" in this particular courtroom. (*See* ch. 7, When Judges Cry: Dealing with a Defendant's Death by Suicide.)

Going back to the time I stopped my active artistic career, and reconnecting to that time in my life enabled me to bring joy now to the elderly when performing for them. The contemplation about the purpose of life, taking responsibility for my actions, even in light of the fact that I had failed tremendously, but also realizing that there can be forgiveness and a sense of lenience were overwhelming positive experiences at the time. All of this allowed me to move forward, rebuild myself, rebuild the relationships to my family, and connect back into a professional career that is now more mature and better developed than it ever was. While I went through therapy to help me cope with my past, the sentence of active therapy allowed me to cope with the present challenges, rebuild my life, and lay a pathway to my own future. It was a positive experience for which I am tremendously grateful to the judge. It is this experience of facing humanity and seeing a future for myself, and those whom I love and who love me, that helped me to move on without bitterness into the years to come.

Chapter

15

Case Study: Transformation

LaReese Harvey

This chapter is a powerful narrative of how the author, LaReese Harvey, witnessed another resident of the jail attempt suicide and how it inspired her to live life as fully as possible, as well as to do a deep dive into the emotions and circumstances which had led to her incarceration. But this chapter also illustrates what is seldom discussed: the rich network of support among the residents found in some jails and prisons. Here, as well as in a later case study by Tracie Bernardi, we see women who try to convince one another that life is indeed worth living, no matter how hopeless it seems.

• • •

Little Donna

It was late in the evening. We were all locked in our rooms for the night. I just heard screams. I jumped up out of my sleep, I ran to the window in my door. I looked out to see if I could see anything down the hall. It wasn't my floor. It was downstairs. I don't remember the time, I never looked at the clock. The only way to get out was if a correctional officer let us out. I waited for five minutes to see if anyone was going to come up the stairs. No one came. I looked at the window across from me. The women in the room looked worried. "Hey, just say a prayer. It will be okay," I said, while putting my hands into the prayer position. I walked away from the window and kneeled before my bed. I didn't know which one of us needed an ambulance. I just knew this woman needed a miracle only God could provide. "Father, God, I come to you as humbly as I know how. I ask that you cleanse me from all sins and cover me in the blood of the Lamb. Lord, this woman is hurting. You know your child. Heal her and comfort us as we help each other through this trial. In Jesus' name I pray. Amen." I put my hand on the bed to help myself up. I got in the bed knowing the morning would bring us sorrow.

I got up at six in the morning. I always start my day on my knees thanking God for the opportunity to serve Him another day. Then I began my yoga routine. At 6:45 a.m. the Corrections Officer (CO) will come by for count. I will ask to go to the bathroom then. I began on the floor with my legs crossed. I breathed deeply in through my nose and exhaled slowly out my mouth. I did this three times. Then I would stretch my arms straight to the sky with palms up. Inhale through my nose. Slowly let my arms come down into prayer position as I exhaled out. I then proceed to stretch my back and legs by doing the downward dog. Then I would move my legs back and put myself in an upside-down V position. I bend my knees and stretch my arms before me with my head down. I did this about four times. I stood up and began to read my Bible. Whatever happened last night, I will know in about 10 minutes. *I must ask God for strength*, I thought to myself.

The first-shift CO came in, opened up the door, and was doing count. I asked him what happened last night. Why was everybody screaming? The CO told me he's doing count and he'll get back to me once he's finished. I sat back down on my bed. I got my toothbrush, toothpaste, and washcloth ready. At 7:30 a.m. the CO came and unlocked all the doors. After this, everybody ran to the bathroom to hurry up and brush their teeth so they can go downstairs to find out what happened. I went to the bathroom after the initial morning rush. I brushed my teeth. I washed my face and I walked back to my room. I shut the door and put a piece of paper in the window so that I can get dressed in private. I got dressed and I proceeded to go downstairs to find out what happened. When I reached the bottom of the steps, I was standing in front of the CO's office. "Harvey," the CO called me. "I need you to go into the Day Room. Tina is having a special meeting for your group." I responded with "okay" and turned to the right to go into the Day Room. We had an emergency group meeting for the youthful offenders. I was the only first-time offender to attend because I was 21. I sat in the chair two seats away from Tina. I watched her as she fought back tears. "Ladies, I have some disturbing news to tell you. Then we are going to process it. We are going to hold Little Donna in love and light." Shakira asked what happened to Little Donna. Tina began to explain to us that Little Donna hung herself last night and now she was in critical condition. The issue is Little Donna was without oxygen to her brain for a period of time. Tina said, "When she survives, unfortunately, Little Donna will not be the same. How do you guys feel about what happened?" The original shock from the news caused most of us to cry. Joy got up and became angry. Joy was breathing heavy. She got out of her chair, screamed, and punched the window. It shattered on contact. The CO ran into the room. "What was that?! You ladies need to control yourself. Joy, sit down or I will write you a ticket." I sat there confused. It was my first time in prison. I was awaiting trial. I didn't understand why the CO was adding insult to injury. Couldn't he see we were all upset? Doesn't he understand these young ladies are teenagers? I don't get it. I shook my head and waited. As I looked around. I noticed the love and compassion. I noticed that these young teenagers did not belong in jail. We all need coping skills to deal with our anger, sadness, and powerlessness. I looked mostly at Joy. Joy was taking it the hardest. After 20 minutes of crying off and on, everyone began to share how they felt.

Joy blamed herself for not checking in on Little Donna last night before we went to bed. Joy said, "I knew Little Donna wanted to talk to me about something. You guys know how annoying she can be. So, I ignored her. I thought she wanted a cigarette or commissary. I even yelled at her to leave me alone or die!" Joy put her face in her hands and started crying. Shakira moved her chair closer to Joy and wrapped her arms around her. The room was silent for a moment. You see, Joy is the toughest amongst us. Well, at least that's what she wants us to believe. To see her cry and be broken tore at my heart strings. I didn't think I could care about these women. I didn't think we would consider each other family. Shakira put her thumb in her mouth, patted Joy on the back, and said, "Shit, I would tell Little Donna to leave me alone too. Especially, when she gets to whining about NOTHING!" We all laughed and began telling stories about Little Donna.

Little Donna is a Black woman who looks like a 10-year-old girl. Little Donna was about four feet two inches tall and weighed 90 pounds, if that. She used this to her advantage to get free stuff from everyone. I remember when a few of us, youthful offenders, wanted to get into the dining room early one morning. We were trying to get extra toast and hard-boiled eggs. It's not often you get a good breakfast. Toast and hard-boiled eggs were a treat! So, all the youthful offenders agreed to send Little Donna into the staff office to ask. She used her little-girl voice to ask the CO to let us into the dining room before everyone else. The staff knew she was being manipulative. However, Little Donna was cute and didn't take no for an answer. So, we got extra toast and hard-boiled eggs that day.

It was during sharing stories about Little Donna I realized I had a choice. I can let this prison—the way the staff talk to me and treat me like I am an animal, and these disrespectful women here—break me to a point where I kill myself. Or I can choose to be positive and know this is just a moment in my life. I chose hope on that day. I chose to be the inspiration of HOPE. I did not want to leave Niantic in a body bag. I want to leave walking out with my head held high, knowing I will never come back. That wasn't the only decision I made that day. As I look around the room, an overwhelming feeling came over me. I knew that I needed to help these young women find hope in this despair. I wanted to let them know that this prison experience was temporary—that this is only a part of their lives and that they will one day be free. I want them to begin to look forward to their freedom, instead of looking at the despair of their everyday life in prison. How do I tell that to these teenagers when five of them are facing 20, 30, and 45 years in prison? How do you tell teenagers, there is life beyond 30? I myself am facing 20 years to life. My sentence is yet to be determined. I just didn't know that teenagers can go to jail for the rest of their lives. How is that possible? How can you be sentenced to spend your twenties and thirties in jail, when you haven't celebrated your 21st birthday? Hell, I didn't even know we didn't have a self-defense law in Connecticut. That's why I am sitting here now. Let me get out of my head and refocus on the group.

We sat in that room talking about Little Donna and our feelings for about two and a half to three hours. We missed breakfast, so staff brought in court-run breakfast bags. I began to eat my banana while listening to one of the girls in the room talk about Little Donna on the streets. She talked about Little Donna trying to get drugs, and drug dealers wanting to card her, and we all laughed. Tina went through some meditative breathing techniques with us to get us to calm down and refocus. She also told us to write Little Donna letters of encouragement. Before group broke up,

Tina told us lunch was going to be on her. So, we all laughed, went to class, and then came back an hour later and had lunch with Tina.

Throughout the day as we walked around, we were talking to people. The older women, who are first-time offenders, tried to counsel us and comfort us throughout the evening. I never did get the whole story of who found Little Donna hanging. No one knew why she did it all. What I do remember most is how I felt hopeless and helpless. Then I remember feeling that I was determined to never ever, ever do anything to go back to jail. So, I sought out counseling for everything I could think of was wrong with me. I started to attend AA meetings. I started talking to a drug counselor, a sexual assault survivor counselor, and I went to those groups. I saw a person-centered therapist and a psychiatrist. It didn't take long for me to realize that in order for me to survive prison, I needed to make my life as comfortable as possible. As if I were working toward a goal, I made up my mind to make prison a college for myself—a break to figure out what was going on with me, so I don't end up like Donna. I didn't want to end up dead in this jail ... in this prison around these strangers.

About a month after Donna hung herself, she came back to the unit. We were all happy to see her. I remember Little Donna walking up to me giving me a big hug and said, "I knew you were praying for me. I felt it and I got better." That made me feel better about why I was there. My decision to be a beacon of hope, instead of a jerk because I was facing life imprisonment, was a great decision. I told myself, "There is more to life, even in prison, beyond your emotional pain. You can be an example and help others. You need to make sure you get better and prepared for your children when you leave here. Don't let this place and the people here force you into taking your own life. You are worth a second chance at life. Remember, Jesus forgives you. That's all that matters."

Little Donna survived her hanging and I survived my trial. *(I was found guilty and sentenced to 10 years imprisonment.)* During my time at York Correctional Facility (formerly Niantic Correctional Facility), I heard about many more women dying or barely recovering from hanging themselves. I had been woken up more times than I care to count listening to women screaming. I've participated in groups where women talked about wanting to die, because of the way staff or their children and families talked to them with disrespect. People do not understand that we did not end up in prison because of the crime we committed. Rather, the crime is the explosive result of underlying emotional and mental issues prior to committing the crime.

Little Donna's hanging stuck with me because it was the first time I heard women screaming in the night. It was the first time I knew someone who tried to hang themselves. It was the day I made a solemn promise to myself. I was going to work hard to make sure people who are incarcerated are treated like human beings and not just tossed aside because of a crime or a bad decision. We know maladaptive behavior is a sign of some underlying mental health or emotional dysfunction. I did not learn coping skills until I went to counseling. Every decision I made was based on survival and emotion. I have lived with killing someone and punished myself more over than the time I spent time in jail. I can never replace that life. I can, however, ensure that my life helps others defeat suicidal ideations and provide help for those who need it most. People who need help don't even know that they need help because everyone around them is working off of survival mode or emotional dysfunction. The worst place you can die is in prison. The worst way to go is by hanging. I'm glad Little Donna made it. She calls my colleague and best friend Tracie Bernardi once in a while. She was never the same after that. There's something missing, but I'm grateful she's alive and I'm grateful that she taught me to value life.

It wasn't until this very moment that I realized why I have been so passionate about criminal justice, prison, and juvenile justice reform. It was the day Little Donna almost died. I never wanted to feel like that again. I didn't want anyone else to either.

I often wondered what Judge Carl Taylor would think of me now, knowing that he tried to put me in jail for the rest of my life. I did have an opportunity to meet Judge Raymond Norko in the summer of 2007. I was just hired by A Better Way Foundation as the lead organizer on drug policy reform. It turned out that my new boss knew Judge Norko very well. You see, Judge Norko officiated at my new boss's wedding! Judge Norko was now the new judge for Community Court in Hartford, Connecticut. Lorenzo Jones was the organizer who helped develop the Community Court with Judge Norko.

I will never forget Judge Norko's face when Mr. Jones asked him if he remembered me. There was caution in his eyes and his posture became defensive. I told Mr. Jones to stop. I introduced myself and let Judge Norko know what I've done while in prison. I also let Judge Norko know how I was doing since I came home. At the time I had four college degrees and I trained adolescent females on racial justice advocacy. Judge Norko sighed in relief. He looked at Mr. Jones and said, "I thought I was going to have to call the Marshals!" Judge Norko continued to laugh, "You gave me a heart attack, man." After a few minutes of hearty laughter, Judge Norko looked at me and said, "I am glad you are doing well. Stick with this guy and you will be great!" I did stick with Mr. Jones for eight years. I was able to advocate, change policies, and make a career out of it! Who knew my second chance would allow me to help others have a more humane second chance? I guess that's what it means to be a HOPE!

• • •

LaResse Harvey is one of the Great Eight inducted into the Connecticut Hall of Change on September 20, 2020, memorializing her 20-plus years of restorative justice, public health, and racial justice modalities and policy changes. Ms. Harvey was a single teenage mother of two when she served a 10-year sentence in prison. As such, she possesses a crucial perspective on community issues and the importance of social reform. She has worked on issues of restorative justice, criminal and drug policy reform, prison and pardon reform, housing, reentry, drug treatment, and custodial parental rights. Ms. Harvey has four college degrees: three associates degrees from Tunxis Community College and a bachelor's in social work from Saint Joseph's College, West Hartford, Connecticut. She is currently attending Trinity Law School, studying for a master's degree in nonprofit law.

Ms. Harvey, along with Tracie Bernardi, founded Once Incarcerated, a nonprofit corporation offering peer support for youth and adults currently and formerly incarcerated. Together Ms. Harvey and Ms. Bernardi host a national weekly Zoom meeting of Once IN Anonymous or OIA, limited to formerly incarcerated people. In 2019, working with OIC-New Britain and ParaDYM youths, Once IN created an Implicit Bias Advocacy and Civics training manual. The manual covers undoing racism, civic engagement, advocacy knowledge, and guidance for building a current issue campaign. Ms. Harvey has published two books on Amazon: *Buttons' Journey: My First Two Years Living with PTSD* and *Buttons' Journey: My Spiritual Foundation Is … Praise!*

As founder and executive director of Civic Trust Public Lobbying Company in Connecticut, Ms. Harvey has helped pass more than 50 pieces of bipartisan legislation. Her firm provides a full range of lobbying support and consultation to community groups and individuals throughout the country. In 2011, after founding Civic Trust Public Lobbying Company, Ms. Harvey had a successful lobbying season, with passage of measures such as marijuana decriminalization, recommendations to eliminate prison rape, and the creation of a Department of Corrections Advisory Committee.

Ms. Harvey was the chairwoman of the Criminal Justice Committee of the New Britain chapter of the NAACP and created the resolution for NAACP's version of BanTheBox. She also works with adolescents and youth ages 10-21 years old on racial justice, advocacy, and life skills. In July of 2010, Ms. Harvey was awarded the Patriot Award from the Bill of Rights Defense Committee for her dedication in ensuring constitutional and human rights for all Connecticut residents. She has also provided a way for young people to receive a college education by partnering with Goodwin College to offer a two-year scholarship for students who intern with the A Better Way Foundation. On September 19, 2019, Connecticut's General Assembly honored her with a citation for 20 years of successful reentry and grassroots lobbying.

Ms. Harvey can be reached at onceincarcerated@gmail.com and her website is www.onceincarcerated.org.

Complete citations are available from the author upon request.

Chapter

16

Case Study: An Insider's View of Suicide in Prison

Tracie Bernardi

If you are disturbed while reading this chapter, you should be. The author, Tracie Bernardi, entered York Correctional Institution at age 19 and was released at the age of 42. Her descriptions of her own suicide attempts, as well as the suicidal ideations of the other inmates, are powerful and searing. As you read about the conditions which drove her to utter despair, and in particular, the behavior of the prison staff, you will wonder how such an environment escapes scrutiny. At the conclusion of her chapter, Tracie reminds us that the vast majority of inmates will be released and be returned to their communities. Thus, the challenge is not only to create prison settings that do not drive people to contemplate suicide within their walls, but also to create prisons that do not release people who are more broken and more dangerous than when they entered.

• • •

My name is Tracie Bernardi and I served 23 long, hard years in prison at York Correctional Institution in Niantic, Connecticut. In the beginning of my prison stay, I was a young girl with an undeveloped brain and no life experience; I was just 19. But more than two decades later, at the end of my sentence I was a 42-year-old, broken woman. I was in disbelief that I was being set free. I mean, who would have thought? I was sure they had locked me up and thrown away the key. I had a 30-year sentence; I did not believe I would ever make it home. To tell you the truth, I feared I would die at my own hand. Most people say they could never have served a sentence like mine. Could you?

Being that I was so young, I was not just angry, I was reckless. As you could imagine, I hated myself for landing in prison. I hated myself for helping take a life. The fact that a little boy had to grow up without a mother because of us sickened me. I was deeply sorry. I can even remember pleading with God, telling him to give back the lost life in exchange for my own. Of course, that never happened.

At the time I desperately needed encouragement and somebody to help me climb out of the pit I was in. But now I was in prison where the only adults in my life were prison guards. There were not people around to invest in me, only people who thought their job was to punish me. What did they not understand? I did not need to be taught any more lessons! A 30-year sentence and the guilt I carried were already too much to bear. I was bursting with regret.

Being locked away from my family, away from society, quickly began to make me crazy. I started dealing with my feelings by cutting my wrists. I would break whatever I could to use to cut myself. In the beginning I would cut myself with the disposable razors sold on commissary. After the Department of Corrections (DOC) wised up and stopped selling them, I would resort to anything I could find to cut. When I had reached that point, I just had to get it out. I would break eyeglasses, I would rip a tin medication tube and cut with that. I would use whatever was available. It was like there was this urgency to hurt myself. I would sometimes get so angry I would try to strangle myself with wire and cords from things like my flatiron or lamp cord. Sounds crazy, right? I *was* crazy. My reality and the treatment during [imprisonment] had taken a grave toll. I once drank cleaning supplies, but lucky for me, DOC waters down inmate cleaning solutions and disinfectants to stretch it. So, all that happened was I had to drink some charcoal stuff at medical and my taste buds were severely burned. (*See* ch. 3, Suicide in Prison.)

Guards speculated I was doing it for attention. I was not! I was doing it because I had nowhere to channel my anger. I had nowhere to channel my guilt. Instead, I etched my pain into my skin. I once wrote all the names of people who hurt me on my left leg.

Gestures like these were the only way I could express my pain. I just wanted the pain to stop. I wanted to undo my reality and live a different existence. But I was stuck in this existence. To me it was a horrid existence. And I wanted all the people in my life who had hurt me and were hurting me to see I was already in pain and stop!

I often wrote poems about my demise and I would list the reasons why I should just end it. But guilt kept me from killing myself. I already broke my mother's heart by landing myself in prison. If I killed myself it would hurt her more. For many years that fear of hurting Mom was enough to keep me alive.

Even though I stayed alive, I still used to obsess over how I would be better off dead. I felt I was a burden on my family and just had no reason to live. With all that was boiling inside me and no outlets, I acted out against myself.

As I said, the guards did not understand. Instead, they punished me with years of self-mutilation tickets. Tickets are disciplines, and after each ticket came sanctions and penalties.

When I would self-harm, I'd be placed in the mental health unit until medically cleared by the prison psychiatrist. The nurses would convey to the captains that I was fine, and the Class A self-mutilation ticket would come sliding under my cell door. So much for if I was feeling better. I was not anymore. I would immediately regress, as I was on my way to solitary confinement to be punished for my transgressions. Not only would I serve 7-14 days in solitary confinement, but I'd receive other sanctions that lasted up to a month. The discipline officers could take three privileges. Usually, they would give me loss of phone or mail. They knew my mom visited faithfully so they would always confiscate my visits. Guess they thought keeping me from being hugged in a visit by someone who loved me would teach me a lesson. They would also take my privilege to buy commissary. I barely ate what they served in the chow hall, so two weeks with no ability to buy food or coffee or a candy bar nearly killed me. I can say without a doubt that these punishments when I was very obviously already in distress absolutely added to my depression and ultimate hate for life.

Eventually someone somewhere grew a brain and realized that they could not continue disciplining people for what are obviously mental health issues. The Department of Correction was becoming slightly more humane.

These were in the early years (1993-1998) of my bid, but by 1999 I was classified to solitary confinement. *Classified* means housed there semi-permanently. I would go on to spend seven long years in solitary, locked down for 23 hours a day, before being released back into general population.

During that seven-year period in solitary confinement my self-harm escalated. I was barely able to resist the urges to tear my wrists apart. I used to fantasize about ways to kill myself right there in an empty cell. I would envision myself standing backwards on my cell sink and just free-falling backwards, cracking my skull on the concrete floor.

For a while I used to try to tongue and cheek my psychiatric meds, planning to eventually OD. Usually though, after two or three days without my meds I'd decide to take them. It was like a vacation from life. I would pop three or four and I would just sleep for days. Anything to cross another day off the calendar.

I remember the worst thing about prison is that the medical unit was always so understaffed. If I was feeling unsafe and I wanted to just talk to someone to keep me from acting on my feelings, it was not an option. One had to say "the magic words" to get to see a mental health staff. In other words, you had to threaten to kill yourself. But threatening to kill yourself came with a price, guards who wanted to teach you another lesson. The guards had a routine that if you did say the magic words, you still would not magically be seen. They would put you in an empty dusty cell on the max side of solitary confinement, Cell J7, with no shoelaces, no underwear, and no bra, handcuffed from behind and shackled for hours before they'd ever even call the medical staff and tell them you were threatening self-harm. Sometimes the guards would wait an entire shift, leaving you to rot for the day in a stripped-down dusty cell.

As a result of this torture when I really needed to talk, I would a lot of times just let it all build up, until one day I would explode and act out against myself.

That one day came. I had had it with life. I don't remember what triggered me, but this time I was going all the way. After five years in solitary, I tried to hang myself.

In the midst of it, as I started to black out from the grip of the sheet on my neck, I realized I did not want to die. I wanted to live but I was already hanging. All I could do was ask God for forgiveness for my sins.

I was dying at my own hand just as I feared. I was not ready to go. Miraculously, a guard burst my cell door open and saved my life.

I remember laying on the floor under a crowd of staff. Some medical, some guards and higher-ranking staff. Most of whom I'm sure had no interest in whether I was OK or not. They were probably more concerned that they would have to do paperwork. They hated paperwork.

Bev the nurse she slapped my face, calling out, "Tracie! Tracie!," begging me to wake. I was conscious, I think I was just in shock so I couldn't respond.

A captain realized I needed help. Being that he was the captain over both solitary confinement and the mental health wing in Medical, he decided I should temporarily be housed in the mental health wing.

Being that I was still on the same solitary status, I was still kept from all other inmates on the ward. Because he was worried about my not having human contact, the captain asked the unit counselor who was a younger woman to spend time with me daily. He told her she could help with coping and stuff. Or she could just talk to me in her office, so I could get out of my cell. I thought this was awesome because to me the counselor was really kind and I needed to not be alone. So, every day she would take me out of my cell for at least an hour and I'd hang out in her office.

But this did not sit well with some of the guards and especially the nurses. They were more worried about crying favoritism than my well-being. The other women on the ward were not solitary status so they got to have group recreation, gym, chow hall, and other activities that allowed them to interact with each other. They were not allowed to talk to me. They would get yelled at for even stopping at my cell door when they were let out of their rooms. The nurses had other ideas. They got jealous and reported to outside higher-ups. They could care less whether I had human interaction or not. They claimed that I was being treated "too well" by this counselor. This caused an entire internal investigation to be launched.

When push came to shove, the captain did not admit that he asked the counselor to spend extra time with me. As a result of the investigation and the conflict with the nurses, the counselor was transferred to another unit. I was transferred back to solitary confinement.

Don't get me wrong: there were guards and prison staff who were not a-holes. They were kind and actually did their job. But most of them, even the kind ones, would disappoint you when they are around their comrades. Treating people in prison with dignity is only done in secret. It's only done only when no one was looking. I never got the treatment I needed in the prison I was in. No one did.

But now I had to figure out a way to live in prison. I needed to know how to cope without hurting myself because I had to get out of solitary. And eventually I did.

I worked on coping skills just to get me through. I started to get better by sharing my story with other women who were in solitary. Laying on concrete cell floors, I talked with other women in solitary under the steel cell doors. Some women would confess that they were thinking of suicide. This was scary because I knew how hard it was to calm me down when I had reached my breaking point. Day after day I'd lay on the floor talking women through stuff. I would make them laugh and ask them questions that would help them remember why they were valuable. I am telling you, no matter how much inhaling that dusty air dried my mouth and made me cough, I would stay on the floor talking. We would verbally pull one another out of pits.

And when I helped someone else, I began to feel good about myself. Not like I was great, but like I had purpose. Like suddenly I could use all the bad in my life for good. I could use it to help others.

After earning my way back to general population and out of solitary, I continued to see the two clinical social workers who had an extreme impact on my healing process in solitary, Jill Sandora and Liz Allen.

Liz Allen is now Dr. Liz Allen, but at the time she created a peer-support program called "Sisters Standing Strong." The program consisted of mentors who were role models. Inmates could apply if they met the criteria. They would be interviewed and then the warden and his brass would decide if you were worthy of becoming a mentor. Because I saw how effective and helpful sharing my story was, this was right up my alley. I wanted to be a mentor. I applied. And it was no easy feat. I was to choose to live discipline-free for the two years. But technically I had just got released from serving seven years in solitary confinement.

At this point not a lot of staff trusted or believed in me. Jill and Liz really had to fight for me, but eventually I was approved and became a mentor. Once designated an official mentor, I was able to go into different housing units and facilitate peer support groups under the direct supervision of Jill, Liz, or other social workers involved in the overseeing of the program. These groups saved my life and had a significant impact on many women. Not just hearing my story, but my hearing the stories of different mentors was healing. It made us realize we were not alone. It showed us that we were not cursed or deserving of the bad things happening. We learned that everyone made mistakes and problems were universal. Facilitating these groups built my self-esteem as I began to feel necessary in this world. As you might imagine, many women in general population felt bad about themselves, and now here I was talking them through. I was helping others by sharing my experiences. In doing this I recognized my purpose.

I was fortunate that I found my reason before death. Some of the women I've known in York Correctional Institution didn't. They died by their own hands. They were not saved.

In March 1999, Bobbie Jo Garcia was in a suicide watch cell in the mental health unit and still managed to hang herself. She was just 18 years old. Bobbi Jo was a good friend of mine who had just lost her mother, who died while giving birth to a sibling.

About a week before Bobbi died, Linda Hogan, another prisoner at York, killed herself.

In July 2009, Cheryl Thrall, age 37, was put in solitary confinement. She couldn't deal with the stress, hung herself, and died.

Cassandra Baker, a friend and fellow Wesleyan student, hung herself. An inmate named Joyce Salters, age 53, killed herself at York. And some year in between all of those (I don't remember which), a woman named Louisa killed herself, too, although I could never find a newspaper article about her.

All these ladies' lives were cut short because prison is too severe a punishment. Some people don't realize how destructive prison life is.

Can you imagine anything so bad that you would want to end your life? That's what we lived day and day out, being harassed by guards and sometimes other inmates who thought it was their job to inflict punishment and help teach us a lesson. But what they didn't realize is they were not helping us. They were only re-traumatizing us. They were only driving us more and more into despair.

There were days I sat in solitary starving myself because the guard that day thought it would be funny to announce to our tier that he may have spit in one of our trays. This was common among guards. Then, if we gave our tray back untouched, they wrote in the logbook that we "might" be starving ourselves. Guards would threaten to call mental health. They would make us sleep with a bright light shining in our faces. Third-shift staff thought it was funny to kick or bang on our cell door as they walked by on their 15-minute tours, startling us out of our sleep. Then there were a few who would wait until you took your medication and were ready to go to sleep, and they'd tell you to exit your cell while they searched it. They'd look through all your stuff, and tie all your sheets in knots.

Once they let you back in your cell, you can't go to sleep for hours because you have to unknot your linen. These things that were done by guards for sport were forms of torture. Forcing you to sleep while a bright light shines in your face is torture. Guards putting a shoe in the tier dryer and turning it on for 70-minute cycles as a means of ensuring seg inmates won't talk under the door is torture. Purposefully forgetting that we are in the recreation yard in the wintertime is torture. Hanging up our phone call five minutes early, knowing we waited weeks—sometimes months—for these 15-minute phone calls was torture. Purposely separating anyone who seemed to make friends was torture. So much of what the guards did as a means of thinking they were punishing us was, simply put, breaking us more.

Thank God I was rescued. But those ladies I mentioned were not. They weren't just inmates. They were peoples' daughters and sisters and aunts. They had friends and loved ones. More importantly, had they not gone to prison they might still be alive.

Endless strip-searches. It's a violation to be commanded to bend, squat, spread them, and cough. To me, who was just 19 when I entered prison and had saved my virginity until I was 17, it was like being raped every time. It left me feeling nasty and ashamed.

I don't know what exactly led each of the women to kill themselves, but I know it was always because of something a guard did or did not do.

In some instances, a woman would complain that she was suicidal, and the guards would offer her a sheet. This was a common joke. Or worse, they would send the suicidal person asking for help back to their cell. They did that with "Lucky" Barbara Mahon. They didn't take her serious and she was.

So, you see, there is definitely a need for change in the culture of Department of Corrections, not just with guards but with all staff, including brass and medical personnel.

Inmates need to be treated with dignity. People who work in corrections must be made to understand that the way they treat prisoners is detrimental and can determine whether people get rehabilitated or not. The reason inmates being rehabilitated matter is because most prisoners come home. Which means we could potentially be your neighbor. Do you want us coming home stable and capable of being productive members of society, or more messed up when we went in?

Imagine the lives better training and treatment can save ...

• • •

Tracie Bernardi is a Certified Recovery Support Specialist. She is co-founder and co-director of Once Incarcerated, a nonprofit organization dedicated to ending recidivism and generational incarceration. She facilitates Once In Anonymous (OIA), an online safe haven for formerly incarcerated people. https://www.facebook.com/TracieBernardi1974.

Tracie is also a dedicated ACLU Smart Justice Leader fighting to end mass incarceration. As a formerly incarcerated woman who entered prison as a teenager and left as a woman, she speaks widely against solitary confinement, based on serving seven of her 23 years in prison in solitary. She has spoken at Yale, Wesleyan, and Capital Community College as well as at numerous churches and libraries. She has taken courses at Trinity College, Capital Community College, Wesleyan University, Quinnipiac University, and Three Rivers Community College.

Tracie blogs at http://23yearsaninmate.wordpress.com and she is planning on publishing a memoir. She is part of the Prison Arts Project, and her work has been displayed at The Brooklyn Museum, The American Visionary Art Museum, the Maier Museum of Art at Randolph College, and the Hartford Public Library. She can be reached at onceincarcerated@gmail.com.

Suggested Works

Following is a list of suggested works arranged according to chapter. These categories are not airtight, and some resources may be used in or applicable to other areas. In addition to exploring the works cited in individual chapters, readers are encouraged to explore the articles and books written by the various chapter authors. The following are the works that correspond to various chapters, along with other works that deal with the criminal justice system and the phenomenon of suicide, as well as works that deal with suicide in general.

The Price of Empathy: Learning to Cope with Trauma in the Criminal Courtroom

Alliance for Safety and Justice. *Toward Shared Safety: First-Ever National Survey of America's Safety Gaps* (Sept. 2020). https://allianceforsafetyandjustice.org/wp-content/uploads/2020/09/NatlSafetyGaps-Report-PREVIEW-20200908-1751.pdf

Bessel van der Kolk, M. D. The Body Keeps the Score: Brain, Mind, and Body in the Healing of Trauma. Penguin Books, 2015.

Simon, Jonathan, & Stephen A. Rosenbaum. *Dignifying Madness: Rethinking Commitment Law in an Age of Mass Incarceration*. 70 U. Miami L. Rev. (2015). https://lawreview.law.miami.edu/wp-content/uploads/2015/12/DignifyingMadness.pdf

Styron, William. Darkness Visible: A Memoir of Madness. Penguin Random House, 1989.

Vera Institute of Justice. *Reimagining Prison Web Report*. https://www.vera.org/reimagining-prison-web-report

Pretrial/Noncustodial Client Suicide and Attorney Impact

Bao, Jenna. *Prisons: The New Asylums*. Harvard Political Review (2020). https://harvardpolitics.com/prisons-the-new-asylums/

Cho, Jeena. *Why Are Lawyers So Unhappy*? https://abovethelaw.com/2016/08/why-are-lawyers-so-unhappy

Gonzalez, Jennifer M. Reingle, & Nadine M. Connell. *Mental Health of Prisoners: Identifying Barriers to Mental Health Treatment and Medication Continuity*. PUBMED.GOV (December 2014).

Hoffer, Tia A., Joy Lynn E. Shelton, Stephen Behnke, & Philip Erdberg. *Exploring the Impact of Child Sex Offender Suicide*. Journal of Family Violence 25, 777-786 (2010).

Mills, Jeremy F., & Daryl G. Kroner. *Predicting Suicidal Ideation with the Depression Hopelessness and Suicide Screening Form (DHS)*. Journal of Offender Rehabilitation, 47(1), 74-100 (May 2008).

Suicide in Prison

Barry, Lisa C., Dorothy B. Wakefield, Robert L. Trestman, & Yeates Conwell. *Disability in Prison Activities of Daily Living and Likelihood of Depression and Suicidal Ideation in Older Prisoners.* International Journal of Geriatric Psychiatry, 32, 1141–1149 (2017).

Dodson, Kimberly D. Routledge Handbook on Offenders with Special Needs. Routledge, 2018.

Myslimaj, Fatbardha, & Eglantina Dervishi. *Suicide Attempts and Self-Inflicting on Prison Custody and Prison.* Academic Journal of Interdisciplinary Studies, 5(2), 175–180 (2016). doi:10.5901/ajis.2016.v5n2p175

National Commission on Correctional Health Care. *Procedure in the Event of an Inmate Death.* (2018). https://www.ncchc.org/procedure-in-the-event-of-an-inmate-death-32-3

National Institute of Corrections. Suicide in Corrections. U.S. Department of Justice, 2017.

Tomczak, Philippa. Suicide in Prison: What Happens Next? Bristol University Press, 2018.

Walker, Tammi, & Graham Towl. Preventing Self-Harm and Suicide in Women's Prisons. Waterside Press, 2016.

Recognizing and Addressing the Problem of Suicide Following Incarceration

Bureau of Justice Statistics. Home page. www.bjs.gov

Fox, Aaron, et al. *Deaths in Custody and Following Release.* Journal of Health and Human Administration, 41(4) (2019).

Freudenberg, Nicholas, & Daliah Heller. *A Review of Opportunities to Improve the Health of People Involved in the Criminal Justice System in the United States.* Annual Review of Public Health (2016).

King, Carlene, et al. *Suicide by People in a Community Justice Pathway: Population-Based Nested Case-Control Study.* British Journal of Psychiatry (2015).

Lim, Sungwoo, et al. *Risks of Drug-Related Death, Suicide, and Homicide During the Immediate Post-Release Period Among People Released from New York City Jails, 2001-2005.* American Journal of Epidemiology (2012).

Luigi, Mimosa, et al. *Shedding Light on "the Hole": A Systematic Review and Meta-Analysis on Adverse Psychological Effects and Mortality Following Solitary Confinement in Correctional Settings.* Frontiers in Psychiatry (2020). https://doi.org/10.3389/fpsyt.2020.00840

National Research Council. The Growth of Incarceration in the United States: Exploring Causes and Consequences. National Research Council, 2014.

PRISON HEALTH CARE: COSTS AND QUALITY. Pew Research Center, 2017.

Prison Policy Initiative. www.prisonpolicy.org.

Sirdifield, Coral, Charlie Brooker, & Rebecca Marples. *Suicide and Probation: A Systematic Review of the Literature*. FORENSIC SCIENCE INTERNATIONAL: MIND AND LAW 1 (2020).

Psychological Autopsies

Joiner, Thomas. MYTHS ABOUT SUICIDE. Harvard University Press, 2010.

Joiner, Thomas. THE PERVERSION OF VIRTUE: UNDERSTANDING MURDER-SUICIDE. Oxford University Press, 2014.

Leenaars, Antoon A. THE PSYCHOLOGICAL AUTOPSY. Routledge, 2017.

Ramsland, Katherine. THE PSYCHOLOGY OF DEATH INVESTIGATIONS: BEHAVIORAL ANALYSIS FOR PSYCHOLOGICAL AUTOPSY AND CRIMINAL PROFILING. CRC Press, 2018.

Rogers, James R., & David Lester. UNDERSTANDING SUICIDE: WHY WE DON'T AND HOW WE MIGHT. Hogrefe Publishing, 2010.

Death Suggested, Cause Abated

Cohen, Randy. *A Suicidal Client?* NY TIMES, Oct. 22, 2006. https://www.nytimes.com/2006/10/22/magazine/a-suicidal-client.html

Klevorick, Caitlin. *Our Unhealthy View of Mental Health (and Mental Illness)*. HUFFINGTON POST, March 2, 2013. https://www.huffingtonpost.com/caitlin-klevorick/our-unhealthy-view-of-men_b_2797892.html

Peterson, Jillian, & Kevin Heinz. *Understanding Offenders with Serious Mental Illness in the Criminal Justice System*. 42 MITCHELL HAMLINE L. REV. 537 (2016).

When Judges Cry: Dealing with Defendant's Death by Suicide

Bough, Stephen R. *Getting to Know a Felon: One Judge's Attempt at Imposing Sentences that Are Sufficient, But Not Greater than Necessary*. 87 UMKC L. REV. 1, 25–33 (Fall 2018).

Delgado, Richard, & Jean Stefancic. *Do Judges Cry? An Essay on Empathy and Fellow-Feeling*. 70 CASE WESTERN RESERVE L. REV. 1, 50 (2019).

Ellis, Alan, & J. Michael Henderson. *Federal Prison Guidebook: Sentencing and Post-Conviction Remedies*. 4th rev. James Publishing, 2017.

Reiss, Christina. GUIDE TO JUDICIAL WELL-BEING. Federal Judicial Center, 2013.

Suicide Prevention in the Criminal Justice System: Breaking the Silence

Altiraifi, Azza, & Nicole Rapfogel. *Mental Health Care Was Severely Inequitable, Then Came the Coronavirus Crisis*. CENTER FOR AMERICAN PROGRESS, September 2020.

Miller, Benjamin F., & M. Jeffrey Coffey. *Understanding Suicide Risk and Prevention* (Health Policy Brief). HEALTH AFFAIRS, January 29, 2021. doi:10.1377/hpb20201228.198475. health-affairs-brief-suicide-risk-prevention-miller.pdf

NCCHC/AFSP. SUICIDE PREVENTION RESOURCE GUIDE: NATIONAL RESPONSE PLAN FOR SUICIDE PREVENTION IN CORRECTIONS, PROJECT2025 (2019).

Substance Abuse and Mental Health Services Administration. (2014). *SAMHSA's Concept of Trauma and Guidance for a Trauma-Informed Approach*. HHS Publication No. (SMA) 14-4884. Substance Abuse and Mental Health Services Administration, (2014). https://ncsacw.samhsa.gov/userfiles/files/SAMHSA_Trauma.pdf

Vallas, Rebecca. *Disabilities Behind Bars*. CENTER FOR AMERICAN PROGRESS, July 2016.

Pretrial, Probation, and Parole

Awenat, Yvonne F., et al. *Improving the Quality of Prison Research: A Qualitative Study of Ex-Offender Service User Involvement in Prison Suicide Prevention Research*. HEALTH EXPECTATIONS 21, no. 1, 100-109 (2018). WILEY ONLINE, June 22, 2017. https://www.onlinelibrary.wiley.com/doi/full/10.1111/hex.12590

Bureau of Prisons. *Suicide Prevention Program Policy Example-Federal Model*, April 5, 2007. www.bop.gov/policy/progstat/5324_008.pdf

Elridge, Coleman. *Our Silent National Crisis*. THE COUNCIL OF STATE GOVERNMENTS, June 24, 2016. https://knowledgecenter.csg.org/kc/content/our-silent-national-crisis

Soronen, Lisa. *Supreme Court Denies Prison Officers Qualified Immunity*. THE COUNCIL OF STATE GOVERNMENTS, November 4, 2020. https://knowledgecenter.csg.org/kc/content/supreme-court-denies-prison-officers-qualified-immunity

Tartaro, Christine. SUICIDE AND SELF-HARM IN PRISONS AND JAILS. Lexington, 2010.

Suicide in the Criminal Justice System

Forefront Suicide Prevention. University of Washington. https://www.intheforefront.org

National Alliance on Mental Illness (NAMI). https://nami.org/home

National Suicide Prevention Lifeline. https://suicidepreventionlifeline.org

Psychology Today. https://www.psychologytoday.com/us

Suicide Risk Assessment for Individuals Involved in the Legal System

American Foundation for Suicide Prevention. www.afsp.org

American Psychiatric Association. https://www.psychiatry.org/patients-families/suicide-prevention

American Psychological Association. https://www.apa.org/topics/suicide/index.html

National Institute of Mental Health. www.nimh.nih.gov

Suicide Prevention Resource Center. www.sprc.org

Suicide in the Criminal Justice System: Ethical Considerations

Attempted Suicide as Evidence of Guilt in Criminal Cases: The Legal and Psychological Views. 1964 WASH. U. L.Q. 204 (1964). https://openscholarship.wustl.edu/law_lawreview/vol1964/iss2/4

Gough, Kimberly A. *The Conflict Between Confidentiality and Disclosure When a Client Announces Suicidal Intentions: A Proposed Amendment to the Model Ethics Codes.* 40 WAYNE L. REV. 1629 (1994). https://repository.library.georgetown.edu/handle/10822/874655

Kruse, Katherine R. *Engaged Client-Centered Representation of the Moral Foundations of the Lawyer-Client Relationship.* 39 HOFSTRA L. REV. 577 (2011). https://scholars.law.unlv.edu/cgi/viewcontent.cgi?referer=&httpsredir=1&article=1659&context=facpub

Lafitte, Elizabeth. *Model Rule 1.14: The Well-Intended Rule Still Leaves Some Questions Unanswered.* 17 GEO. J. LEGAL ETHICS 313 (2004). https://repository.library.georgetown.edu/handle/10822/993834

Uphoff, Rodney J. *Role of the Criminal Defense Lawyer in Representing the Mentally Impaired Defendant: Zealous Advocate or Officer of the Court*, 1988 Wis. L. Rev. 65, https://scholarship.law.missouri.edu/cgi/viewcontent.cgi?article=1387&context=facpubs

Case Studies

Benedek, David M., & Gary H. Wynn. CLINICAL MANUAL FOR MANAGEMENT OF PTSD. American Psychiatric Association, 2011.

Bonhoeffer, Dietrich, et al. LETTERS AND PAPERS FROM PRISON. Fortress Press, 2010.

Frankl, Viktor. MAN'S SEARCH FOR MEANING. Beacon, 1959.

Kafka, Franz. THE TRIAL. Oberon Books, 2015.

Koslow, Stephen, et al. A CONCISE GUIDE TO UNDERSTANDING SUICIDE. Cambridge University Press, 2014.

Mandela, Nelson. LONG WALK TO FREEDOM. Little Brown, 2008.

O'Brien, Thomas, & Scott Paeth. RELIGIOUS PERSPECTIVES ON BUSINESS ETHICS: AN ANTHOLOGY. Rowman & Littlefield, 2006.

Rathbone, Christina. A WORLD APART: WOMEN, PRISON, AND LIFE BEHIND BARS. Random House, 2007.

Index

Note: Page numbers followed by *f* denote figures; by *t*, tables; by *n*, notes